A Series of Ups and Downs

A Bicycle Journey Across the World

pedalled by

ROB YOUNG

Published by Muddy Ink Publishing

First published in 2025 in the United Kingdom by Muddy Ink Publishing.

Edition: First Edition
Publisher: Muddy Ink Publishing

ISBN: 9781068477706

Muddy Ink Publishing, 32 Gunton Road, London SW17 9EL

For Molly

CONTENTS

Chapter 1: The Goodbye 1

Chapter 2: To the Cliffs 13

Chapter 3: Ferries & Canals 19

Chapter 4: Hills, Forests & Beer 29

Chapter 5: The Long Ride to Vienna 41

Chapter 6: Along the Danube 45

Chapter 7: The Carpathian Test 61

Chapter 8: Crossing into Turkey 71

Chapter 9: The City In Between 83

Chapter 10: The Black Sea: Together 89

Chapter 11: The Black Sea: Alone 101

Chapter 12: Vodka & Kindness 107

Chapter 13: Between the Caspian & the Carpet 123

Chapter 14: Roads & Revelations 139

Chapter 15: Five Days of Dust 161

Chapter 16: Bukhara and Beyond 167
Chapter 17: High Roads to the Border 179
Chapter 18: Arrival in Kashgar 189
Chapter 19: The Descent into Pakistan.......... 205
Chapter 20: Escorted South.......... 215
Chapter 21: Amritsar & Northern India.......... 227
Chapter 22: Punjab to Rajasthan.......... 243
Chapter 23: Desert to City 261
Chapter 24: Southern Shores 267
Chapter 25: The Quiet Peninsula 283
Chapter 26: Satun to Bangkok 287
Chapter 27: A Friendly Visit 303
Chapter 28: China Revisited 319
Chapter 29: Korean Cuisine 333
Chapter 30: The Beginning of the End.......... 345
Chapter 31: Bridges & Shrines 353
Chapter 32: The End: Fuji & the Pacific.......... 369

Author's Note

When I set out from my front door in London with two wheels, a tent, and more nerves than experience, I wasn't chasing records or headlines. I was chasing something harder to pin down: freedom, silence, maybe even a version of myself I hadn't met yet.

This isn't a guidebook, and it certainly isn't a glossy travel brochure. Some days were glorious, others were brutal. I laughed, I swore, I broke down, and I kept pedalling. What you'll find here are the raw ups and downs of a road that carried me thousands of kilometres away from home, and in many ways closer to myself.

What kept me moving weren't strong legs or tough gear, but the small moments of kindness along the way: a wave from a driver, a smile in a tea shop, a message from home arriving just when I needed it. They reminded me that the world, for all its challenges, is full of good people.

So this is my journey, as it really happened. The good, the bad and the ugly. I hope in these pages you'll find not just the mountains, deserts, storms and cities I passed through, but also the strange mix of struggle and wonder that comes from chasing a road with no end in sight.

Rob

CHAPTER 1

The Goodbye

Number of days on the road: 0
Total distance covered: 0 km

I woke up with a knot in my stomach.

For a moment, I lay still, staring at the ceiling, listening to the muffled groan of the city outside—the distant rumble of buses, the occasional siren, the restless shuffle of life outside.

Beside me, Ellen—my girlfriend—lay silent, her breathing slow and steady, her dark hair spilling across the pillow. She looked peaceful, unfazed by the storm raging inside me for months. I reached out towards her instinctively, then stopped. A hollow ache settled in my chest.

How could I leave her?

Then again, how could I stay?

Sliding quietly out of bed, the cool morning air wrapped around me. I moved through the flat in silence, the faint creak of the floorboards being the only audible sound. Everything felt slightly out of sorts—from the magnolia-hued walls, the framed photographs, the chipped coffee mug on the kitchen counter. I grabbed a bowl of cereal and ate it without tasting.

I glanced through the kitchen window. It was summer and London's skyline was blurred by the early morning light—but I could still make out the rows of rooftops in shades of slate and rust. Somewhere outside, a bus hissed to a stop, the sound swallowed by the morning mist. The city was starting the day without me.

She appeared a few moments later, wrapped in her familiar white dressing gown, padding barefoot across the floor. She hesitated at the doorway before sitting beside me, silence filling the space between us.

Her voice was barely a whisper. "So, this is really happening?"

I swallowed hard. "Yeah."

She nodded, lips tightening. Her eyes glistened, but she didn't cry. I wanted to say something, anything, to soften this moment, but what was there left to say? We hadn't broken up in a storm of anger; there had been no shouting or betrayal. We had simply faded, eroded by time and silence, until the distance between us felt permanent.

I had asked her to come with me.

She wanted to stay.

Neither of us could give the other what they needed.

She pulled me into a hug. A single tear rolled down her cheek onto my skin. I pressed my face into her hair, breathing in the familiar scent of home. For a moment, I wished it were enough to make me stay.

But we both knew it wasn't.

She pulled away first. "You should go before it gets harder."

I nodded. She had always been stronger than me.

In the living room, Shirley—my bike—leaned against the wall, bathed in the slanting morning light. Her steel-blue frame wasn't flashy—she was sturdy, dependable, and built to last. I assembled her piece by piece, tightening each bolt and selecting each component with care. Seven waterproof panniers clung to her frame, bulging with everything I owned for this journey: clothes, camping gear, tools, a journal, and for reasons I couldn't quite justify, a tiny travel guitar strapped to the back.

She was beautiful. She was ridiculous. She was my escape.

I'd always wanted to travel the world. Not in fragments. Not two weeks at a time. I wanted to see the whole thing—slowly, and on my own terms.

That idea had lived with me for years, whispered in traffic jams, half-joked about over beers. I wasn't trying to run away from anything. I just couldn't accept that the 9-to-5 routine was all there was.

The job wasn't a disaster. Life wasn't falling apart. But somewhere deep down, I knew I didn't want to spend the rest of my life rehearsing the same version of adulthood, day after day. I was too young to feel that settled.

When the firm offered redundancy, it wasn't the reason I left, it was the excuse I needed to finally go.

I had a plan. I'd ride from London to Tokyo, overland, across Europe, Central Asia, China, and beyond or wherever the road would take me.

I wanted to know what the world felt like under my wheels. I wanted to see if I could cross a continent the way I used to cross a city. To move through the world slowly enough to feel it change around me, and change me with it.

And yet, doubt crept in. Had I prepared enough? Had I forgotten something critical? Would Shirley really carry me across continents, or was I about to fail in the most spectacular way possible?

I swallowed back my doubt as I put on my clothes before realising I didn't even have a map of London, and quickly dashed out to buy one.

Outside, Islington's Upper Street was already awake. The scent of fresh coffee and petrol mingled in the air. Buses hissed, shop shutters rattled open, and people rushed past clutching takeaway coffees, lost in their morning rituals.

Did they know what it felt like to leave everything behind?

I bought a map from a corner shop, returning to the flat one last time. I spread it out on the couch and traced a possible route, searching for the easiest, least painful way to leave. But there was no easy way to do this. No shortcut through emotion.

I folded the map and turned back to Ellen.

"So, I guess this is it," I said, my voice cracking despite the false cheer.

She forced a small smile. "I guess so."

Something meaningful was being severed.

I shivered—not from the cold, but from the fear pressing deep in my bones.

I wheeled Shirley into the yard. She felt heavier than I'd expected, all 48 kilograms of gear pressing down, not just in weight but in meaning.

One final embrace. One last kiss.

"Goodbye," she whispered.

I opened my mouth to reply, but no sound came out. I swung my leg over Shirley, gripping the handlebars until my knuckles turned white and pushed off.

The first pedal stroke wobbled. The second steadied. By the third, I was moving.

I didn't look back.

I wouldn't leave if I did.

And just like that, my journey began.

***

Shirley and I rolled quietly through London's streets. Her wheels hummed against the tarmac, steady and reassuring beneath me.

Soon, the commuter rush swallowed me—buses trundling along, black cabs weaving, cyclists darting forward like nervous fish in a predator-filled sea.

On London Bridge, I stopped. With one foot resting on the pavement, I stared at the River Thames below. The water was sluggish and grey, reflecting the shifting sky above. The weight of my decision settled heavily on my shoulders.

A bus thundered past, jolting me back to the present. I took a deep breath, tightened my grip on the handlebars, and pushed off. I didn't know what I was chasing—only that I couldn't stay still any longer.

There was no turning back now.

The bus suddenly pulled sharply into a bus stop. I put on a spurt and pedalled past it, only to be overtaken again a few moments later. We continued this dance until I finally turned off toward Blackheath.

By the time I reached Blackheath Hill, I had already cycled over 10 kilometres and, my thighs burned and sweat trickled down my back. Shirley felt solid beneath me; she was an extension of my body, absorbing the city's chaos as we climbed higher.

At the top of the hill, I stopped and looked back. London sprawled out below. It was already starting to feel distant.

As I set off again, office blocks gave way to rows of Victorian terraces, their bay windows catching the midday sun. These turned into neat semis, then detached houses with sprawling hedgerows and gravel drives. As suburbia thinned out, the landscape finally opened into the patchwork fields of rural Britain.

Urban grit had softened into country roads and I breathed in the air, cleaner, fresher, a little less toxic perhaps.

In one village, a freshly painted red post box stood proudly outside a row of crooked cottages. A Tudor-themed pub with hanging baskets leaned into the narrow road. Was it too early for a pint? Probably.

Hours later, I took refuge at a small village café, Shirley propped on the wall outside. My legs were aching.

I sat at a little iron table in the uneven courtyard. One leg was shorter than the others, and it wobbled every time I shifted. It felt oddly perfect—an accurate reflection of my emotional state, perhaps.

"Tea and a slice of cake, love?" The elderly owner smiled, wiping her hands on her apron.

"Yes, please," I exhaled, realising how much I needed the break.

She placed a steaming mug and a thick slice of Victoria sponge in front of me. "So, where are you off to, then?"

I hesitated. Stirred my tea. Watched the ripples fade.

"I'm not entirely sure," I admitted. "Just... away."

I expected her to press me, but instead she smiled knowingly and said, "Sometimes, 'away' is exactly where you need to be."

I took a sip of tea.

Maybe she was right.

Back on the bike and by late afternoon, the warmth of the sun had softened, stretching long shadows across the road. My legs were tiring, my body sluggish, the initial thrill of the morning now dulled by fatigue. The quiet drum of tyres on asphalt was the only sound for miles.

I stopped to slap on a generous layer of factor 30 sunscreen. It didn't help much—by evening, my arms were an ominous glowing pink. Maybe in time I'd build up some kind of tolerance. Or just get used to looking like a boiled lobster.

As I continued into the evening, the road wound through rolling fields, the golden light catching on tips of wheat that swayed lazily in the breeze. A part of me wanted to stop, maybe even turn around. But something stronger pulled me forward.

The last few kilometres into Faversham felt endless. I had now covered 90 kilometres and I scanned for somewhere—anywhere—to set up for the night. A small sign for a campsite flickered into view, half-hidden among the hedgerows, and I turned onto a gravel track leading towards a cluster of farm buildings.

The owner, a stout man in his sixties, eyed Shirley approvingly. "You cycled here?" he asked, as I handed over the £8.10 fee to pitch for the night.

"From London," I replied, as if saying it aloud would make it sound less absurd.

He let out a low whistle. "You'll sleep well tonight, lad."

I wanted to believe him, but first, I had to battle the tent.

It was a spectacle of incompetence. The poles were in rebellion, and the canvas lining flapped in the wind like a matador's cape. By the time I got the tent standing, I was damp with sweat and covered in grass and mud. I had practised the assembly a few times, but I clearly hadn't tamed the beast yet. Little did I know that this would become my routine for the next year of my life after many long and gruelling days in the saddle.

As I unpacked, somehow, everything I needed was buried deep in the last pannier that I checked. I crouched in the grass, cursing softly, surrounded by a pile of gear that looked like it had been thrown from a moving vehicle.

Collapsing onto my bright orange sleeping mat, I made my first meal of the journey—boil-in-the-bag meatballs and macaroni cheese. It was lukewarm, gloopy, and vaguely synthetic, but after a day in the saddle, it tasted like Michelin-star dining to me.

Nearby, a family sat outside their massive campervan, their children laughing as they played a game of football. I envied their comfort, the ease of their well-equipped setup. But, as I lay back staring at the deepening sky with the crisp air settling onto my skin, I felt something stir inside me.

I allowed the thought to surface for the first time—I really had done it. I'd left. The departure had been a struggle, both emotionally and physically. My belongings lay in chaos, a perfect reflection of my thoughts. But I was slowly adjusting and learning, in every sense.

I pulled out my copy of Paulo Coelho's *The Alchemist,* and flicked through its well-thumbed pages. It felt like the right book for this moment—one about journeys, listening to omens, and seeking something you don't quite understand yet.

Then, I was out like a light.

CHAPTER 2

To the Cliffs

Number of days on the road: 2
Total distance covered: 133 km

H*ad someone punched me in the face while I slept?* The campsite mirror suggested yes. My eyes were puffy and swollen—I looked like I'd been caught between a heavyweight boxer and a hangover.

I would never take a job that would have made me get up at the crack of dawn and work until either exhaustion or sunset, or whichever came first, but that's exactly what I'd signed up for. A cycling nomad, by choice, and without payment. Was I mad? Probably.

It was 5:30 a.m. The sunrise had already turned my tent into a suffocating oven, and I had prised myself out of my sleeping bag and waddled, stiff and sore, to the shower block to wash.

The mirror was unforgiving. My cheeks were flushed, and my hair was stuck to my forehead.

I splashed cold water onto my face, muttering to my reflection. "You wanted adventure. Here it is."

Porridge and tea felt like the right way to start what promised to be a spectacular day. The warmth crept through my limbs like central heating. Even in this unfamiliar setting, it almost felt like home. I wasn't a morning person, but I was bouncing around, eager to get Shirley rolling again.

By 7 a.m. I was back on the road, winding towards the Kent coast.

The roads were freshly tarred and blissfully empty. I passed ivy-choked verges bursting with wildflowers, and sleepy villages that seemed untouched by time. A few tractors trundled past, their drivers giving the kind of slow, approving nods reserved for madmen and missionaries.

The kilometres ticked by steadily.

But the hills came thick and fast.

With every climb, my legs screamed, my 48 kilograms of gear dragging me backwards. I gritted my teeth, pushed down on the pedals, and ground my way up each incline.

The first glimpse of Dover came in a break between the hills—a smudge of white cliffs on the horizon.

My legs slowed.

Those cliffs weren't just a landmark. They were the edge of something, of home, of comfort, of everything I knew. I had dreamt of this moment. But now that it was here, all I felt was the weight of it.

When I crossed the water, I couldn't pretend anymore. This was real.

It didn't feel real yet.

But soon the road dipped and, suddenly, the town spread out below me.

I coasted downhill, the wind making my eyes water, the sea glittering in the distance, the imposing structure of Dover Castle watching over the harbour.

I'd made it.

Locating the ferry terminal wasn't hard—the towering ships gave the game away. I hadn't looked at a map since I left London, and my expensive A-to-Z had been a dead weight. I tossed it into a recycling bin near the terminal, feeling both relieved that I made it to the coast and mild guilt that I had not even taken the map out of my bag since purchasing it.

I wheeled Shirley up to the counter in the cavernous terminal building, parked her where I could keep an eye on her, and scanned the list of destinations. Calais was the obvious choice, but the next departure wasn't until late afternoon. Dunkirk at 2 p.m.? *That'll do nicely*, I thought, and booked my passage.

With time to spare, I headed to the terminal café with its plain white walls, basic plastic chairs, and a menu stuck to the counter with peeling tape. I ordered a ham and cheese toastie and a cup of tea. As I ate, the cheese oozed out and dribbled down my chin. I wiped it with a napkin and looked around—there were families on holiday and lorry drivers eating their lunch in silence. I didn't belong to either of these groups, but I felt strangely connected to them all the same.

At the boarding gate, a bored-looking woman barely glanced up.

"One bicycle, one passenger," I said, handing over my passport.

She stamped my ticket and waved me through. "Lane six."

I navigated towards a sea of waiting vehicles, feeling oddly exposed. Amongst the rows of lorries and SUVs, Shirley and I stood out—a tiny blue bicycle, bags strapped haphazardly to her frame, a rider crusted in salt, his skin a bright pink from the sun.

People in their air-conditioned cars peered out at me, and I grinned back at them.

The ferry horn sounded; it was deep and commanding. The ramp lowered with a metallic groan, and the rows of vehicles began moving.

“Just lock it up against that rail there, mate,” a ferry worker in a high-vis jacket said as he directed me towards a metal bar.

I secured Shirley beside the rail as instructed. She looked strangely heroic there, standing proud among the hulking cars and lorries. I gave her a gentle pat on the handlebars. “We made it.”

I climbed the stairs to the upper deck and, as the massive steel ship groaned and lurched into motion, I stood and watched the chalk-white cliffs recede into the distance.

They looked different from this angle—more dramatic, towering, their edges rougher than I’d ever realised.

My father’s voice echoed in my memory. “Those cliffs have seen centuries of farewells.”

For the first time, I understood what he meant.

I was leaving.

Not just England.

Not just my old life.

But the person I had been.

I took a deep breath, let the wind whip through my hair, and turned my gaze towards France.

My adventure had finally begun.

CHAPTER 3

Ferries & Canals

Number of days on the road: 3
Total distance covered: 137 km

Leaving Dunkirk felt like trying to escape a maze designed by someone with a cruel sense of humour. The roads twisted and turned, leading me in circles past typical warehouses and industrial complexes until I was convinced I'd passed the same rusting cargo container at least three times. My map of Western Europe that I had packed was useless, its neat lines and symbols no match for the chaotic sprawl of France's third-largest port. Sweating and exasperated, I finally spotted a policewoman standing at a crossroads, her uniform crisp and her expression calm amidst the chaos. I approached her, my voice tinged with desperation.

"Excusez-moi, madame. Je suis perdu."

She raised an eyebrow, her lips curling into a knowing smile. "Lost, are we?" she replied in English, her accent thick but her tone warm.

"Hopelessly," I admitted, gesturing to Shirley and my overloaded panniers. "I'm trying to get to Belgium, but your roads seem determined to keep me here."

She chuckled, pointing northeast. "Follow this road until you see the sign for Furnes. You can't miss it—unless you're as good at getting lost as you seem to be."

Grateful, I thanked her and pedalled off, her laughter ringing in my ears.

I soon found my way to the Route de Furnes, following the grassy canal edge on pristine, flat, and almost entirely traffic-free roads—I'd be following this path almost the entire way to Bruges. Noisy engines were replaced by the whirring of Shirley's wheels as they pounded the path. Birds skittered across the canal's glassy surface, startled by my passing.

With every kilometre, I felt less like I was leaving somewhere and more like I was arriving.

Now that I was travelling in the right direction, I was finally able to appreciate the glorious day. I was pleased I had set out in June. If I lasted until autumn, I hoped that I might make it closer to Greece or Turkey, where the weather would still be warm.

Whilst the temperature was warm, the breeze against my face was cool. I inhaled deeply, letting it fill my lungs as Shirley's wheels purred along. Trees lined the banks, their branches arching toward the water. Around me, the world seemed to move at a slower pace—cyclists pedalled leisurely, their baskets filled with groceries or flowers, while walkers strolled with dogs trotting happily at their sides. I smiled at a woman walking a terrier, and she nodded in return. I felt a quiet sense of peace settle over me.

I decided to stop for a takeaway since I wanted to make good progress, and the time spent firing up the stove was not what I needed. When I crossed into Belgium—my third country of the day—after a good day's cycling, the sun began to slouch and fall from the sky. Looking for somewhere to sleep turned into a hilarious first experience of wild camping. I say "wild", but what I really mean is "unauthorised".

Just short of Nieuwpoort town, only about 15-20 kilometres from the French border, a small iron footbridge crossed over the canal. On the far embankment, nestled amongst trees, I found a grassy verge with just enough space for my army-green two-man tent. It was reasonably level, hidden from the path and—based on no expertise whatsoever—good enough for me. I pitched camp and clambered down the embankment, salty and sweaty from a warm day in the saddle, clutching my shower gel and a towel. I had no idea how clean the water was, but kayakers had been in the same stretch of canal earlier that day, so I figured it must meet some basic health standards. I hadn't thought it through, but the water looked inviting, and I was already halfway down the bank. Splash. Cold, glorious, ridiculous.

Feeling cleaner and fresher, yet tired from a full day's cycling, it was time for more sleep. My trip was already developing a routine, and it was only the end of day two.

But something had shifted. I lay there in the dark, half-listening to the quiet of the canal, and it struck me—this wasn't just an escape anymore. It was a way of being.

I didn't miss a ceiling or a mattress, and I didn't mind the damp socks or the distant rumble of lorries.

I felt—in the smallest, strangest way—free.

Shirley and I effortlessly covered the remainder of the distance to the outskirts of Bruges. Seeking directions, I stopped a cheerful man outside a corner shop.

"Excuse me, sir—can you tell me how to get to Bruges?"

He looked at me, baffled. "You're in Bruges."

"Oh. Right." I laughed. "In that case—any idea where the Belfry is?"

"Aah, the Belfry! Not quite Pisa, but she leans a little. Left at the next turn. Follow your ears—it usually sings."

His humour matched the city's charm.

I rolled through the yellow stone arch of the Smedenpoort Gate and into the quiet cobbled streets. Narrow alleys wound past crooked brick buildings and over tranquil canals. I stopped at a little café, ordered a rich, dark coffee, and sat outside watching the world drift by. The bitter warmth was grounding–it was a small comfort in a foreign place. I sipped slowly, letting myself exhale. It was the first time since leaving London that I'd let myself slow down.

Climbing the Belfry Tower, each step up the spiral stone staircase was a victory for my calves. At the top, the view stretched across terracotta rooftops and green fields far beyond the city walls. I stood there, flushed and breathless, surprised by how content I felt.

Wandering up and down the canals, I discovered charming little squares and hidden corners. The scent of freshly baked pastries wafted through the air, tempting me to indulge, and I couldn't resist stopping by a quaint café to savour a warm, buttery Belgian waffle topped with strawberries and a dollop of whipped cream. The heavenly treat melted in my mouth.

After two days' rest enjoying the city, my body grateful for a real bed and clean sheets, it was back to the road.

As Shirley and I rolled out of Bruges, I found myself thinking about the life I'd left behind. A few months earlier, I'd been a commercial real estate lawyer—attending meetings and burying my head in complex legal documents. On paper, I had it made. But every day felt like I was rehearsing a version of adulthood I didn't believe in. When my firm offered redundancy packages in the post-2008 shake-up, something inside me shifted. A door cracked open. I stepped through.

Just outside Ghent, I pulled over at a bike shop to fix a slow leak in my front tyre. The place looked like a passion project—wooden walls covered in maps, a rainbow of tyres and tools on every surface. The couple who ran the store and introduced themselves as Jan and Martine greeted me like an old friend.

"Greetings, traveller!" Jan beamed. "Where are you headed?"

"As far as I can get before my legs fall off. So... probably another 2 kilometres."

Martine laughed. "Come inside—we've got snacks for cyclists and a public pump."

Their generosity floored me. They gave me energy bars, pasta, and even a small tin of chain oil.

I thanked them—sincerely—but I also felt something deeper. In my old life, kindness often came with strings attached. Here, it was given freely, without an agenda. It made me wonder how many times I'd walked past people like this without even noticing.

Over the following days, the landscape began to roll gently upward. Belgium became Luxembourg, then eastern fields hinted at Germany.

Thick woodlands punctuated the landscape—dark green conifers standing tall and proud. The woods were alive with the sounds of nature, with birds calling from the treetops, leaves rustling underfoot, and the occasional creak of ancient branches in the breeze.

Then came a wobble.

Flying downhill at close to 60 km/h, the wind howling in my ears and the conifer-lined road blurring beneath me. Suddenly, I felt a sickening jolt. Something had shifted on the bike. There was a grinding screech from behind me.

My heart stopped. I gripped the handlebars, instinctively lowering my weight and easing into the brakes. The rear wheel juddered, refusing to spin cleanly. If I crashed now...

No time to think.

I pulled Shirley to the side of the road, breath ragged and my hands trembling. The rear rack had sheared loose—one of the bolts had vibrated out, and the steel frame had collapsed onto the wheel.

I stared at the hole where the bolt had been, my breath still shallow. I'd been riding as if I were invincible. I realised, then, how fragile this whole adventure was. A single missing bolt, and it could've been over. There'd be no applause, no movie montage—just a mangled bike and an ambulance, if I were lucky.

It wasn't just about strength anymore; I needed to be careful, streetwise, pragmatic, and resourceful.

Shakily, I dug out my multi-tool and a spare bolt, refastened everything slowly and methodically, my hands still twitching with adrenaline.

I sat on the verge longer than I needed to, my heart thudding. Not from fear, from clarity. This journey was built on assumptions—that roads would hold, that bolts would stay tight, and that I would stay upright. One missing piece, and it could all collapse. I wasn't riding across the world. I was surviving it, one turn at a time.

Lesson learned. Check the nuts and bolts every few hundred kilometres so that you don't end up in hospital.

The next few kilometres passed in silence. I didn't wave at the villagers. I barely noticed the scenery. The forest had closed in again, but this time it felt watchful, even cold.

I checked every bolt twice that evening, hands moving slower than usual. I wasn't scared exactly, but something had changed. This trip was fragile. It was about attention, caution and survival. It was asking more of me than I'd expected.

CHAPTER 4

Hills, Forests & Beer

Number of days on the road: 9
Total distance covered: 859 km

The smooth flat roads of northern Europe gave way to the crackle and groan of forest roads as I passed through Luxembourg towards Germany. Here, coarse gravel crunched under my tyres. There were pine needles strewn around like confetti after a woodland wedding. The climbs were constant and winding, but at least they were shaded. Despite this, sweat pooled in the small of my back and the air smelled of sap and promise.

Crossing the Moselle River into Germany felt like a tangible milestone. Borders had a way of reminding me I was moving forward—and not just geographically, but emotionally too.

The sun was fierce again. Despite another generous coat of factor 30 sunscreen, I was already developing a sunburn that could end up having me mistaken for an Oompa Loompa.

The hilly green landscape had transitioned into wine country, with lush vineyards gracefully replacing the dense forests that had accompanied my ride. Neat rows of vines followed the contours of the hills, their symmetry strangely calming after the jumbled sprawl of border towns.

I was settling into a rhythm now. The early aches had faded. The road still bit at my legs, but I'd started to believe I could outlast the discomfort and grow stronger.

To pass the time—and to justify the long hours spent on my own—I started listening to a German language audiobook. Anyone who passed me that day had quite a spectacle. Picture the lone cyclist zipping through undulating countryside, shouting *"Ich möchte einen Kaffee!"* (I want a coffee! at the top of their lungs. It was a sight and sound to behold. It felt ridiculous—but it made the hours pass quickly.

A delightful moment arrived amid my comedic linguistic outbursts as I pedalled into the sleepy town of Mettlach on the loop of the river Saar, and decided to stop for lunch. Here was my opportunity to test out my newly acquired linguistic prowess. Confident in my newfound language skills, I settled down in the family-owned *Café und Bäckerei.*

"Ein Kaffee, bitte?" I ventured, trying to muster the best accent I could.

"Certainly, sir. Would you like milk and sugar?" replied the friendly waitress, her English only tinged with the slightest German accent.

Embarrassed by my unmistakable Englishness, I found solace in the fact that at least I was understood. Sipping my coffee, I jotted down a few more essentials in my notebook: *Brot, Bier, Wasser,* plus a few pleasantries and directions for good measure. Armed thus, and with a caffeine-induced boost of confidence, I felt well-equipped to continue the journey.

Venturing deeper into southwestern Germany, I quickly discovered that it wasn't the easiest place to navigate on a bicycle. Fast-flowing highways with trucks zooming by posed a constant threat to cyclists like me. Cycling was prohibited on these main roads, leaving me with diversions through housing estates and out-of-the-way B-roads. The roads themselves were often cracked and bumpy, the kind that jarred your bones and rattled every inch of Shirley's frame. The signage for these cycle routes was often confusing or absent altogether.

Even when the scenery soared, I couldn't quite relax. The road surface buzzed through the handlebars like static. One jolt too many, and the whole operation might come unstuck.

This all started around the cities of Saarbrücken and Stuttgart, where major trunk roads dominated the landscape. Despite my heightening frustration, I persevered—assisted by my barely passable German and the occasional kind local who pointed me back on course.

Eventually, the traffic thinned, and the world opened up again. The oppressive heat of the cities gave way to the cool shade of towering pine forests. Nature had woven a drapery of towering trees. The scent of warm asphalt was replaced by earth and resin. I was no longer dodging trucks—I was riding into the heart of the Black Forest and the sparsely populated Swabian Alps, where the road climbed ever upwards as I headed eastward.

The landscape here was vast and deeply green, each corner revealing more forest and more silence. The road twisted relentlessly upwards, every bend unveiling another brutal incline. My breath came in ragged gasps; my legs burned as though molten lead had been poured into them. Sweat dripped into my eyes, which stung as I blinked furiously. I could feel the weight of Shirley and my gear; it felt like I was dragging an anchor behind me.

Just as I thought I couldn't push another pedal, a gust of mountain air hit me—it was cool, crisp, and laced with the scent of pine. I was almost there. Gritting my teeth, I forced my way up the 800 metres to the summit.

When I reached the top, I unclipped my pedals, staggered off Shirley, and collapsed onto the grass, arms spread wide, lungs gulping in air. It was another personal triumph—

my highest climb on a bicycle. For a moment, everything was still. The panoramic view was intoxicating: the forest sprawled outwards for miles, its canopy of green rolling to the horizon. I revelled in the quiet achievement.

I descended into the forest's embrace, and the surroundings transformed. The dark woods closed in, their towering trunks forming a living colonnade. It felt like riding up the aisle of a cavernous cathedral that was formed entirely of trees.

In this enchanted forest, I discovered a secluded camping spot. The solitude was profound. There were no distant car horns, no murmurs of civilisation, just the subtle movements of nature: the wind brushing through branches, the crack of a twig underfoot, the occasional bird call echoing in the canopy.

People asked if I felt scared camping alone in the middle of nowhere. Yes, at first it was a bit nerve-racking. But reverse psychology helped. I thought, *What if some crazy person spots my tent and comes to investigate?* Until I realised that perhaps I *was* the crazy person wandering around the forest. Once I had embraced that fact—my own weirdness—I slept just fine.

Here, in the Black Forest, under the watchful gaze of trees older than any building I'd lived in, I thought about home. About Ellen. About everything I'd left behind.

She was no longer my girlfriend. She was my ex-girlfriend. The term felt wrong. It felt awkward, final.

The nights were the hardest. As I lay in my tent, cocooned in darkness, the thoughts I outran during the day caught up with me. I wondered how she was. If she were happy. If she missed me, or if she had already begun rebuilding her life without me.

I told myself this journey was the right choice. That I needed it. We both knew I couldn't stay. But in the quiet moments, I wasn't always so sure. Loneliness has sharp edges. But so does growth. The constant stimuli of new places, people, and small physical tasks helped distract me—what to eat, where to go, where to sleep. The days were full. The nights were hard. Perhaps she was finding it harder. That thought cut even deeper. I hoped she wasn't—mostly out of love—perhaps partly out of guilt.

Eventually, the forest thinned. Hills softened. I pushed on. Each day became a little easier than the last. My legs grew stronger, my lungs more efficient. I crested hill after hill with growing confidence. I was changing. I was growing. And I knew it.

Munich finally emerged. The sound hit me first—trams rattling on steel tracks, voices echoing between buildings, a distant street musician strumming a blues riff near a fountain. After days of silence, the city was roaring with life around me as I finally rolled into the heart of the *Altstadt,* the historic old town.

Arriving at *Marienplatz,* I was greeted by a spectacular sight: the *Neues Rathaus,* the city's grand neo-Gothic town hall. Its façade was lined with spires and sculpted figures, and, as luck would have it, I had arrived just in time for the famous Glockenspiel show. A crowd had gathered, eyes turned upwards as life-sized mechanical figures twirled to the tune of chiming bells. I stood among them, Shirley propped against a lamppost. I momentarily forgot my exhaustion.

From there, I wandered through *Viktualienmarkt,* Munich's sprawling open-air food market, where stalls overflowed with fresh bread, juicy sausages, and cheese wheels the size of tractor tyres. I indulged in a traditional *Weißwurst mit süßem Senf,* delicate white sausages served with sweet mustard and a side of freshly baked pretzels. A cold Bavarian beer completed the meal, and as I sat beneath the shade of a chestnut tree in a beer garden, I felt a wave of satisfaction wash over me.

In the *Englischer Garten,* Munich's vast urban park, locals sprawled on the grass, soaking up the afternoon sun, while others gathered at the *Chinesischer Turm,* another lively beer garden. It was a city brimming with life and warmth.

I had planned for a quiet evening—perhaps another pretzel, beer, and an early night before setting off again.

Instead, I found myself seated across from a breathtakingly confident German woman in a dimly lit Bavarian tavern, where wooden beams lined the ceiling and waiters in *Lederhosen* bustled between tables.

Her name was Annalena, and we had met entirely by chance. She'd been admiring my fully loaded bicycle outside a café when she struck up a conversation.

"Where are you headed?" she asked, curiosity twinkling in her sharp blue eyes.

"Japan," I replied, still disbelieving it myself.

"That's ridiculous," she laughed, "but I like it."

She had that same calm certainty I used to envy in Ellen—the kind that made you feel seen, even while you were drifting away. Except Annalena didn't ask me to stay. She didn't ask anything of me at all.

One moment, we were strangers; the next, we were sharing dinner and a second beer as if we'd known each other for years.

We ordered *Schweinshaxe,* a roasted pork knuckle with a crispy golden crust, served with rich gravy and tangy sauerkraut. The meat fell off the bone at the first touch of a fork, and paired with a cold local beer, it was one of the most satisfying meals I can remember.

We talked about travel, books, love, the people we'd lost, and the quiet reasons some of us need to keep moving.

"So why are you doing this?" she asked, leaning in.

I hesitated. How could I sum up the tangled mess of restlessness, heartbreak, and longing?

"Because I have to," I said finally. "Because if I don't, I'll always wonder."

She nodded, as if she understood completely. And maybe she did.

After one last drink, we stepped outside into the cool Munich air. The streets were quiet, bathed in warm light. For a moment, I thought about asking her to come with me for a few days. But I didn't. Some encounters are meant to be fleeting—perfect in their impermanence.

"Good luck, crazy cyclist," she said, kissing my cheek before disappearing into the night.

I stood there for a while, watching the spot where she vanished. Annalena was light, warm and fleeting. Maybe that's why, just for a moment, I let myself feel something again.

I turned to Shirley. The road was still calling.

***

Over the next few days, I rode through Bavaria and into Austria at the town of Passau before linking up with and following the serene banks of the Danube. It was in Tulln an der Donau in Austria that I was taught a significant lesson in campfire-making.

The campsite was neat and family-friendly, with all the modern amenities. I chuckled as I watched a group of kids struggling to light a fire after recent heavy rain. Feeling confident—perhaps *too* confident—I approached with a grin.

"Hi guys! Want to see how it's really done?"

I pulled fuel from my camping stove and generously poured it over the damp wood.

A match. A spark. An explosion.

The fire roared to life, triumphant—for all of two seconds. Then a spark leapt into the open fuel bottle behind me.

Panic.

I kicked the bottle. Fuel spilt. Flames shot across the ground. The kids screamed. I frantically shovelled dirt onto the fire, stomping and swearing.

After a few minutes of chaos, I got it under control. What remained was a perfectly lit campfire—and a large patch of scorched earth.

Trying to maintain a calm façade, I lit a cigarette and turned to the startled kids.

“Good fire, eh?”

We all burst into laughter—nervous, relieved, ridiculous.

That night, I lay in my tent, heart still thumping, and thought about what could've happened if I'd been even a little more careless.

Adventure was exhilarating.

But I really needed to be less of an idiot with petrol.

CHAPTER 5

The Long Ride to Vienna

Number of days on the road: 16
Total distance covered: 1,305 km

The border came and went with barely a sign, but the landscape signalled a change. Fields grew tidier, towns more orderly, and the randomness of the countryside gave way to something more curated.

Vienna announced itself with grace. The road straightened, trees aligned like soldiers, and the rattling of trams began to replace birdsong. The air changed too—it was crisper, cooler, cleaner, as if the city scrubbed itself each morning in preparation for the day ahead.

Traffic increased steadily. I found myself cycling beside cars and buses rather than tractors and touring cyclists. Then came the architecture—rising stone by stone, style by style—until I was pedalling among grand façades and wide boulevards. The temperature changed again, cooler, scented faintly with chestnuts and something sweet I couldn't name. The cobbles thudded under my wheels like a welcoming drumroll.

I arrived in Vienna on two wheels, dusty and sunburnt. I felt like a misfit among the sharp suits and elegant skirts of the *Innere Stadt*. Even the traffic seemed better dressed.

Vienna didn't just wear its history—it wore it proudly, like a medal. Palaces loomed above the streets, their façades bursting with sculpted cherubs, marble columns, gilded balconies, and floral motifs. I passed beneath wrought-iron balconies twisted into elegant patterns, their shadows dancing across pastel walls glowing in the afternoon light. It was all too perfect—the architecture, the symmetry, the composure. I should have been in awe. And I was. But I also felt like an intruder in a world that didn't belong to me. I had been on the road for the best part of a week since Munich, and I was now a grubby smudge on the city's canvas. Vienna gleamed. I flinched.

For two days, I let the city carry me. I wandered without purpose or direction, letting the boulevards and alleyways lead the way. The *Innere Stadt*—the historic heart of Vienna—felt like stepping into a living museum. I wandered through the Hofburg courtyards, where the echo of horses' hooves lingered in the stone. Gothic spires and Baroque details towered above me. Everything here had scale and dignity.

One afternoon, I ducked into a coffeehouse and ordered a slice of *Sachertorte* and a coffee so strong it kicked like a mule. The cake arrived on a silver tray, its glossy dark chocolate glaze catching the glow of a chandelier overhead. It was rich, dark, and impossibly dense—a Viennese hug I hadn't realised I needed. The thin layer of apricot jam gave it just the right tang. The coffee, bold and bitter, was the perfect counterbalance.

The indulgent Sachertorte was only the beginning of my education in Viennese cuisine. From the coffeehouse, I headed for the *Naschmarkt*—Vienna's bustling outdoor market, where spices, sausages and ripe fruit jostled for space beneath striped awnings. The air buzzed with chatter and the mingled scents of roasting chestnuts, fresh bread, and sizzling *Käsekrainer*—an oozing cheese-filled sausage full of flavour. I devoured one on the spot while eavesdropping on students arguing about politics in three different languages at once.

That evening, I ended up in a hostel bar with a group of backpackers, and we danced late into the night to some awful 90s pop music. For a few hours, I didn't feel like a solo cyclist or a wandering nomad—I felt like a university student again, carefree and slightly drunk. The music was terrible. The hangover was worse. But the moment was golden.

Even with a beer in hand and dancing like an idiot, I felt a tug. A shadow of absence. I kept laughing, but part of me was already listening for silence again. Staying in one place for too long didn't feel natural—but moving on did.

As the city swirled around me, I couldn't shake the feeling that I didn't quite belong. Vienna was magnificent—but it felt like stillness, there was no motion. It was like walking into a painting: breathtaking and timeless, but frozen. I needed to move.

The river pulled at me.

CHAPTER 6

Along the Danube

Number of days on the road: 23
Total distance covered: 1,961 km

After two days of pause in Vienna, I packed Shirley, clipped on the panniers, and wheeled her out onto the cycle path that hugged the Danube. The city dissolved behind me. The grand façades faded into farmland and wooded banks. The hush of the river returned.

The *Donauradweg*—the Danube Cycle Path—is one of the most famous in Europe, a well-maintained ribbon of asphalt stretching from Germany to the Black Sea. At times, it felt like I was floating along it: lulled by the rhythm of the pedals, the murmur of the river, and the dappled shade of trees overhead. Other days brought wind, rain, and long, punishing headwinds that turned every kilometre into a grind.

But always, the river was there. Wide. Steady. Indifferent.

It reminded me of something, something I hadn't allowed myself to fully admit: I wasn't just here for adventure; I hoped the motion would lead to peace. Part of me thought that the further I travelled, the closer I'd come to understanding why I'd left—and what I was really looking for.

The air shifted—it was cooler, touched with the earthy scent of the Danube and the faint whisper of coming rain. I pedalled on. The road unfolded gently. Time stretched. The silence deepened.

Other cyclists appeared now and then—locals on day trips, fellow tourers, Lycra-clad speed demons. We exchanged nods or waves. Small flickers of connection in a mostly solitary ride. And the solitude felt right. I was beginning to trust it.

At the beginning of my journey, the silence would have unnerved me. Now, it felt like company. The road no longer asked for chatter or distraction—it just wanted presence. With each quiet kilometre, I could feel something in me beginning to settle. I wasn't running anymore. I was riding toward something, even if I didn't know what that was yet.

The terrain wasn't always kind. Some stretches were smooth and breezy. Others were cracked and patchy—wounds in the path where tree roots had broken through the surface or floodwaters had gouged trenches into the tarmac. One section reeked of decay—on the roadside, a pile of sun-bloated fish had been abandoned near a weir. The stillness returned soon after, but it made the peace feel earned. There was tranquillity in the motion, in the simple forward rhythm of it all.

One evening, as the sun dipped low and gold across the river, I found a small campsite tucked just behind a thicket of trees. The Danube moved slowly nearby, the current gentle and rhythmic—like breath. I pitched my tent by the water's edge and sat cross-legged, dinner steaming in my lap, watching the light fade. The breeze teased the leaves above.

I ate slowly, the steam from my meal curling into the cooling air. A thought surfaced: I *hadn't spoken aloud all day*. The silence didn't feel empty. It felt honest.

This wasn't excitement or thrill. This was something else. Something quieter. A kind of belonging I hadn't known before.

By the time I reached Slovakia and then Hungary, I had begun to slow down. I was no longer pushing to get somewhere—I was starting to let the journey guide me instead. That felt new. Foreign, even. I'd spent so long outrunning silence that surrendering to it felt like a risk. But somehow, it didn't scare me anymore. The road was teaching me something I hadn't expected: to stop trying to outrun life, and instead, move with it. Like the Danube itself—never still, never rushed—just steady, and always moving forward.

Budapest gave me a soft landing—a city I'd visited before. It offered a real bed, a long shower and clean clothes. I took two nights off, wandered the city's familiar streets, and rested in its ruin bars and thermal baths. Then I was back on the path, riding south along the Danube once again.

One afternoon, I stopped in a small village—just a scatter of pastel-painted houses, a sun-drenched square, and a café with rickety wooden tables set outside it. The owner, a kind-faced woman with silver hair, greeted me with a smile and brought out a bowl of goulash and a cold beer.

The goulash came steaming in a cracked ceramic bowl, thick as lava, the paprika oil pooling in rust-red circles on top. I burned my tongue on the first bite, but I didn't care. The beer was crisp and cold. I sat for a long time, watching life unfold—children chasing a ball, an old man trimming his roses, laundry fluttering on a line. The simplicity was humbling. These people weren't rushing anywhere. They were rooted. It stirred something in me.

I pedalled away full, grateful, and strangely content. I wasn't heading anywhere in particular.

And for the first time since I'd left London, that felt like enough.

Then came the crash.

It happened without warning. A patch of sand had been poured lazily over a stretch of damaged cycle path, hiding deep ruts beneath. I hit it at speed.

Shirley's front wheel skidded. My balance went.

"Oh shit!"

One second, I was gliding. The next—slam.

Pain shot through my shoulder as gravel tore at my skin. My lip throbbed. My hands stung. The impact knocked the wind from me.

I lay there, stunned, staring at the sky. The sun blinked through the trees, indifferent. The breeze stirred the grass. Silence.

"Fuck. Fucking hell. Fuck," I muttered, half into the dust.

I didn't move for a minute. Then, slowly, I sat up, wincing. My left arm was grazed, blood trickling. My lip was bleeding—I wasn't sure if it was from impact or from biting it. I turned to Shirley, fearing the worst.

But somehow, miraculously, she was intact. She had a few scrapes but nothing major.

I got back on the bike, shaky but functional. The rest of the day dragged—every bump jarred my shoulder, every kilometre heavier than the last. But I kept moving.

That fall stayed with me—not just the bruises, but the realisation. This journey wasn't a guaranteed arc of beautiful moments and growth. It could turn on me at any moment. All I could do was be ready—or at least willing—to get up and keep going.

Late that evening, I crossed into Serbia. This border crossing wasn't like the others. Gone were the invisible EU borders. I was met with gates, guards, and a passport stamp that landed with a satisfying thunk. Finally, proof that I was further from home. Further out in the world.

I cycled the last stretch to Sombor under a hazy sky, past sunflower fields and villages as the day slowly slipped into evening. At a roadside station, I collapsed into shade, slurping warm water and watching the road shimmer in the heat. Despite the ache from my recent crash and the weight of the day, I felt strangely optimistic. I couldn't quite say why—but Serbia felt right.

The road south offered relief. Good tarmac, mostly flat, with the occasional breeze cutting across the plains of the Pannonian Basin. Despite the heat, I'd made good time. After 150 kilometres, I rolled into Novi Sad, my legs cramping, my shoulder still tender from the fall.

If the border had felt like a frontier, Novi Sad welcomed me like an old friend—no fanfare, just soft light, swaying trees, and a quiet confidence. The city didn't shout. It didn't need to.

I found a guesthouse tucked down a side street, ivy crawling up its whitewashed walls like it was trying to keep the place hidden. A hand-painted sign read *Dom Priatelja* —House of Friends. Fitting.

Marija, the owner, opened the door with the kind of tired smile that said she'd seen hundreds of road-weary travellers like me and still thought every one of us mattered. "*Dobrodošli,*" she said softly, waving me inside. She led me up a narrow wooden staircase to a small room with pale blue walls, a creaky wardrobe, and a bed topped with a hand-stitched quilt that smelled faintly of lavender and old paperbacks. Exactly what I needed.

After a long, scalding hot shower that seemed to rinse off not just the sweat but the stubborn tension that had gripped my shoulders for days, I changed into clean(ish) clothes and ventured into the city.

My legs ached, but something compelled me to walk—to move, to keep momentum. That was my only rule now.

Novi Sad had an ease to it, like it wasn't trying too hard. Locals strolled lazily along the pedestrianised boulevards, and café tables spilt out onto shaded squares. I walked to Petrovaradin Fortress—a 17th century fortress located on the banks of the Danube built to fend off the Ottomans. I clambered past moss-covered walls and graffiti-tagged bastions until I reached the city's ramparts. The Danube unspooled below—broad, slow, eternal. Somewhere in the distance, a saxophone played softly through the early evening air.

I breathed in. Not just air. Relief. Stillness. Progress.

Later that evening, I ate at a *kafana*—a local bistro Marija had recommended. The air inside was thick with the smell of grilled meat and wood smoke. I ordered *ćevapi,* classic minced meat sausages served with flatbread, raw onions, and a generous helping of *ajvar*—a tangy, smoky red pepper relish I was quickly falling in love with. A cold *Jelen Pivo* —a Serbian pale lager—washed it all down. Around me, locals talked and laughed, raising toasts and arguing about football. I felt invisible, but not in a lonely way. More like I'd slipped between the cracks of my old life and something new.

Back in my room, the quilt pulled up to my chin, I ran my fingers across the bandage on my shoulder. The fall had rattled more than just bones. But I was still here. Still riding. And for the first time in days, I felt light.

Where Novi Sad had offered softness, Belgrade hit me like a freight train.

I approached the capital on tired legs and frayed nerves, the road narrowing, traffic thickening. Horns blared. Buses swerved. Towering concrete blocks loomed beside crumbling Ottoman façades and fading Austro-Hungarian grandeur. The whole city buzzed with urgency—defiant, chaotic, electric.

Navigating my way into the centre felt like being dropped into a blender. I dodged trams, potholes, and pedestrians who walked like they were invincible. Shirley clattered and groaned beneath me, tyres bouncing over uneven cobbles. But strangely, it matched my mood. After weeks of gentle riverside calm, I was ready for something raw.

I found a traveller hostel tucked off a cobbled side street. A tall townhouse with cracked pastel paint and flower boxes straining with geraniums. Inside, it smelled like travellers do—of damp towels, cheap aftershave, instant noodles, and the faint optimism of people passing through. I liked it immediately.

That night, I wandered Belgrade's heart. Kalemegdan Fortress stood above the confluence of the Sava and Danube rivers like a weathered sentinel. I leaned against the ancient walls and watched boats drift along the rivers, their wakes folding into the water like whispered stories. Serbia didn't whisper, though—it hummed.

I passed through Knez Mihailova Street, where cafés sprawled out onto the pavements and buskers played melancholic Balkan jazz. I sat at a terrace with a tiny, bitter espresso and scrawled in my notebook, catching a fragment of thought that had been circling since Austria:

Can motion ever really replace meaning? Or just distract from its absence?

Back at the hostel, I met Zorana.

She sat behind the reception desk with legs crossed, dark hair over one shoulder, a novel resting in her lap. She glanced up and gave me a smile.

"Long ride?" she asked, eyeing the handlebar bag in my hand.

"London to here," I said, wiping sweat from my brow.

"On that thing?" She nodded toward Shirley, slouched awkwardly in the corner beneath a rack of umbrellas.

"That thing has a name, thank you very much. Shirley's temperamental, but loyal."

Zorana laughed, and just like that, we were talking like old friends. She poured me a shot of *rakija*—Serbia's national spirit—as if it were protocol.

Later, we sat on the rooftop under a sky heavy with stars and city haze. She told me about her hometown, Smederevo, its history and how it was changing. I told her about the crash. About how loud the silence can be after a fall. And what it's like to keep moving because you're afraid of what might catch you if you stop.

"So why are you really cycling across the world?" she asked.

I paused. I had answers for strangers—pre-packed ones. But hers didn't feel like a stranger's question.

"Because maybe…hopefully, by the time I get there—wherever *there* is—I'll recognise myself again."

She didn't respond right away. She just nodded slowly.

As I got up to leave, she handed me a scrap of paper with a phone number and an address.

"Come to Smederevo," she said. "My family will feed you. We'll show you the town. You can rest for a while. You look like you need it."

I tucked the note into my journal. I hadn't expected to find connection here in this noisy, beautiful, unrelenting city. But her invitation felt like more than kindness. It felt like an anchor.

A few days later, I arrived in Smederevo, where Zorana and her family greeted me with open arms. Their home was everything she had described and more—a sun-washed house with a wraparound balcony that overlooked the Danube. The railings were laced with potted herbs in chipped terracotta pots, and the scent of rosemary and grilled peppers drifted through the open kitchen window.

Zorana's parents welcomed me like an old friend. Her father poured a shot of *rakija* before I'd even put my bag down, and her mother ushered me inside with a warmth that made my chest ache with gratitude. It felt like being momentarily adopted—by people who had no reason to open their door other than simple, boundless kindness.

After a home-cooked lunch of stuffed peppers and soft white bread still warm from the oven, Zorana took me on a walking tour of her hometown. We wandered through the streets of Smederevo, past crumbling stone walls, fruit stalls bursting with late-summer colour, and locals chatting on benches beneath shady trees.

The highlight was the Smederevo Fortress—once the capital of Serbia, now a relic standing proud by the river. We climbed the old stone towers, where weeds push through cracks in the battlements, and looked out over the Danube, shimmering under a soft, late-afternoon haze.

"Beautiful, isn't it?" Zorana said, brushing her hair from her face.

"It really is," I replied, meaning it.

That evening, we joined her friends at a small local bar. The place throbbed with music and laughter—low ceilings, rattling speakers, candle wax pooled in old wine bottles. Her friends were lively, fast-talking, and full of mischief and warmth. We drank too much *rakija,* danced to Balkan pop, and shouted over each other with stories. Somewhere between the shots and the music, I felt a strange, fleeting sense of belonging.

"Come back one day," Zorana said as we walked home, her voice barely louder than the rustling leaves.

"I might," I said. But we both knew I wouldn't.

The next morning, I said goodbye. I didn't want to leave. Not just because of the comfort, or the food, or the company. But because it's hard to walk away from people who made you feel like you mattered—even for just a little while.

I rejoined the river, and the Danube continued to guide me east, slow but insistent, flowing between banks that were beginning to change again—it was less tame now, less cultivated. The terrain grew wild and brooding—as if the earth itself were bracing for something. So was I. Something was building in me, though I didn't yet know what shape it would take.

I was riding toward the Iron Gates. This is where the Danube meets the Carpathian Mountains, carving a 100-kilometre-long narrow gorge that forms part of the border between Serbia and Romania and rises up like a big gateway. It's a place where nature no longer whispers—it roars.

The road clung to the cliffs—it was so close to the edge in places that it felt like one wobble could end the whole journey. Tunnels, carved straight into the mountainside, swallowed me whole and spat me out blinking on the other side. The air was cool and sharp, and tinged with river water and stone.

Above me, the jagged limestone peaks leaned inward as if trying to meet across the water. Below, the Danube churned through the narrowing gorge—a ribbon of blue-green muscle, defiant and alive.

I pushed Shirley hard through this terrain. The climbs were brutal, the descents nerve-jangling. My legs screamed on the ascents, and my hands ached from squeezing the brakes on the way down. On one stretch, the tarmac had eroded into a web of cracks, and I had to dismount and walk Shirley carefully along a hard shoulder no wider than a gutter. My heart pounded—not from effort, but from exposure. One wrong step and I'd be tumbling toward the rocks.

It wasn't just about navigation anymore. It was about nerve.

And then, just as I rounded the final bend, there he was.

Decebalus.

Carved into the sheer rock face on the Romanian side, the face of the last Dacian king stared out across the Danube. Forty metres tall and chiselled directly into the cliff, his eyes were deep-set and fierce, his brow furrowed in eternal defiance. It was both ancient and strangely modern—a monument to resistance, watching over the passage of centuries.

I stopped and rested Shirley against the guardrail. And I just stood there.

There was something humbling about it. Something anchoring. Decebalus had once ruled these lands, defied Rome and carved his own path into history. And here I was—just a sunburnt man on a bicycle, trying to make sense of a broken heart and a longing for something more.

At that moment, I felt connected to him.

Not because I was a warrior. But because I, too, had chosen to resist the tide.

The rock face, the churning river, the quiet weight of it all—this didn't feel like sightseeing. It felt like witnessing. This was a reminder that everything I'd left behind—the job, the routine, the girl—was part of a former world. Now, I was somewhere else entirely. I was somewhere raw and real.

I lingered longer than I meant to. Long enough for the light to shift, long enough to feel some ancient quiet rise in my chest. I wasn't praying, but something in me was listening.

When I finally turned back to the road, the gorge began to widen. The cliffs softened. The Danube spread out again, relaxed, like a wild thing that had finally stopped fighting.

I looked for a ferry crossing point. It was time to change banks. To switch from Serbia to Romania. To keep moving east, to where new stories waited.

Under the watchful stone eyes of a long-dead king, I felt the quietest sense of peace I'd known in a long time.

CHAPTER 7

The Carpathian Test

Number of days on the road: 51
Total distance covered: 3,061 km

Romania unfolded before me like a journey back in time. Each turn revealed a landscape untouched by haste—rolling hills with shepherds silhouetted against the sky, guiding their flocks across land that seemed to move to a different rhythm. Then there was the clatter of wooden carts on gravel streets, the smell of freshly cut hay—this was a place where tradition still shaped the day.

In villages, dishevelled dogs roamed freely, their matted fur and wary eyes telling stories of hard living. Some were wild, others semi-domesticated, but all seemed to move with the same casual authority as the locals. They owned the streets as much as anyone else—they were a part of the fabric of the place, like the sagging cottages and ancient churches quietly holding their corners of time.

Occasionally, the dogs would chase me. It was annoying at first as I couldn't tell if they were being aggressive or playful as they barked and ran alongside me. Most of the time, this would last just a few moments before they would give up and turn back.

The weather turned against me as I pedalled along. First came the wind, gusting with a spiteful persistence, then the rain, which was cold, drenching and relentless. My waterproofs proved laughably optimistic. The road became a grind, the kind that gets inside your bones. I hunched over the bars, squinting through sheets of rain, counting down the kilometres like prayers.

By the time I reached Calafat, soaked and shaking, I was in survival mode. Everything had narrowed. My goals had shrunk to the next shelter, the next hot drink, the next hour without breaking. I wasn't adventuring anymore—I was enduring. And somewhere in that grind, I realised this wasn't just about kilometres. It was about a resilience I hadn't known I had.

A modest roadside hotel offered a hot shower that felt like salvation. It's funny how quickly the bar for happiness can drop and then, just as suddenly, be revived.

Later that evening, Calafat surprised me. A Romanian folk festival had taken over the streets—violins, tambourines, sizzling meat stalls, dancers in traditional dress, and the sound of joy all rang through the town.

The music caught in my throat. After so much grey and grit, the colour felt overwhelming. One minute, I was standing at the edge of the crowd; the next, I had let myself be pulled into their celebration.

I wandered around, drawn in by music and the smell of grilled bread, and was swept up by a group of young locals heading to a makeshift campfire on the banks of the Danube.

We sat in a loose circle, sharing drinks, stories, and songs on a battered guitar. The river moved quietly beside us, a silent witness to our revelry. It was one of those rare moments where connection doesn't need translation. We shared a common language of laughter and firelight.

Three days later, I was cutting through vast plains beneath a sky that stretched wider than I thought the sky could stretch. This was agrarian Romania—fields worked by hand or with horses dragging ploughs through the soil. Villages looked almost improvised, cobbled together over generations. Farmers moved through their routines with the kind of quiet efficiency that comes from years of repetition.

In one village, young boys herded cattle across open pastures, shadowed by massive guard dogs that eyed me with polite suspicion. The boys waved, their faces smudged with dirt, their eyes bright with curiosity. I waved back, oddly comforted. I was just another moving part in their day. No one cared where I was from. I was simply passing through, and that was enough.

However, as the light began to fade, I realised I'd made a mistake. A wrong turn somewhere.

I rolled into a small village where smiles gave way to curious stares. Not unfriendly, just... bemused. I stopped at a junction and pulled out my soggy map, trying to decipher where I'd gone wrong. A few villagers emerged to help—or just to watch the show. Between my "Franspanian" (a desperate blend of French, Spanish, and hand gestures) and their cheerful patience, we managed to work out a new route. A toothless man traced the path with a gnarled finger and nodded firmly, as if to say: *there—you're good now.*

Before leaving, I ducked into a crumbling shop. A tiny woman in a headscarf appeared from the back room, looking me up and down. After another round of miming, she handed me a bottle of milk, patted my shoulder, and smiled like I was her wayward son returning home.

As darkness fell, I followed a narrow track that ran alongside a tributary winding its way back toward the Danube. I found a perfect camping spot—flat ground, a line of trees for shelter, and silence stretching in all directions. I dragged Shirley off the road and set up camp by the riverbank. The cool air was a welcome change from the humidity of the day. I cooked a simple dinner, then sat by the water's edge, watching the sky fade to black. It felt like the whole day had folded into that one still moment. Just me, the river, and the soft hush of night.

But the silence was too complete. The usual night sounds—crickets, rustling leaves—had faded into something else.

Then, a howl. Low and unmistakable. Definitely a wolf. My blood turned to ice.

Another sound followed. Closer this time. A low growl.

Something was circling the tent.

I froze. I grabbed the only weapons I had—my bike pump and a tiny ultrasonic dog dazer. Neither exactly battle-ready, but better than nothing. I lay perfectly still, listening. Minutes passed. The rustling stopped. Silence returned—but I was tense, coiled.

At 2 a.m., I heard it again. Growling, scraping. At 5 a.m., one last slow circle around the tent. Closer this time. I didn't sleep. I just waited.

By dawn, the wolf had gone—but the fear lingered, curled tight in my stomach. When the light had softened the landscape and I'd finally let my eyes close, something slammed into the tent.

I shot upright, pulse racing, certain that this was it.

I grabbed the pump, unzipped the tent and lunged out—half-naked, wild-haired, and ready to defend my life—

—and came face-to-face with a dairy cow.

It blinked at me. I blinked at it. Then, utterly unfazed, it chewed on a corner of my tent and wandered off. A few more cows ambled by, totally indifferent to the drama.

From a nearby ridge, a herdsman waved.

I exhaled—and laughed. Long, loud, ridiculous laughter.

I'd survived wolves, rainstorms, and getting lost in three languages—only to be taken out by a dairy cow with attitude.

Romania, it seemed, had a sense of humour.

Having made a lengthy and unnecessary detour, I spent the next day or so catching up with my schedule to reach Bulgaria. The road followed the River Jiu until it rejoined the Danube, and from there I crossed back over the river, heading south toward the city of Veliko Tarnovo—a more direct route to Turkey and Istanbul.

I was still slightly haunted by the previous night's encounter. I started to wonder if I had imagined the wolf scenario, but I reminded myself that the sound was unmistakable. I remembered the roaming shepherds who usually had several large Kangal or mastiff sheepdogs to protect them from wolf attacks. I took solace in the fact that, despite the comical ending, I had dealt with the situation, and that gave me strength.

When I pedalled into the ferry terminal to cross the Danube, it was already unloading, so I didn't wait long to board.

As I disembarked on the Bulgarian side, I met six Polish cyclists—three girls and three guys in their early twenties—who were travelling from Poland to Istanbul. They were bound for the capital, Sofia, and I decided to ride with them for an hour or so, even though I was heading in a different direction.

When we reached my fork in the road, they pleaded with me to stay. I hadn't planned to visit Sofia, but I decided to stick with my new friends. I wasn't disappointed. On our way, we stopped in the city of Vratsa and picked up water and a few beers for a night's camping in the foothills of the Balkan Mountains.

They set about making enough spaghetti carbonara to feed a small army of hungry cyclists, and we devoured it enthusiastically, beers in hand, as we chatted by the fire and I played songs on my guitar.

I turned to Natalia. "So, what made you guys pick Istanbul?"

She grinned. "Seemed like a good excuse to ride through half of Europe."

Tomasz laughed. "And because we're all slightly mad."

"Cheers to that," I said, and we raised our cups.

We spent the next few days riding together towards Sofia, and I felt grateful for their company as we climbed into the mountains, which turned out to be among the most spectacular scenery of my trip. The road wound through cliffs and pine forest, offering views across valleys thick with trees and scattered with farmhouses. We stopped at cold-water springs and lit fires that, mercifully, didn't explode. We cooked sausages on sticks, laughed around the flames, and felt far from civilisation in the best possible way.

I was in my element. I've always loved the wilderness. This time, I loved sharing it.

The group treated me as one of their own. As a perfect example of their thoughtfulness, they made a pact to speak only English while I was with them—even to each other. They didn't need to, but it meant more than I could say.

We rolled downhill toward Sofia, where we spent a few days sightseeing and resting up. Saying goodbye wasn't easy.

I headed south, alone again, climbing into the Rila Mountains, which are set between five valleys and form a national park. I was aiming for Samokov. The route passed roadside springs where I could refill with fresh, ice-cold water whenever I needed it.

That night, I camped in the trees and took a moment to reflect.

Riding solo again after being with such a lively gang hit me hard. I loved being a solo traveller—mostly. But sometimes, especially somewhere awe-inspiring, I felt a pang of sadness that nobody else was there to feel it with me. Some moments are meant to be lived, not re-told. Lying on my back, staring up at the star-studded sky, I realised that, sometimes, gazing up at the night sky is something that should be shared too.

I turned my thoughts to the next leg of my trip—the road to Istanbul—and packed for a quick getaway, praying for an undisturbed night's sleep beneath the trees.

My prayer was answered. No wolves or cows attacked my tent that night.

The next morning, I climbed steadily toward the ski resort of Borovets, perched at 1,350 metres. It was the highest point I'd cycled to—though I hadn't realised until I saw a sign at the resort. I should've known: it was midsummer, and I needed a fleece.

The beauty of a long climb is the reward that follows. From Borovets, I enjoyed 40 kilometres of uninterrupted downhill, stopping now and then to cool the brakes and take in the views. The descent wasn't without incident—two enormous dogs chased me for several terrifying minutes. I pedalled like my life depended on it, which, frankly, it might have.

I pushed on toward Plovdiv, Bulgaria's second-largest city covering 138 kilometres in one day. When I reached the city, a fruit seller offered me a bag of peaches and refused to take any money. Another small act of kindness. Another reminder that the road was still good to me.

Plovdiv—often called "the city of the seven hills"—is one of Bulgaria's oldest and most enchanting cities. In the old town, cobbled streets weave past 19th-century houses with colourful façades and carved wooden bay windows. I explored the stunning Roman theatre, a partially restored amphitheatre once used for gladiator fights and performances. Not far away, the Roman stadium of Philippopolis nestled beneath the city—built by Emperor Hadrian of Hadrian's Wall fame.

I lingered in Plovdiv for two days, soaking up its charm before setting off once more—this time toward the Greek border.

As I crossed into Greece, the landscape shifted, and I felt the change instantly. The countryside softened. Greek houses, reminiscent of sleepy Spanish villas, began to appear. Olive groves basked under the late-summer sun, the silvery leaves shimmering in the breeze. The villages were rustic, with whitewashed walls and cobbled alleyways, each one more picturesque than the last.

Then, I made a mistake.

CHAPTER 8

Crossing into Turkey

Number of days on the road: 60
Total distance covered: 3,951 km

Taking a quiet road out of a Greek village, I suddenly found myself in Turkey. No guards. No fences. Just a gentle bend—and I was across the border.

My heart slammed into my chest. It was the absurdity of it—a border crossed without knowing it. A nation entered by accident. The moment should have felt monumental, but instead, it felt like I'd slipped between the cracks. My journey had just shifted continents, and I didn't even have a photo to show for it.

There were no signs, no patrols, no one watching. But I didn't want to push my luck. I spun Shirley around and pedalled faster than I had in days, praying my accidental crossing wouldn't turn into something more serious.

I made it back to Marasia, a sleepy Greek town nestled by a tributary of the river Arda. There, I found a café and a quiet park—the perfect spot to rest before attempting to cross the border properly the next day.

The café owner brought me a plate of grilled *souvlaki*—tender marinated pork skewers, served with fresh salad and warm crusty bread. After dinner, I set up camp on the riverbank and took a long, cool dip to wash off the dust of the day.

As I lay back on the grass, the water flowing nearby and the stars beginning to blink into view, I felt calm again. Balanced. Between borders. Between moments. Between where I'd been—and whatever came next.

The following morning, I eased Shirley through the narrow lanes of Kastanies, the Greek border village felt half-awake—stone walls glistening with moisture, geraniums nodding in windowsills, the air thick with the scent of wet leaves and soil. Old men in wool cardigans sat beneath a café's blue awning, sipping tea and eyeing me with expressions that were part curiosity, part quiet amusement. One man raised two fingers in greeting without lifting his gaze from the local newspaper.

Then came the border. Not one of those invisible, EU-era suggestions, but a real one—wire fences, checkpoint booths, a stretch of tarmac watched by men in boots with guns. As I rolled to a halt, a Turkish guard stepped from his booth, squinting at me like I'd arrived by penny-farthing. His uniform was immaculate, his moustache enviably sharp.

"Passport," he said flatly. No smile.

I handed it over, offering the sort of weary grin that only works in some countries. He studied the pages, then looked up at my sun-worn face, then back down. A nod. A stamp. A curt wave.

"Welcome to Turkey."

The crossing itself was a no-man's-land of cracked tarmac and chain-link fences, but 100 metres in, the world changed. The road widened. The colours deepened. The signage grew angular and unfamiliar. A call to prayer rang faintly in the distance, rising above the low thunder of trucks.

The city of Edirne was chaos wrapped in sunlight. The scent hit me first—grilled meat, cumin, exhaust fumes, and fresh bread. Then the noise. Horns, hawkers, the flutter of pigeons as they scattered from a plaza. The Selimiye Mosque loomed ahead like some celestial anchor, its minarets piercing the sky, its dome holding court over the city.

I leaned Shirley against a bollard and stood in the square for a moment, completely still. Around me, everything moved: shoppers with plastic bags, veiled women chatting outside bakeries, men hawking lottery tickets or polishing shoes beneath striped umbrellas. A child tugged at his mother's sleeve, pointing at me. The woman gave me a polite, tight-lipped smile—the kind reserved for oddities, not threats.

I ducked into a worn-out shop with a rotating rack of postcards out front and bought a SIM card. The teenager behind the counter wore headphones connected to a CD player and barely looked up from the magazine he was reading. When I asked if the SIM card would work, he shrugged.

"It works," he said, then paused. "Unless it doesn't."

A few kilometres beyond the bustle, I pulled into a roadside café tucked beneath a striped awning, its colours faded by years of sun. Grape vines crept along the edge of the roof, their leaves twitching in the warm breeze. The air was thick with the smell of tobacco. Inside, a group of elderly men sat at low tables, hunched over backgammon boards, their fingers worn smooth from decades of dice rolls. The only sounds were the clinking of glasses and the scrape of chair legs on stone.

I took a plastic seat under the awning and lit a cigarette. A teenager in a grey t-shirt approached with a notepad and a tray of small, empty hourglass-shaped tea glasses. I asked for an *Ayran*—a savoury yoghurt drink, and he returned almost instantly, beads of condensation clinging to the cup.

Minutes later, a plate of lamb köfte arrived, steam rising from the charred meat. The smell—a mix of cumin, smoke, and something faintly sweet—hit me first. Grilled onions, sliced tomato, and warm bread rounded out the plate. I ate slowly, savouring each bite. The meat was tender and peppery, the onions caramelised. Everything tasted like it had been made with care.

The old men glanced up now and then. One of them nodded once, then turned back to his game.

When I reached for my wallet, three of them stood at once, waving me off. "*Misafir*," one said. Guest.

I paused, hand on my wallet, but there was no arguing. This was settled. I sat back, stunned.

There was no fuss, no conversation. Just quiet generosity on a dusty roadside in a country I'd barely entered. I watched them return to their game, tea glasses clinking gently, dice tumbling across the board.

For a moment, everything stilled. I didn't feel like a stranger. I had never felt welcome like this before.

***

The land changed quickly. The rich green gave way to dry scrub and dusty hills. The air thickened and calmed. Villages became sparser, and water harder to find. The road was cracked in places, laced with gravel, and the climbs were relentless—never steep enough to brag about, but long and nagging and endless.

By mid-morning each day, the heat was oppressive. Sweat soaked my shirt, ran down my legs and collected at the small of my back. The headwind arrived not with drama, but with steady resistance—a constant shove that made every kilometre feel like five.

My speed dropped. Eleven kilometres an hour. Ten. On some climbs, it felt like I was barely moving. I cursed the hills. I cursed the wind. I cursed Shirley and every decision that had led me to this point. The joy of the road began to erode, and it was replaced by something closer to obligation.

One night, I pitched my tent on a scrap of dry land behind a cluster of thorn bushes. The air was dead still and alive with flies. I lay flat in the tent, fully clothed, limbs sticky with sweat and dust, and I was unable to sleep. The buzzing, which sounded like static, never stopped.

By morning, I was brittle and felt hollowed out. I moved slowly, packed mechanically and climbed back on my bike like it was something I was being forced to do.

The road narrowed, shouldered by loose gravel. I pedalled in silence, lost in a haze of discomfort and a little unaware of what was going on around me.

I heard the lorry before I saw it—a low, growling engine that didn't slow. The horn came late, loud and sudden. The blast of air that followed knocked me sideways. My front wheel dipped off the tarmac into the gravel, and there was no time to correct it.

My body hit the ground hard, all momentum gone in a heartbeat. The impact jarred through my right side—elbow, hip, knee—and I rolled once before coming to a stop. Shirley clattered into the ditch, metal on stone.

I lay there, blinking up at the sky, stunned. Not again, I thought. Not like Hungary.

This time it was worse. My right hand throbbed in a way that made my stomach churn. My thumb had already started to swell, and I couldn't move it. The pain was sharp, deep. This wasn't just a knock; this was something more.

I sat up, swore under my breath, and checked Shirley. She had a bent front rack and a scraped bar end. But, miraculously, she was still rideable.

I taped my wrist to the handlebars using a roll of duct tape from my pannier, just enough to keep control. My hand hung limp. Every bump sent a fresh jolt up my arm.

I rode on. One-handed. Angry. Embarrassed. On the edge of tears. It felt like I'd come to the end of something.

The idea of quitting crept in for the first time. Of throwing in the towel and calling for help. Istanbul felt impossibly far. My energy reserves were gone. There was no one to say, "You're okay. You've got this." On the contrary, I am sure at one point, a stray dog muttered the words, "*go home you loser*". It was all in my head of course, tiredness can do that to you.

A few kilometres down the road, I passed a small roadside shack with a faded sign advertising ice cream. I pulled over, more instinctively than from desire. Two young lads behind the counter looked up, wide-eyed. I must've looked like I'd been in a fight. And I had been—with the road, and I'd lost.

They grinned and handed me a cone and refused payment. I sat under a sun-bleached umbrella, licking the ice cream slowly, letting the cold numb the pain in my mouth where I'd bitten my lip in the crash.

The boys asked about the bike, pointed at my bandaged hand, and mimed crashing with mock horror. I laughed despite myself. Their good humour was infectious.

That ice cream was a turning point.

It wasn't a fix. But it gave me the impetus to get myself to Istanbul. My heart had refilled—just a little.

I got back on my bike.

The road into the city began innocuously enough—flat, almost forgiving, with long straight stretches and a faint breeze nudging at my back. But that illusion didn't last.

Within 30 kilometres of the Bosphorus, everything changed.

The traffic thickened, gradually at first, then all at once—as if someone had twisted the dial from "country lane" to "urban hellscape." Trucks thundered past me with inches to spare. Horns blared constantly, not in warning but out of habit. It was a language of impatience that didn't care whether you were in a car or astride a bicycle with a taped-up wrist and a thousand-yard stare.

I kept my head down and pushed on, following signs for the city centre, the flow of vehicles funnelling me into tighter lanes, narrower shoulders, and faster traffic. There were no cycle paths here—just crumbling kerbs, potholes, and sheer bloody-mindedness.

I shouted once—loud and wordless—at a taxi that nearly clipped my panniers in a near miss. The driver didn't flinch. He was already onto his next near miss.

I was riding on adrenaline and anger. My legs ached. My hand was screaming. My clothes were soaked through with sweat. But I was close. So close, and my determination and will were returning like a warmth from within.

Istanbul's skyline appeared in fragments at first—minarets rising like needles, a distant glint of blue sea, a jumble of rooftops cascading down the hillside. Then the road crested, and suddenly, there it was:

Istanbul.

The Bosphorus glimmered beneath the midday sun, slicing the city in two like a ribbon of steel and salt. Ferries crossed its surface like ants on a picnic cloth. To the east: Asia. To the west: Europe. I had ridden across a continent.

I pulled over at a wide promenade near Sarayburnu, a point marking the tip of the peninsula where the Golden Horn estuary meets the strait. I dismounted slowly, stiffly, and unwrapped the tape from my wrist with a wince. I let Shirley slump against a bench.

Then I walked—limped, really—to the water's edge.

I knelt and dipped my hands into the Bosphorus.

The water was cold. It stung the cuts on my fingers. The sensation made me gasp, made it real.

I had made it. Four thousand one hundred and forty kilometres. Over 50 days. From London to the edge of Asia, by bike, by willpower, by whatever was left in the tank after everything else had been spent.

I sat on the concrete, my head bowed, letting the moment sink in. My clothes were caked in salt. My thumb was turning purple. My heart was thudding, not with exertion anymore, but with something deeper. Something like peace.

And then the tears came.

They weren't dramatic. Just slow, involuntary, tired tears.

They tasted like seawater. Like triumph. Like grief. Like joy.

I laughed through them—I was half-mad, probably. I must have looked completely deranged to passers-by. But I didn't care.

This wasn't for them.

This moment was mine.

A man limped past, saw my bike, saw my face, and gave me a thumbs-up. I nodded back. No words needed.

I stayed there a long time. Letting the chaos of Istanbul swirl around me. Letting it be noisy and smoggy and beautiful.

Then, eventually, I stood. Picked Shirley up. Wheeled her along the waterfront, slow and steady.

The line had been drawn. One continent crossed. I was excited about what lay ahead.

CHAPTER 9

The City In Between

Number of days on the road: **62**
Total distance covered: **4,140 km**

Istanbul wasn't just a pause; it was a jolt, a sensory riot. The city thrummed with a mesmerising collision of East and West, of ancient stone and neon signage, of centuries-old mosques pressed up against late-night cafés. Boats bobbed along the Bosphorus, ferrying passengers between continents like it was the most ordinary thing in the world. It was not ordinary. Nothing about Istanbul is ordinary.

The hostel district was buzzing. Backpackers sprawled on cushions with beers in hand, swapping tales of border crossings and food poisoning and love affairs on mountaintops. I checked into a modest place in the Sultanahmet neighbourhood with a rooftop terrace. It overlooked the Bosphorus, the Hagia Sophia, and the Blue Mosque —the domes and spires catching the last pink-gold light of day. The call to prayer drifted across rooftops like smoke.

That evening, I was sitting on that rooftop, sipping a cold Efes beer, when a bearded man in his forties with long grey hair and a battered cotton shirt appeared like he'd been searching for me.

"You've gotta be Rob," he said.

I blinked. "Er… yes?" I wasn't sure where this conversation was heading.

"I'm Bill," he grinned. "Everywhere I've been for the last month, people have been talking about this other British cyclist who's always a couple of days ahead of me. Ferry operators. Locals. Other cyclists. I had to catch up with you eventually."

As it turned out, Bill wasn't your average traveller. Years earlier, he'd backpacked through Africa and driven across the Sahara in a half-owned Peugeot 504 that he'd bought in Marrakech. He'd bandaged gunshot wounds in Zaire, bribed Algerian border guards, and picked up dysentery in the process. The cycle to India that he was currently on had started, inevitably, as a drunken idea in a pub.

As Bill and I discussed our experiences further, we realised it wasn't just our journeys that aligned. Like me, Bill had been handed a redundancy payout when his employer closed its UK office, and so Bill had decided to turn his drunken idea into reality.

We hit it off immediately. It had been weeks since I'd had a real laugh with someone who truly got what it was like to be on a two-wheeled nomadic adventure. Not just the roads or the weather, but everything in between. I hadn't realised how much I'd missed the camaraderie of shared madness.

The next day, we visited a bike shop together to carry out some essential maintenance. We barely made it five minutes from the hostel before disaster struck. Bill caught his front wheel in a tram track and performed an acrobatic faceplant that sent him tumbling through the air.

"It was like watching a slow-motion Superman audition," I said, helping to peel him off the cobbles.

He dusted himself off, grinning. "That's one way to make an entrance."

The smell of grease and oil filled the small, cramped shop, mingling with the scent of old rubber and camaraderie. We set to work repairing our bikes. Shirley was in dire need of some attention. I replaced the chain, fixed the brake pads, and re-oiled every moving part, taking my time to ensure everything was in working order. I checked all the nuts and bolts on the racks and made sure everything was as tight and fastened as it should be. By the time we were done, Shirley was gleaming, and I couldn't help but feel a surge of pride at how far we had come together.

Heading further east from Turkey meant travelling through Iran or into Georgia or Armenia. Accordingly, in a dimly lit internet café that smelled of sweat and ancient circuit boards, Bill and I filled out the forms for our Iranian visas—knowing full well they might never come. If rejected, the only way for either of us to travel further east, other than by plane, would mean detouring north to Azerbaijan and taking the ferry across the Caspian Sea to Kazakhstan.

Istanbul was the perfect place to pause and regroup. But it was more than that; it was magnificent. A city with the weight of empires in its stonework and the pulse of youth in its streets. The Grand Bazaar was a sensory overload with its labyrinth of narrow alleys and crowded stalls, each one more colourful and chaotic than the last. The air was thick with the scent of spices—cumin, cinnamon, and saffron mingling in a heady blend that was almost intoxicating. The sounds of haggling filled the air, the voices of vendors and customers rising and falling in a constant rhythm. I bought a few essentials—fresh underwear, a vest, and a new cap for sun protection. I ate grilled meat by the Galata Bridge, the smoke rising from food stalls blending with diesel fumes and sea salt.

One evening, while sitting in a square near Sultanahmet, I watched the Blue Mosque and Hagia Sophia trade shadows as the sun dipped behind them. Each minaret, each dome, felt sacred. Not just for what they were, but for where I was—4,000 kilometres from home and a whole continent behind me.

Bill and I spent our days exploring: Beyoğlu, Galata, the New City. At night, we drank rakı on rooftops and shared dinners with friends we'd met in the hostel. One night, we met two Turkish women, Manolya and her friend Simge, who took us on a whirlwind tour of the nightlife at Taksim Square: rooftop bars and tiny *meyhanes*—Turkish taverns, tucked behind shuttered shop fronts. The music was so loud it reverberated in your bones. I danced like someone who didn't care what tomorrow looked like.

Over the next day, on the hostel's rooftop terrace, Bill and I planned the next leg of the ride. We spread maps between bottles of beer and bowls of peanuts. The Black Sea coast called to us. It promised fewer tourists, more hardship, wilder roads.

It was decided. We would ride out of Istanbul together the next day.

CHAPTER 10

The Black Sea: Together

Number of days on the road: 68
Total distance covered: 4,140 km

When the time came to leave Istanbul, we were waved off by our new friends from the hostel. Bikes weren't allowed on the bridge across the Bosphorus, so we took a small, crowded ferry across the strait. The boat ride was a welcome respite. I looked back at the stunning view of the city bathed in sunlight as we sailed away from Europe and towards Asia. The breeze off the water was refreshing, a pleasing contrast to the hot, humid city we were leaving. Despite only being a 30-minute ferry ride away, the small village of Anadolu Kavağı, where we disembarked, was a world away from the bustling metropolis of Istanbul. Nestled on the banks of the Bosphorus, it was a quiet, peaceful place, with narrow streets lined with stone houses.

Our first challenge was the steep climb up to Yoros Castle, a fortress perched high on a hill overlooking the

Bosphorus and the Black Sea. The road up was brutal, with a 20 per cent gradient that tested every ounce of strength that Bill and I had. But the view from the top was worth every drop of sweat. From the castle, we could see the point where the Bosphorus met the Black Sea, the waters of the two merging in a swirl of blue and green. The castle itself was a relic of ancient times, its crumbling walls and weathered stones a reminder of the many empires that had fought to control this strategic point.

We were so heady with delight that, when leaving the site, we made a critical error in judgement. We took what we thought was a shortcut. Instead, we found ourselves on a nightmarish detour—a stretch of road that was nothing more than a jumble of rocks and so narrow that it rattled our bones and made cycling almost impossible. Bill would later call it "a slight navigational miscalculation". It took us two hours to cover 10 kilometres, our bodies aching from the constant jarring. But eventually, we stumbled onto a deserted beach, hidden behind a crumbling goat track. The sand was soft and cool underfoot, pocked with driftwood and sea glass. The tide was low, the waves gentle. We peeled off our shoes and stood in silence for a beat, letting the sheer, unexpected beauty of it wash over us. It was a perfect camping spot.

That night, as we sat around a campfire on the beach, the smell of saltwater in the air and the sound of the waves a constant lullaby, we talked about the journey so far and the road ahead. Bill was a kindred spirit, someone who understood the thrill of travelling the open road on his own—and the challenges that came with it. We shared stories, laughed, and cooked a simple meal over the fire, the warmth of the flames warding off the chill of the night.

"Did you hear that?" Bill asked, breaking the comfortable silence.

"What?" I replied, straining to listen.

Then it came again, a distant howl that sent a shiver down my spine. The sound was unmistakable—the call of a wolf. Bill, who had not yet encountered such wildlife on his journey, looked uneasy. But with memories of my own close encounters, I was strangely calm. The howls seemed far off, and I reassured him, confident that we were safe for the night. We laughed it off, but the presence of those wild creatures, somewhere out there in the darkness, added an edge to the night. Something about the flickering fire, the wolf howls in the distance, and Bill as a companion made me feel comfortable. I wasn't a lonely cycling nomad anymore. Now we were two. We crawled into our tents, the exhaustion of the day quickly pulling us into sleep.

Morning came with the gentle light of dawn filtering through the fabric of the tent, casting a warm glow over everything. I awoke to find paw prints in the sand around our tents. But there was no sign of any wolves, only the serene beauty of the beach and the vast expanse of the

Black Sea before us. As I lay on my inflatable camping mattress, gazing out at the water, I felt a deep sense of contentment. This was what the journey was about—these quiet moments of connection with nature, where the world felt both vast and intimate at the same time.

Breakfast was a simple affair—bread, cheese, and the last of our tea. The air was fresh and salty with the aroma of the forest that bordered the beach. As we ate, the sun rose higher in the sky, its warm rays chasing away the last of the morning chill. I found myself daydreaming about sharing these moments with someone special, someone who would appreciate the quiet beauty of this place as much as I did. But for now, that person would have to be Bill, my long-haired, goatee-bearded, hippy road buddy.

We set off, the road rough and bumpy, each jolt a reminder of the harshness of the terrain. The previous night's rest had done little to ease the aches in our muscles, and the road seemed determined to shake us from our saddles. But, despite the physical toll, the beauty of the landscape made it all worthwhile. We passed through small villages nestled in the hills, their red-tiled roofs peeking out from the greenery, the air filled with wood smoke. The road hugged the coastline, offering breathtaking views of the cliffs that jutted out into the sea, their jagged faces weathered by centuries of wind and water.

We stopped for lunch in the old town of Şile, a small fishing village with a rocky beach and a lighthouse that stood sentinel over the coast. We parked the bikes near a row of fishing boats that had been pulled up on the sand, their nets drying in the sun. A salty breeze stirred the awnings of a tiny tavern where we ordered grilled fish and a lemony salad. The smell of charcoal and fishing nets mingled in the air as we sat on creaky wooden chairs, boots off, our feet sore and sand-dusted.

It was a few days later in the town of Ağva, whilst having breakfast, that Bill spotted Emrys, a blond Australian cyclist in his mid-twenties. Rather than panniers, Emrys had been towing all of his belongings in a small trailer connected to his bike since he had started his trip in Germany. It was efficient.

We quickly fell into conversation, sharing stories of our travels and the challenges we had faced along the way. Emrys was easy-going, with a quick smile and a laid-back attitude that fit well with our little group. Together, the three of us cycled on, passing through fields of hazelnut orchards and fruit that dominated either side of the road; the air smelled of ripening fruit and freshly tilled soil.

The road took us over steep cliffs, with climbs of 200 to 400 metres that tested our endurance as we climbed higher and higher, only to be rewarded with stunning views of the sea far below. Each headland was a challenge: the roads snaked upwards in a series of switchbacks that left us breathless and drenched in sweat. But the downhill rides were exhilarating, the wind whipping past as we hurtled towards our next destination. The sound of the sea crashing against the cliffs below was a constant companion, a reminder of the power of the natural world.

We covered 60 kilometres that day, a slow and gruelling pace from the incessant inclines that left us exhausted by nightfall. The setting sun cast long shadows across the landscape, the sky painted in hues of orange and pink, the air warm and hazy. As we set up camp on a secluded beach, the familiar smell of the sea and sand filling our nostrils, I couldn't help but marvel at the beauty of the world around us. The day had been tough, but it was moments like these that made it all worthwhile.

A few days later, after stopping at a local eatery for lunch, I felt a sudden wave of nausea wash over me. The meal, which had seemed so appetising at first, now sat like a lead weight in my stomach. By the time we set off again, I was feeling decidedly off-colour, and it wasn't long before I had to stop. I told Bill and Emrys to carry on without me, insisting that I would catch up later. They reluctantly agreed, leaving me to rest in my tent as the heat of the day baked me like a turkey in an oven.

The afternoon passed in a blur of discomfort, the nausea turning to full-blown vomiting that left me weak and shaking. I spent the night tossing and turning, unable to find any relief from the sickness that gripped me. The smell of the food I had eaten earlier lingered, an uncomfortable reminder of my condition. By morning, I was exhausted and dehydrated, but determined to carry on.

After a delayed start, I felt considerably better and put in a long shift on the bike. At the end of a gruelling day, I spotted a familiar red blob in the distance. It was Bill and Emrys, setting up camp in a field. They had made a wrong turn earlier in the day, taking a long detour that had allowed me to catch up.

"Well, well, well! Look who's here! Lost and found, huh?" I teased as I approached.

"Hi! That worked out okay, didn't it... we ended up on the scenic route without even realising it," Bill said, grinning back.

"Outsmarted by the roads again. But, hey, at least we found a nice spot to camp," Emrys added with a chuckle.

We laughed together, despite our shared exhaustion, finding humour in the challenges we'd faced over the past few days. I brewed a pot of tea with the last of my English tea bags. Bill played "Have a Cuppa Tea" by The Kinks on a small speaker, and we sat and then danced around the campfire, sipping our drinks and enjoying the warmth of the flames. The smell of the burning wood and the salty air was a comforting aroma that made me feel at home, even in this far-flung corner of the world.

The following days were a mix of physical highs and lows as we continued along the coast. The road was rough and bumpy, testing our endurance as we navigated the uneven terrain. But the scenery remained breathtaking.

We covered 700 kilometres in a week—a punishing pace that left us weary but satisfied. Our goal was a small cove near Doğanyurt. It was a charming little harbour, tucked between forested bluffs, but the final approach nearly broke us.

The road had been freshly tarred and, in theory, gritted. But somewhere along the line, they'd clearly run out of grit. What should have been a smooth descent turned into a slow-motion slog. Hot black tar glued itself to our tyres like molasses, which then slung upwards in foul streaks that splattered our bikes, legs, and panniers. With every crank, our drivetrains sounded more like coffee grinders.

Every few minutes, we stopped to scrape off the buildup with twigs, keys, and even tent pegs—but the road fought back. The heat softened everything. Our pedals stuck, and the air smelled like melting tyres.

Then Emrys went down. One second, he was upright, the next, he was sliding through the muck like a rag doll in an oil slick. When he finally stood, drenched from chin to boot in tar, we didn't know whether to check for injuries or just burst out laughing. He looked like he'd crawled out of a chimney.

As we limped into Doğanyurt after 20 kilometres on the tar road, a kind Turkish man took pity on us. He emptied his chainsaw of petrol, offering it to us so we could clean off some of the worst of the tar. Further along the road, we found a petrol station where we bought more fuel to continue the cleaning process. It was a long, messy task, but by the end of it, we had managed to get our bikes back into some semblance of working order. We set up camp on a beach, using a nearby tap to wash ourselves and our clothes, grateful for the chance to rest after the ordeal.

By the time we reached the weathered seaside town of İnebolu a few days later, the air felt different—it was cooler, quieter, and tinged with something like finality. Bill was heading inland to Ankara, where his girlfriend would be flying in to meet him. We had ridden together for almost two weeks. We both knew the parting was coming, but neither of us had said it aloud until that morning.

We found a patch of grass behind his hotel, overlooking the harbour. Fishing boats bobbed in the swell, their nets hanging like tired flags. The garden was simple—plastic tables, a few crooked parasols, the clink of glasses from somewhere inside. We sat on a wooden bench that still smelled faintly of varnish, our bikes leaned together nearby, paint-scratched and tar-speckled.

A cold beer sweated in my hand. We didn't say much. Just let the sounds of the town wash over us—the calls of gulls, a child shouting in the street, the distant thrum of a scooter engine climbing a hill.

"I'll miss the tea dances," Bill said, finally, with a wry smile.

"Don't die in a ditch," I replied, raising my bottle in mock solemnity.

He chuckled, took a last swig, and wheeled his bike into the road. And just like that, he was gone.

The journey continued. But something had shifted. Bill had been a kindred spirit—a road philosopher, a chaos magnet, a friend. Without him, the road felt a little quieter.

Emrys and I turned east. The cliffs waited.

The next few days brought a change in the landscape—the mountains began to diminish, and the road flattened out, allowing us to pick up speed. But just as we began to make progress, the weather turned against us. A sudden thunderstorm lashed us with rain, soaking our equipment and leaving us cold and miserable. My tent, already on its last legs, suffered a final blow when I broke a tent pole while setting up camp in the rain. It was a frustrating end to a long day, and I knew I would need to find a solution before continuing on.

Sinop was our next major stop, a small town perched on the narrowest point of the Black Sea. We checked into a cheap hotel, grateful for the chance to shower, dry off and warm up. I washed my clothes in the shower and set about updating my journal with the smell of wet clothes filling my room.

In Sinop, after enjoying a satisfying brunch of *börek*—the Turkish pastry that had become a staple, this time filled with creamy feta—I parted ways with Emrys. We had been travelling together for several weeks, but I was ready to be on my own again. I thought that I needed solitude and the chance to reflect on my journey so far, and to find my own rhythm once more.

CHAPTER 11

The Black Sea: Alone

Number of days on the road: 81
Total distance covered: 4,945 km

W*hoosh*! A truck zoomed past me far too close for comfort.

I had reached a series of tunnels that bored straight through the cliffs, some stretching over three kilometres long. There were no pedestrian walkways. Just two narrow lanes, no lighting, and a speed limit nobody obeyed.

The next truck tore past me like a freight train, its horn detonating in the confined space. The sound ricocheted off the concrete walls, a thunderclap that hit me in the chest. My ears rang. The pressure wave sucked at my panniers and made Shirley wobble. Diesel fumes clung to the inside of my nose and throat.

Another truck. Closer this time. The headlights carved through the gloom like blades. If any of them drifted a few inches towards me, or didn't see me in time, I'd be smeared against the tunnel wall like roadkill.

I stared dead ahead and kept pedalling, gripping the bars in blind faith. Every time I burst out into the daylight, I let out a wild "Whoo hoo! I'm Alive!"—half joy, genuine relief.

It had now been three months since I'd left home. The days —with all the early starts and aching legs—were starting to blur together. Occasionally, I missed the quiet intimacy of familiar voices and the ease of having someone beside me to say, "Look at that."

Sometimes I wanted to fly home for an hour. One hug. One pint. One ordinary evening. Then return. Just a pause. Not an ending. But time doesn't pause.

At night I lay there, staring through the mesh at the stars, trying to find Orion or the Plough, something that connected me to home. They were always there, those constellations. Silent, unchanged and somehow comforting.

Life was simple. Brutally so. And in that simplicity, even the tiniest joys felt magnified. Whenever things just started to feel like they were getting tough, a moment of magic seemed to arrive: a wave from a lorry driver, a child shouting hello, the fizz of a cold sugary drink when my legs were shot. Men in tea shops who offered smiles and endless refills. Sunrises that arrived like promises, and sunsets that felt like closure. Messages from home that landed at just the right time.

Just as my emotional tank of energy was running dry, a kind act or gesture would top me right back up again.

Somewhere between Sinop and Trabzon, the road flattened out, and I started making progress again—100-kilometre days with my legs grinding steadily forward.

Ramadan was now in full swing, people were excited and the waves and smiles continued. The only downside for me, was that the cafés I relied on for sustenance were shut during the day. I made do with petrol station snacks and corner shop biscuits. I quickly had a new found respect for those that fasted during this magnificent holy month. I only wished I was able to harness the same willpower.

After a number of days, I arrived in the city of Trabzon where I took a few days rest.

I visited the majestic Sümela Monastery, built high up into the cliffs of Mount Mela. To Access this UNESCO World Heritage site I embarked on a long and arduous walk up the hillside on narrow trails and stairways. Also known as the Monastery of Virgin Mary, it is a religious and cultural landmark that has been perched on this sheer cliff face of the Zigana Mountains since 385 AD. Its construction is attributed to two Greek monks who discovered an icon of the Virgin Mary in a nearby cave. Since then, the Sümela Monastery has served as an important centre for Greek Orthodox Christianity. The monastery's stunning architecture captivated me as I explored its multiple chambers, chapels and caves. From the top, the view stretched across the lush evergreen forests of the Altindere Valley. I felt small, like a passing traveller looking up at something that had endured for centuries.

While in Trabzon, I also undertook some necessary domestic tasks. I sorted out a makeshift tent pole by duct-taping a piece of piping to the broken pole, effectively like a splint. I picked up a slightly better raincoat, long trousers, a battery-powered MP3 player with new music on it in the market, and ordered new tyres to be delivered to the Georgian capital, Tbilisi, since mine were now bound together with strips of cloth.

There was something deeply comforting about putting things back in order. A raincoat that I hoped wouldn't leak, tyres that would hold together, a few new songs to keep me company. They weren't luxuries, just small reinforcements—but they made me feel ready again. Every adjustment, every fix, felt like quietly telling myself: you can keep going.

I also gave Shirley a deep clean, scrubbing away the layers of grit that had built up over weeks on the road. Watching the frame shine back at me, I felt as if I'd knocked some of the weight off my own shoulders too. Small rituals like that reminded me that progress wasn't only measured in kilometres.

With the onset of better weather, I was ready to make progress. Trabzon had been an invaluable stop in keeping me fuelled physically and mentally, and able to continue onwards.

But Turkey had one final farewell in store for me. As I cycled through the rain-soaked streets towards the border, I hit a tram line at 25 km/h and went sliding down the road. The fall was painful, but thankfully there was no other traffic to collide with, and the slickness of the wet road saved me from losing several layers of skin.

I picked myself up, shaken but unbroken, and continued on my way, determined not to let a small mishap spoil my memories of Turkey and its incredible people.

Turkey had taken a lot out of me, but it had also given me so much

CHAPTER 12

Vodka & Kindness

Number of days on the road: 90
Total distance covered: 5,632 km

Night had already fallen as I crossed the border into Georgia. Despite the late hour, the guards greeted me with warm smiles and a surprising enthusiasm. They peppered me with questions, curious about my journey so far and my plans ahead. Their friendliness was a balm for my tiredness, giving me the energy to push through the darkness toward Batumi.

The anticipation of entering a new country had spurred me on and, before reaching the border, I had managed to cover 130 kilometres. I left the friendly guards behind and continued to Batumi, the cool night air adding a refreshing element to the ride.

By the time I arrived in Batumi, it was late and Georgia's second-largest city was shrouded in darkness.

I found lodging at a family-run guesthouse, the kind that exudes warmth and hospitality from the moment you step inside. The man who opened the door was tall, barrel-chested, and bald-headed, and he was smoking a cigarette that had burned down to the filter. He looked me over, squinting through the smoke, then gave a single nod and stepped aside without a word. A woman appeared behind him, wiping her hands on a floral apron, her hair tied back in a scarf patterned with sunflowers.

The man's name was Gaucha. His wide smile and cheerful demeanour put me instantly at ease. His family welcomed me with a hearty spread of cheese, vodka, and beer—a sportsman's dinner, if ever there was one. The vodka burned like fire but melted the day's fatigue. The cheese was sharp, and the bread was still warm. Laughter came easy, as if I'd stepped into someone else's life—one where strangers become family by the second glass. He mentioned that he wanted to take me to his children's school the following day to speak some English to the students and help out with the English lesson.

In the morning, I was roused by the sound of children playing outside. I came out to the kitchen for a breakfast of eggs and Georgian coffee. Finely ground and unfiltered, the coffee was a thick and aromatic brew. It was bold and bitter—and exactly what I needed to get myself up for the day.

Before I had time to relax any further, I was being dragged by Gaucha to his kids' school. The building was a typical government structure—it was concrete and functional, with little thought given to aesthetics. It was built for purpose, not beauty. There were no decorations, no softness, just grey walls and right angles.

Inside, I was met by the school director, a tall, stern-looking man whose very presence demanded respect. He towered over me, his authoritative voice echoing in the empty corridors as he questioned me about my qualifications. I felt like a schoolboy again, caught in front of a headmaster for some minor infraction, only this time the stakes felt a bit higher. My lack of formal teaching qualifications became glaringly obvious, and I half-expected to be shown the door. But to my surprise, the director seemed satisfied that my mere ability to speak English was qualification enough.

Soon enough, I was standing in front of a classroom full of disinterested teenagers, their chatter filling the room with a cacophony of sound. I cleared my throat, feeling a wave of nervousness wash over me. "Hi, my name is Rob. I am from England, and I just cycled here from London." My words hung in the air for a moment, and then, like a wave, silence swept through the room. I had their attention. And in that silence, something clicked. These kids didn't care about distance or gear ratios. They wanted a story. And I had one. I started talking—and not just about cycling, but about what it felt like to leave everything behind. Eyes widened. Heads tilted. I saw the moment I stopped being a novelty and started being real.

For the next half hour, the students bombarded me with questions. Their curiosity was infectious, and I found myself enjoying the impromptu session. By the end of it, I was shocked when the director offered me a permanent position. I could have stayed in Batumi, teaching English and settling into the rhythm of life here if I'd wanted to. The thought was tempting—after all, the people I had met were warm and welcoming, and the city had a unique charm. There was something alluring about the idea of putting down roots there. But I had a mission and, despite the pull of this place, I knew I had to continue my journey. It took some persuading, especially with Gaucha, who was convinced I could make a small fortune by setting up a private English school in town.

That evening, I found myself back at the table with Gaucha, his familiar broad grin as warm as the crackling fire nearby. He placed a steaming bowl of Georgian stew before me. Its rich tomato base was thick and tangy, and brightened with garlic and fresh coriander. I scooped it up with torn hunks of warm bread, each bite a reward. Between mouthfuls, we talked about the day—his work at the guesthouse, the quirks of his kids, and my travels. "You have strong legs, my friend," he chuckled, gesturing toward Shirley, who was leaning against the wall. "But even strong legs need strong food." I laughed and nodded, savouring the meal. I felt entirely at home.

In the days that followed, I wandered through the city under grey skies. The amount of development here was dramatic. Roads were being dug up all around the city, presumably to pave the way for new infrastructure and roads. Cranes working on new developments punctuated the skyline all around. Batumi Boulevard had been redeveloped with palm-lined paths offering views of the sea on one side, with construction sites on the other. The plans for the city were as ambitious as anything I had seen anywhere before.

I eventually set off from Batumi, waved off by Gaucha and his children in rain that seemed relentless, soaking me through as I cycled on. The roads were slick and treacherous, the sky a constant grey. Yet, the people I met along the way were unfailingly kind, full of enthusiasm for my journey—and for life itself. One evening, after a particularly gruelling day of cycling through endless drizzle, I found myself outside a rustic wooden restaurant tucked against a backdrop of dense, rain-drenched greenery. It was closed, but I could smell that something hearty was cooking, the aroma wafting from the open doorway and mingling with the scent of the soaked ground. With no better option on where I might be able to put my tent for the night, I approached the owner, a short, slim man with a toothy smile and twinkling eyes, and asked if I could pitch my tent in his garden.

"Of course, of course!" he exclaimed, waving me inside with a welcoming hand. "But first, you must eat.

No one should sleep on an empty stomach, especially not in this weather!"

I hesitated at the threshold, rain pooling at my feet on the scuffed wooden floor. "Are you sure? I don't want to impose."

"Impose? Ha!" He laughed heartily. "You are a guest! Now, sit!"

He ushered me to a corner table, where the warm light of a single hanging lamp cast a soft glow over the room. On the walls hung wooden carvings, and the fireplace crackled invitingly in the corner. He brought out some fresh bread still warm from the oven.

As I tore into the bread, he sat opposite me, his arms crossed in curiosity. "So, tell me, my friend," he began, "what brings you here, cycling through this endless rain? Are you chasing something?"

I chuckled through a mouthful of bread. "Maybe I'm chasing adventure—and myself, I suppose."

He nodded sagely, pouring us both a glass of tea. "And what have you found?"

"A lot of rain," I joked, eliciting another booming laugh from him. Then I added, "But also kindness, like yours. And a reminder that the world isn't as big or as scary as it sometimes seems."

He raised his glass to mine.

***

As I pedalled steadily toward Tbilisi, my routine roadside stops for water or food frequently turned into unexpected social events. Roadside cafés became hubs of Georgian hospitality, where locals welcomed me with open arms—and bottles of vodka. The tradition seemed almost sacred; no sooner would I park Shirley up and sit down than the toasts would begin. Despite my protests, the shots would keep coming, each with a cheer and a push to drink. Five or six shots would be downed before I knew what had happened, the warm burn of vodka spreading through me. Then, I would ride off slightly unsteady but smiling. I couldn't help but marvel at this curious custom.

The vodka loosened my thoughts and added a surreal charm to this leg of the journey, though I made sure to keep a firm grip on my handlebars and a steady pace. Somehow, even in this state, I was still covering over 100 kilometres a day, the road unfolding ahead as both a challenge and an invitation to embrace the unexpected quirks of Georgian life. I only worried that the truck drivers screaming past were drinking just as much as I was.

Shirley was starting to show signs of wear. I had done almost 6,000 kilometres and been on the road for 94 days. Both of her tyres were in terrible shape, and I was down to patching up punctures with alarming regularity.

I had managed to get a message home and my father had arranged for some tyres to be sent to the Georgian capital, Tbilisi for me to collect. I pressed on along potholed roads toward a 1,000 metre-high pass over the mountains. The air thinned and cooled as we climbed the massive hill.

As I neared the town of Gomi, looking for shelter from more rain, I was welcomed into the wooden stilted house belonging to Levani, a shepherd, and his mother. Their home was simple, with an iron wood-burning stove at its heart, used for everything from cooking to heating the house. Cows and chickens roamed freely in the garden, and Levani and his mother's meals were as straightforward as their lifestyle—milk, cheese, eggs, tomatoes, cucumbers, and bread. Yet the simplicity of the food made it all the more satisfying. Levani didn't speak much English, but he proudly produced an old English-Georgian dictionary from his school days, and we communicated as best we could.

"You… from England?" he asked slowly, his finger running over the page.

"Yes, England. London," I said, miming the shape of a map with my hands.

Levani grinned and nodded enthusiastically. "London… football! Chelsea?" His eyes sparkled with amusement.

I laughed. "No, no. Liverpool!"

His face scrunched up in mock disapproval before he chuckled. "Ah, Liverpool! Gerrard!"

It was a strange but oddly comforting way to bond—football, it seemed, was a universal language.

The most surprising moment came when Levani opened his bedroom cupboard to reveal an AK-47 assault rifle, a box of ammunition, and a rocket-propelled grenade launcher. He explained, through the dictionary and gestures, that every trained man in Georgia was armed in case the Russians invaded again—a sobering reminder of the war that had taken place only a year before in 2008. It was a glimpse into rural life in Georgia that I wouldn't soon forget.

The next day I rode 120 kilometres to the capital. Tbilisi wasn't what I expected. I had pictured a rugged, Soviet-tinged city—off the well-worn path, untouched by travellers. But reality, surprisingly, was far better. The streets were alive with colour and energy. Cobbled alleyways twisted between elegant balconies, cafés buzzed with chatter, and the scent of cheesy bread filled the air. I stood at the entrance to the Old Town, taking it all in—

And then, I saw them.

Two fully loaded touring bikes leaning against a café wall.

I stepped inside, half in disbelief, and was immediately greeted by a thick French accent.

"You are also cycling?"

"Yeah," I said, grinning. "I thought I was alone out here."

He laughed. "You are not alone, my friend. There are now six of us in town."

Indeed, there were. I located the hostel that was to accommodate all six of us and our bikes. There were the two Frenchmen—Romain and Ben, and three Englishmen: a bearded man called Keith and two lads, Matt and Jack.

Later that afternoon, as we settled into the hostel, two more cyclists arrived—Chris and Sara, a couple who had started their journey in Spain. And then, to my surprise, Emrys, the Australian from Turkey, turned up.

I grinned as he walked in. "You again? Thought I lost you back in Turkey."

"You can't get rid of me that easily," he shot back.

It was a strange feeling, meeting so many other long-distance cyclists in a place that I had imagined would be devoid of such company.

I bonded with them over the next few days, and in various mixes of groups, as we spent time exploring Tbilisi together and obtaining ongoing visas for Azerbaijan.

Our first stop was the city's famous sulphur baths, natural hot springs that offered a much-needed respite for weary bodies. The sulphuric smell was strong, but the warm, therapeutic waters melted away the aches and pains from the road.

We wandered through the old town, its cobblestone streets winding between ancient buildings that seemed to whisper stories from centuries past. The Narikala Fortress, perched high on a hill, offered a breathtaking view of the city and the Kura River, which flowed serenely through the heart of Tbilisi. We marvelled at the Georgian Orthodox churches, particularly the Holy Trinity Cathedral, its golden dome gleaming in the sunlight.

The city's streets led us into bustling markets, where vendors sold everything from crafts to second-hand goods. The smell of sizzling meat and freshly baked bread filled the air, drawing us to street food stalls where we sampled *khachapuri*, a warm, cheese-filled bread that oozed comfort with every bite, and *khinkali*, dumplings stuffed with spiced meat that burst with flavour.

Tbilisi was not just a city of history, but of life. Street musicians played Georgian songs, their voices mingling with the sound of clinking glasses from nearby cafés. In the evenings, we found ourselves in cosy, dimly lit courtyards, listening to live music. These nights were filled with warmth and friendship.

At one point, Matt leaned over to me and raised his glass. "So, what's next for you?"

I hesitated. "Azerbaijan… then, if I get the visa, Iran."

His eyes widened. "Iran? You're brave."

"Or stupid," Sara quipped with a smirk.

I shrugged. "Guess I'll find out."

It was 22nd September when my Azeri visa was approved by the embassy in Tbilisi. It was my first full-page visa, a significant milestone in my journey, and I couldn't resist photographing it and proudly displaying it in my passport. To top it off, Shirley's new tyres arrived from the UK. These weren't just any tyres—they had a ceramic lining that made them practically unpuncturable. I felt a surge of confidence, knowing that Shirley was ready for whatever lay ahead.

Days later, I was back on the road, this time with Keith. Our little group had planned to cycle together from Tbilisi into Azerbaijan, but the others weren't exactly early risers, and Keith and I were eager to get going. We agreed to meet up again as a group in Baku.

The first day's ride took us out of Tbilisi. We tried to avoid being swallowed whole by manholes in the road, their covers missing—presumed stolen and sold off for scrap.

We made it about 100 kilometres to the town of Sighnaghi, a picture-perfect hilltop town in Georgia's Kakheti region. As we approached, the town revealed itself—perched atop a hill, it was surrounded by rolling vineyards with the distant silhouette of the Caucasus Mountains.

"You sure this is Georgia?" Keith muttered, taking in the Tuscan-like scenery.

"Apparently," I said, snapping a photo, "it is beautiful."

The first thing that caught my eye was the defensive wall encircling the town, a relic from the 18th century, highlighting Sighnaghi's strategic importance in years gone by. We walked along the fortress walls, taking in the panoramic view of the Alazani Valley below, bathing in the afternoon light, and the vineyards stretching out to the horizon.

Stepping into the town felt like stepping back in time. The architecture was a blend of Georgian and European influences, with colourful façades, ornate balconies draped in flowers, and narrow, winding cobblestone streets that begged to be explored. We wandered through the town at a leisurely pace, soaking in the tranquillity that seemed to hang in the air.

Later that night, Keith told me the story of his father's ashes. He had been on the road for several years, cycling through Europe, North Africa, Syria, and Egypt.

His journey had been marked by tragedy when his bike, which was carrying an urn with his father's ashes in it, was stolen at a train station in Turkey. Despite the loss, the Turkish people had rallied together to buy him a new bike, allowing him to continue his journey. I was grateful to have the chance to ride with him, sharing stories and experiences as we cycled together.

We rolled into Lagodekhi, a Georgian town on the Azerbaijan border, just before midday. The crossing was quiet; there was only a sun-bleached, low-slung building flanked by two sleepy guards lounging in plastic chairs. One of them perked up as we approached, waved us through the gates, and gestured toward a narrow checkpoint booth that looked more like a village post office than a portal to another nation.

"Where you from?" asked the older of the two, squinting at our passports as if they might bite.

"The UK," Keith and I said in unison.

He nodded, then surprised us with a grin. "We must have tea!"

Before we could reply, we were ushered into a cramped, fan-cooled customs control room with posters of mountains on the walls and a half-drunk pot of black tea on the desk.

Another guard—barely older than a teenager—poured us tiny glass cups, added sugar without asking, and began firing off questions in eager, broken English.

"Where from?

How many kilometres?

You have... girlfriend?"

We sipped politely, answered questions between laughs, and repeated the handful of Azeri words they attempted to teach us. For a moment, it felt less like crossing a border and more like stumbling into someone's living room.

Eventually, they stamped our passports, shook our hands with enthusiasm and waved us through.

We camped that night just beyond the last outpost of Georgian red tape, under a row of walnut trees at the edge of a field.

As we lay there, Keith and I discussed our reasons for being on the road; the people we met, and the experiences we had encountered. Keith articulated it far better than I ever could:

"Everyone claims to have their own reasons for being on the road—whether to reinvent themselves or to break free from the chains of day-to-day life that may have restrained them.

But there is something else inside those who opt for the saddle. Something more. It's the profound sense of freedom one gains when cycling.

One is not pinned down to a single route, as you are by coach, plane, or car. You stop when and where you want —head off the road, park in the middle of a city, or hitch a ride if you need to.

Directions are yours to choose. You are not boxed in by your pocket, only by your muscle and will.

But more important than this is the connection you have to the land—the sights, the sounds, the scents that surround you; the people who meet and greet you, who want to help, put you up, and feed you."

CHAPTER 13

Between the Caspian & the Carpet

Number of days on the road: 102
Total distance covered: 6,193 km

The following days were challenging, as we tackled the hilly terrain leading us through the Azeri regions of Balakan, Qax and then Sheki. The road climbed steeply, and the scenery became more dramatic. For three days we rode through the northern folds of Azerbaijan, each switchback offering new angles on the Caucasus Mountains—towering, ancient, and utterly indifferent. The lower slopes were a riot of green—walnut groves, poplar stands, apple orchards—but above them, snow lingered stubbornly on the jagged ridgelines, a stark reminder that Russia lay just beyond the peaks.

I found myself stopping often—not out of fatigue, but because it was impossible not to. Every bend offered another breathtaking view: shepherds guiding flocks across wildflower meadows, rivers threading silver through the valleys, clouds dragging their bellies along the treetops. I took more photos in that stretch than I had in weeks, though none of them felt quite enough to do justice to the experience.

The rain came without warning. One moment, the sky was bruised but holding; the next, it let go. Torrents hammered down with the kind of intensity that rewrites your understanding of the word "wet". Roads became rivers. Fields vanished beneath a sheet of grey. The world was all water and motion and noise.

Somewhere in the downpour, I lost Keith.

One second, he was ahead, his green bicycle a blur through the mist. The next—gone. I kept riding, heart pounding more from uncertainty than effort, blinking away rain and trying to spot him around each bend. But by the time I rolled into Gabala, soaked to the bone and shivering, the light had drained from the sky. I checked a few cafés, shouted his name into the dark, then surrendered to a cheap hotel on the edge of town.

The shower was hot, and I stood beneath it for a few long minutes, watching brown water swirl around the drain. I lay on the bed in damp clothes, staring at the ceiling, listening to the rain hammering the window.

The next morning brought a break in the weather and the first reluctant hints of blue in the sky. I left a message for Keith—written on a piece of paper and then taped onto a rock. I left it balanced carefully on the kerbstone at the edge of town. Just a name, an arrow, and a crude smiley face. Primitive, but hopeful.

By afternoon, the sun had returned and so had Keith. He'd found the rock.

We reconnected in Shamakhi, some 90 kilometres from Gabala, where we both admitted we were knackered. The rain hadn't just soaked us—it had worn us down. We found a guesthouse and took a two-day break. Local news showed footage of villages waist-deep in floodwater. Our decision to pause wasn't just sensible. It was survival.

The hotel in Shamakhi was a boxy roadside relic from the Soviet era—faded carpets, a flickering hallway light, and a smell of boiled cabbage that clung to every curtain. It was busy though, so it must have been good.

In the dining room, a slim waiter approached with a notepad and an unlit cigarette dangling from his lip. He launched straight into a question in rapid Azeri.

Keith and I blinked.

He repeated it in Russian. We still blinked.

I tried my best diplomatic shrug. Keith offered one of his usual disarming smiles, the kind that usually bought us time.

"Uh... food?" I said, pointing at the table and then to my mouth.

The waiter frowned. He said something again—louder, this time. I tried a new tactic: miming. I pointed to my stomach, then drew a pretend plate in the air, mimed a spoon going to my mouth. He raised an eyebrow, unconvinced.

I doubled down: exaggerated chewing, a look of bliss, a hopeful thumbs-up.

He sighed and vanished through a swinging door.

A few moments later, an older man emerged from the kitchen—apron streaked, hair wild, a theatrical glint in his eye. Without a word, he lifted the lid off a metal tray and presented it like a game show prize: a bubbling stew thick with meat and onions.

"Cow?" I said, then mimicked horns with my fingers. "Moo."

He looked confused for a second, then his face lit up.

"Ahhhh mooo!" he chimed in, nodding enthusiastically and chuckling.

Keith nearly fell off his chair laughing, and I was crying with laughter by the time the man stood up and wiped his hands theatrically on his apron.

"Perfect," I said, wiping my eyes. "I'll have... one of those."

Keith, still chuckling, tried to explain that he was a vegetarian, and it seemed he might have finally got through to them.

The waiter returned later with two steaming plates—mine piled with beef stew, Keith's with a mountain of rice... and a lone chicken leg perched on top like a trophy.

He stared at it. "I don't think they count chicken."

"Not in this postcode," I said.

We ate anyway, still laughing, still slightly mystified but full, and oddly grateful for the strange, clucking dance of dinner diplomacy. It seemed kindness arrived in the form of stew and impersonations in Azerbaijan.

The highlight of our stay in Shamakhi came in the form of an unexpected encounter. After a visit to the outside toilet, Keith asked me if I had seen anything unusual. I shook my head, puzzled.

"You didn't notice the bear?"

"What bear?"

Keith pointed.

There it was. A huge brown beast ambling around the car park like it owned the place.

Keith was already posing in front of it, grinning like a tourist outside Big Ben.

"You absolute lunatic," I muttered.

The bear sniffed the air. Took a few slow steps forward.

"Keith. Move."

"It's fine!"

"KEITH. MOVE. NOW."

He finally took the hint, backing away as the bear reached for his backpack.

It lost interest and wandered off. Keith beamed. "Got the shot."

I stared at him. "It'll be a great obituary photo."

After our two-day rest, the sun returned, and the landscape shifted beneath our wheels. The mountains fell away behind us, replaced by a vast, sunburnt desert—red hills rolling out in every direction, the road a tight ribbon unspooling through nowhere.

There were no buildings, no trees, no signs of life. Just wind, heat, and the horizon.

With the tailwind behind us and music blasting through my headphones, I opened it up—no hands on the handlebars, only my legs pumping, the road slipping past at 78 km/h. I filmed as I flew, the scenery blurring into streaks of ochre and gold. It was the kind of ride that makes you forget the weight of panniers, miles, and doubts. Just me, the bike, and the burn of freedom.

Then Keith got a puncture. He waved me on. "Go on. I'll catch up."

I took the bait, grinning, legs churning. If I could beat him to Baku, I'd have bragging rights for weeks.

But a few kilometres later, karma struck—my own back tyre hissed then gave out, flattening with a final sigh. I rolled to a stop, shoulders slumping.

Keith coasted up behind me, smirking.

"You got everything you need?"

"Yeah," I muttered, already reaching for the tools.

"Well then," he said, pulling out his camera. "Say cheese. See you at my winner's dinner."

And with that, he rode off, whistling.

***

I found Keith in Baku sipping tea in the shadow of a sandstone wall, legs stretched out like he'd claimed the city for himself. His clothes were dustier than mine, his face sun-kissed and grinning. "You made it then," he said, lifting his cup. "I'll have another one of these, please."

Jack and Matt arrived with Chris and Sara a few days later, their bikes creaking and faces half-dazed from the heat. We were a ragtag bunch—road-worn and saddle-sore—standing in the middle of Baku's polished centre like someone had dropped a caravan of Bedouin into Knightsbridge.

Baku hit me like a mirage—part Silk Road, part oil boom, part fever dream. Minarets and Maseratis. Ancient walls shadowed by flame-shaped skyscrapers. The call to prayer echoing between boutiques selling €600 sunglasses. I wandered the wide boulevards in my sun-bleached trousers and salt-stained fleece, feeling like a vagrant who'd taken a wrong turn into a Vogue shoot.

Still, it was mesmerising.

To find the heart of the city, I slipped through the walls of the *Icherisheher*—the Old City. The noise dropped. The light changed. Cobbled alleys curled like question marks, and stone buildings leaned in over narrow lanes. The air smelled of limestone dust, old wood, and incense. I ran my hand along the wall. It was cool and pockmarked. Centuries were embedded in its skin.

Inside, the past was visible everywhere: Persian domes, Ottoman windows, Russian balconies. Its history layered like sediment. I followed the alleyways until they opened into the Palace of the Shirvanshahs, the old royal seat perched on a knoll, its walls the colour of sand after rain.

Keith was already reading the plaque, quietly reverent. “Fifteenth century,” he said. “The dynasty ruled for nearly 700 years.”

We walked the courtyards and archways in near silence. The *Divankhana*—an ancient pavilion, with its octagonal dome and whispering acoustics, felt like a room designed to hold secrets. You could almost hear the scrape of sandals, the murmur of debate. In one corner, a niche still bore the faint trace of Arabic script—part prayer, part proclamation.

Beyond it, the hammam stood quiet and cool, its tiled floors once slick with steam and power. I tried to picture the Shah reclining there, robe askew, discussing borders between mouthfuls of pilaf.

The real jewel, though, was the rooftop view: the city stretched out in all directions, old and new locked in an uneasy embrace. The wind skimmed across the city, swept in from the Caspian Sea.

As the day drew to a close, Keith and I found a small, lively restaurant tucked away in one of Baku’s older streets. The smell of sizzling kebab meat and savoury spices wafted through the air, mingling with the low hum of conversation from other diners. The city's dining scene offered a mix of Azeri dishes and international cuisine, but we both gravitated toward something local.

I ordered an aromatic lamb kebab and Keith a halloumi-filled one, sizzling on metal skewers, their juices dripping onto charred flatbreads beneath them. A side of tangy pomegranate salad glistened in the dim light, its ruby-red seeds bursting with sweet and sour intensity. Freshly baked tandir bread, warm and pillowy, arrived with a generous smear of creamy, herb-filled yoghurt.

Keith took a bite and groaned in satisfaction. "Alright, this might be the best meal we've had in weeks," he declared.

"Agreed," I said, tearing a piece of bread to scoop up some of the yoghurt. "Who needs energy bars when you have this?"

I spent almost two weeks in Baku—far longer than I had wanted. Much of that time was spent relaxing with my fellow cyclists and trying to get visas for potential onward countries. We all secured visas for Uzbekistan and we had tried in earnest to get Chinese visas but were denied when they became aware that we were travelling into the Urumqi region. There had been some recent unrest, and it appeared that they did not want tourists heading into the region. It was a painful wait for what turned out to be very little reward.

The good news, however, was that I was able to secure an Iranian visa. I had applied for this back in Istanbul with Bill, and it had taken over a month for this to be processed. I therefore collected this with some excitement from the Iranian embassy in Baku.

As I was the only one with an Iranian visa, I headed off on my own once again the next morning, leaving the rest behind to take the ferry from Baku, across the Caspian Sea to Uzbekistan. It was possible, but unlikely, that we would meet up with each other again somewhere else along the Silk Road, but only time would tell.

The initial ride out of Baku toward the Iranian border was uninspiring, a barren stretch of desert that seemed to go on forever. Perhaps it was the disappointment of my failed attempt to obtain a Chinese visa weighing on me, turning the landscape into a reflection of my mood. The road ahead was uncertain, and the challenges seemed to be mounting. If I couldn't secure visas for China and Turkmenistan, I would have to travel through Iran to Pakistan and then cross Pakistan's notorious Balochistan Province to reach India. At the time, the region was known for lawlessness, unrest, bombings, and targeted killings due to heightened political unrest, insurgency, and militarisation. It was a daunting prospect, and I felt the weight of it pressing down on me as I cycled through the endless desert.

But the vast sandy landscape had a way of surprising me. As I rode, the vast emptiness began to take on a beauty of its own. The barren landscape was breathtaking in its starkness. Being in the middle of nowhere, with nothing but the open road ahead, filled me with a sense of real adventure. It was just me, Shirley, and the endless horizon. The silence was profound, broken only by the crunching sound of my wheels on the asphalt and the occasional gust of wind.

At one point, a family pulled up next to me in the middle of the desert. They asked for a photo with me, then quickly piled back into their car and drove off, leaving me alone once more. The encounter was brief, but it cheered me up immensely. I could only imagine what they must have thought—seeing a lone cyclist in the middle of the desert must have seemed like an oddity, something worth documenting. Perhaps they wanted proof to show their friends that they had encountered a crazy European cycling through the vast emptiness of the Azeri desert.

I was about 350 kilometres, or a three-day ride from the Iranian border when I decided to camp for the night by a railway line. The desert scrub provided some shelter and, though I was woken a few times by passing trains, it was a peaceful spot, the kind of place where the stars shone brightly in the absence of city lights.

But the tranquillity of the desert was shattered the next day when I found myself confronted by a pack of dogs. These were no ordinary dogs, they were Kangal sheepdogs—massive creatures bred to protect livestock from wolves and other predators with a bite force of 743 pounds per square inch. Their sheer size and fierce demeanour sent a jolt of fear through me as they appeared out of nowhere,

The first bark was low and guttural, carrying across the barren landscape like a warning shot. Then, out of the scrubland, they appeared. Three. No, four. No... six. Massive, muscular, and moving with the confidence of apex predators. Their fur was a mix of dirty white and grey, their thick necks wrapped in metal collars with sharp prongs—a defence against wolves. Their eyes locked onto me.

I stopped pedalling. My breath was shallow, my pulse thundering in my ears. I knew better than to run. But standing still didn't feel like an option either.

The largest of them, a brute the size of a small horse, took a step closer. Then another. His lips curled back, revealing yellowed fangs as thick as my fingers.

I gripped Shirley's handlebars, my mind racing. What do I do? Keep eye contact? Look away? Climb something?

Then a deep, bone-rattling growl rippled through the air. The pack fanned out, cutting off my escape routes. They were in hunting formation now.

And I was the prey.

There was no shepherd in sight, no one to call them off. The dogs were in charge, and I was on their territory. They circled me, their growls growing louder, more menacing. I knew I couldn't outrun them —Kangals are fast, and their powerful jaws could easily tear me apart. I dismounted my bike, hoping to show them that I wasn't a threat, but it didn't work. They closed in, their circle tightening around me, and I could feel my heart pounding in my chest, adrenaline surging through my veins.

The biggest of them took a step closer.

Then, just when I thought it was over for me and Shirley, salvation arrived in the form of a battered Kamaz truck.

The driver—a man with a cigarette clamped between his teeth—swerved toward the dogs, horn blaring. They scattered. He rolled down the window, waved frantically: *Go!*

I pedalled frantically, as quickly as I could at a speed that would have put Lance Armstrong to shame—even in his enhanced days—and when I finally stopped to catch my breath, a group of truckers who had witnessed the ordeal came over to check on me. They didn't speak much English, but their concern was evident. They offered me coffee and croissants, a simple act, but it steadied me.

The encounter with the Kangals left me shaken, a reminder that the road was full of unexpected challenges. But it also reinforced my determination to keep going, to face whatever came my way with courage and resilience. After all, this journey was about more than just reaching a destination—it was about embracing the highs and lows, the good and the bad, and finding strength in the face of adversity.

CHAPTER 14

Roads & Revelations

Number of days on the road: 123
Total distance covered: 6,382 km

Slippery, pale eggs with runny whites shivered on a plate in front of me. It was the next morning, and I was in the border town of Astara on the Azeri side. It had been two days since the Kangal encounter, which remained fresh in my mind. I stared at the eggs, my fork hovering while I did the mental calculus between hunger and hospital. Hunger won. I ate the eggs grimly, expecting consequences. Luckily, none came. That made two ill-fated experiences that I had narrowly escaped in just a few days.

My next challenge was crossing into Iran, which turned out to be one of the more surreal border experiences of the trip. It began, improbably, by walking through a café. Not *past* a café—*through* it. Then out the back door, across a dusty yard strewn with cigarette butts and half-buried bricks, and through what looked suspiciously like someone's garden gate. It felt like slipping into a neighbour's barbecue.

The crossing itself was brief—absurdly so. I was the only foreigner in sight, and I was waved to the front of the queue with barely a glance. But the ease ended there.

On the Iranian side, I was pulled aside by customs officials and shepherded into a low-slung police building. No explanation. No welcome. Just firm hands and rapid-fire Farsi. Within minutes, I was being fingerprinted, photographed, and handed several pages of paperwork—all in a language I couldn't read and certainly couldn't sign in good faith. I tried to explain, but mime only gets you so far in a police station. For two hours, we went around in circles—questions fired, my blank face in return. I refused to sign what I didn't understand, and, eventually, they gave up.

Released without ceremony, I stepped into the sunlight dazed and dehydrated, having successfully made it into Iran. I changed some money at a roadside kiosk and set off from the border city of Astara, hoping the rest of the day would be less *Kafka*, more kilometres.

I was relieved to be back on the road when, having barely ridden 17 kilometres, a man waved me down from the roadside. He was middle-aged with thick glasses, neatly combed black hair and an eager smile.

"Do you speak English?" he asked, stepping forward with both hope and authority.

"I do," I said, cautiously.

"Wonderful! I am an English teacher," he declared, beaming. His name was Reza, and within moments, he'd invited me to visit his "school".

Given his impeccable English and unimposing stature, I figured it was safe enough to follow him down a narrow alley. We emerged into a modest but genuine classroom: wooden desks, a blackboard scrawled with English phrases, and a pile of battered textbooks in the corner.

"You will teach," he said, not quite asking.

I laughed. "When's the class?"

"Five o'clock," he said, delighted. "But first, you come to my home. You eat."

His home was next door. Inside, the floors were blanketed with Persian rugs, and the air was thick with the scent of stewed meat and saffron. His wife greeted me with warm eyes and a gentle smile beneath her headscarf. Their young son watched me silently from the hallway, curious but wary.

We sat cross-legged on the floor and ate rose-scented rice, lamb stew, and warm lavash bread, torn by hand and used to scoop up each bite. Reza beamed as he spoke of his family's plywood factory next door—built by his father from the ground up, he said with pride.

At 5:00 p.m. sharp, we returned to the classroom. I took his advanced English group: teenagers and twenty-somethings—all eager and curious, some shy, some fluent.

"Tell me about something fun you did last year," I prompted.

A girl at the back of the class raised her hand hesitantly. "Last year, my family go to Isfahan."

"Went to Esfahan," I corrected gently.

"Ah, yes—went," she said, nodding. "Last year, my family *went* to Esfahan."

"Perfect," I said. She smiled widely.

By the end of the lesson, they were laughing, joking, and their confidence was growing. We took photos together before saying our goodbyes, and I realised it had been as much an event for them as it had been for me.

That evening, Reza took me out for kebabs—charred lamb skewers with herbs and pillowy naans. The small restaurant was loud with chatter, the air thick with smoke and spice.

"I think you can stay for one month," he grinned between mouthfuls. "Teach more."

"Tempting," I said, "but I've got a long road ahead."

He nodded, though I could tell he didn't love the answer.

That night, I slept at his home, and I woke at dawn to the call to prayer drifting through the window and echoing across the rooftops.

Breakfast was a quiet joy: warm sangak Iranian flatbread, fresh from the oven, with feta, honey, and strong and fragrant black tea with cardamom. I lingered over it, not quite ready to leave.

Back at the school, I packed up my bike. Reza hovered nearby.

"Are you sure you have to go today?" he asked.

"I do," I said, "but I won't forget this."

He smiled, placing a hand on my arm. "Then... good journey, my friend."

And just like that, I was rolling again—past the factory, past the alley, back into the unknown. But the tone for Iran was set: generous, unpredictable, utterly unforgettable.

A reasonably early start meant I had done a respectable 40 kilometres by 11:00 a.m. and decided to stop for elevenses. My rear rack had become loose, and a pannier had fallen off, so I also carried out some essential maintenance. *Check the nuts and bolts so you don't die,* echoed in my head.

As much as I was falling in love with the kindness of the Iranian people, the shadow of bureaucracy loomed large. Every time I stopped to take in a city, share a meal, or chat with a stranger, the thought was there —quiet and insistent. My future was a puzzle of permits and paperwork. The road welcomed me; the paperwork did not.

Further along, a car slowed beside me, and out leaned a familiar face—a German traveller I'd met weeks earlier in Trabzon, now hitching his way east. We grinned, and he pulled over and we swapped road stories, and inevitably, fell into the topic that consumed all overland travellers: visas.

He didn't have good news.

Word was that the Pakistani border was volatile. A recent bombing in Balochistan might mean closures—or worse—death. An Indian visa now reportedly required a return flight booked in advance, and as for Turkmenistan and China—forget it. My route, so carefully imagined, was beginning to dissolve underfoot. There were only three ways further East: Afghanistan—which was currently at war, Turkmenistan—where getting visas was an issue, or Pakistan—through Balochistan.

By the time he drove off, I was deflated. Utterly deflated.

I'd been pushing hard since Baku, burning through kilometres in the desert heat, trusting that a clear path to India would present itself. Now, all of it—every pedal stroke, every dusty sunrise—seemed to be crashing into a bureaucratic brick wall.

The rest of the day unravelled. Horns blared endlessly. Every stop invited a crowd, the same questions on repeat: "Where are you from?" and "Where are you going?" Normally, I welcomed curiosity. Today it felt suffocating. Strangers fiddled with my bike, pawed my panniers, and interrupted meals. I snapped at them in English, and then cursed myself for doing so. I was tired, frustrated, and fed up with myself for being ungrateful.

I ducked into an internet café, hoping for answers. I researched visa requirements, scanned forums for news on the Khunjerab Pass, the northern entry point into Pakistan from China, and the date of its seasonal closure. My mind raced through contingency plans: a bus to Tehran, a flight to India, maybe I could start again from there. For a moment, I even considered the daftest idea yet—buying a beat-up local bike, dressing like a local, and cycling stealthily across Pakistan while Shirley flew ahead to India. It made sense in my heat-addled brain.

Later that day, a queue of cars stopped me on the roadside. Every driver insisted I come to *their* house for dinner. The offers were touching—until they turned into a shouting match. Hands waved, voices rose, accusations flew. I thought they might come to blows over who got to host me. I declined them all and quietly pedalled away.

A few kilometres down the road, I stopped at a small café run by two brothers, Arman and Darius. They had kind eyes and easy smiles. Within minutes, they'd invited me to stay in the spare room above the shop—for a price so low I felt guilty accepting it. And it wasn't just a room. It came with conversation, and shared tobacco pipes, a walk through town where they introduced me to neighbours as if I were royalty. I even played guitar for them after dinner. I was in better spirits than I'd been all week.

The next morning, I somehow ended up in front of a class of eager English students, coaxed into another impromptu lesson. The enthusiasm in the room was infectious. Their questions were thoughtful, their smiles genuine. One boy asked if I was a spy. Another told me her dream was to visit London and ride a red double-decker bus.

When I returned to the café, Arman and Darius refused to take any money. "Your English lesson," they said, "is enough." Breakfast followed: thick yoghurt drizzled with honey, fresh walnuts, steaming tea, and warm *sangak* bread pulled from the oven, its crust still crackling.

Iranian hospitality wasn't just generous, it was cultural bedrock—an unspoken law, as deeply rooted as the cypress trees lining the roads. Guests weren't guests. They were a responsibility, a privilege, and family.

I passed through Rasht, a surprisingly cosmopolitan city where I found a cheap hotel, ate well, wandered shaded streets where the rules of the regime seemed to soften slightly. Women wore skinny jeans under their hijabs. Makeup glimmered on faces that met mine with quiet curiosity. It wasn't what I'd expected from Iran—but then, nothing had been.

I left Rasht recharged but still wary. And I was right to be. The road to Tehran was chaos. Trucks belched black clouds and thundered past with barely a metre to spare. The fuel was cheap, the roads crumbling, and the pollution fierce. Every few minutes, I'd emerge from another diesel plume looking like a chimney sweep.

Then, just outside a nameless village, I was pulled over by a plump man in a military uniform, moustache thick enough to have its own postcode. No gun. No badge. No vehicle. Just a uniform, a sour look, and a questionable sense of authority.

He barked questions I did not understand. When I kept smiling and repeating "Hello!" he began rummaging through my panniers, muttering about a fine and looking for my passport. I had no idea what I was supposedly guilty of.

He gestured down a side street—clearly expecting me to follow.

I didn't like it.

No radio. No backup. Just a shady moustache and a belly. I played dumb, waved cheerily like I'd misunderstood, and pushed off down the main road with a breezy "Goodbye!"

He shouted after me. I smiled and waved again. He didn't follow.

After this encounter, life got more serious. The next day was one of the hardest of my entire trip.

The visa chaos had drained me. I should've felt proud—I'd cycled all the way to Iran from London. Instead, I felt crushed. I'd been defeated not by distance, but by bureaucracy. I was riding hard with nowhere to go, and only seven days left on my Iranian visa. I couldn't shake the feeling that I was pedalling myself into a dead end.

Negativity took hold. I had no route forward. The only available direction seemed to be backwards—to Turkey. I didn't want to go back to Turkey.

Traffic swelled on the outskirts of Tehran. The roads grew thick with lorries, engines howling, horns blaring, and every passing truck belched more fumes into my face. One passed within inches, coughing a thick black cloud that clung to me like shame.

That was it.

I threw Shirley down by the roadside and dropped beside her. Head between my knees. Broken. I cried —loud, hard, unguarded. Everything I'd kept bottled up for weeks poured out. The exhaustion. The uncertainty. The fear that my dream—my reason for being here—was collapsing.

What am I doing here?

The thought hit like a punch.

I'd come so far—7,000 kilometres. I'd pedalled every one, and crossed a continent under my own steam. And yet here I was, on a strip of tarmac somewhere near the insignificant town of Qazvin on the outskirts of Tehran, sobbing in the dirt beside a choked-up motorway.

It was pathetic. And I knew it. And I didn't care.

Eventually, I stopped crying—not because I felt better, but because I ran out of the energy to do even that. I just sat there, empty. I was exhausted in a way that had nothing to do with cycling.

The road stretched ahead, indifferent.

Then, slowly, with a deep breath and the gentlest flicker of resolve, I made a deal with myself: just one more kilometre.

I got back on the bike.

One turn of the pedals. Then another. Then a few more.

And somewhere in that small act of stubbornness, a sliver of determination crept back in. I couldn't fix everything. But I could keep moving.

There was no crowd cheering. No lightning bolt of inspiration. Just me, coaxing myself back from the edge, one slow breath at a time.

Finally—dusty, defeated, but not quite done—I reached the edge of the Iranian capital.

Tehran.

***

I'd managed to pull myself together by the time I reached Tehran. A new sense of focus had replaced the fog of frustration. No more moping. I needed a plan.

It was already dark as I cycled through the sprawling, smog-laden capital. For anyone unaccustomed to chaos, it would've been a nightmare. The roads were madness—lanes existed in theory, but in practice, drivers used whichever space they fancied. Buses and motorbikes rode *against* traffic, headlights blazing straight at me. Contraflow, full speed. It made no sense.

I hadn't seen this level of vehicular anarchy since Istanbul, and even then, Tehran had its own flavour of mayhem. But I'll admit, I quite enjoyed the challenge—dodging taxis, racing red lights, weaving through the confusion in search of the city centre.

I found a reasonably cheap hostel and cut costs by bunking with a Spanish traveller. After a quick köfte and kebab dinner, I collapsed into bed, emotionally wrung out but determined to reset. Tomorrow would be a full-on assault against the mountain of visa issues I still had to solve.

My Iranian visa was set to expire in under a week. On top of that, I still needed Turkmen, Chinese, Kyrgyz, Pakistani, and Indian paperwork. A full house of headaches.

Kyrgyzstan was off the table for now, but I'd heard it might be doable from Uzbekistan. India required a booked return flight, which made it too expensive to prioritise. A Pakistani visa might be available on arrival at the border at Sost, near China, if the border were open and the route safe. That left China and Turkmenistan—both notoriously tricky.

I ruled out cycling through southern Pakistan. It was just too dangerous. To add to the stress, I couldn't withdraw money in Iran due to Western sanctions and the nearest viable ATM was hundreds of kilometres away.

In desperation, I arranged a workaround through the hostel manager. A third-party Iranian with dual nationality and both UK and Iranian bank accounts helped me transfer money. It wasn't cheap. But it was necessary.

Leaving Shirley behind at the hostel, I took the overnight train to Esfahan. There, I managed to extend my Iranian visa by two weeks— it was just enough breathing room to get visas and get moving

The train pulled into Esfahan around 8:00 a.m. and, as I stepped onto the platform, a sharply dressed businessman struck up a conversation. He was curious about my journey and offered to buy me breakfast. My stomach growled at the invitation. I accepted.

What I didn't realise was that his idea of breakfast was a boiled sheep's head.

I'd expected bread. Maybe eggs. Not a full, gelatinous skull—eyeballs, tongue, and brain intact.

He sliced off a slab of tongue and placed it on my plate with a generous spoonful of brain. Then, as if saving the best for last, he gently nudged one of the eyeballs toward me. It stared up like it had unfinished business.

I tried the tongue first—surprisingly tender, almost pleasant—until I realised it felt disturbingly like chewing my own tongue. Then came the brain.

I mashed it into some bread, hoping to disguise the texture, but it coated my mouth like lukewarm cement. Thick. Metallic. Wrong.

I reached for water, but he was watching me, smiling expectantly. I nodded, swallowed hard, and made a sound that vaguely resembled appreciation.

Then came the eyeball.

He pointed at it, beaming. "Full of strength!" he said, flexing his arm.

I stared at it. It stared back.

"You first," I grinned, pushing the plate toward him.

He laughed, shaking his head. "For you! For guest!"

We had reached a standoff.

I'd done my bit. I'd eaten the tongue. I'd suffered the brain. But I wasn't going to blink first with the eyeball. I smiled, admitted defeat, and thankfully, he didn't seem offended. We toasted our cross-cultural bond over coffee and bottled water, the eyeball quietly ignored.

The trip to Esfahan had been worth it. I'd had my Iranian visa extended, and the time to think about my plan. I couldn't get into China if I stated that I was going via the Kashgar border—Azerbaijan had taught me that much. So I pinned my hopes on specifying a different entry point.

I booked a flight to Beijing, printed off the itinerary and went back to the embassy to submit a new application. But Tehran's Chinese Embassy wasn't making it easy. They turned me away on the first visit and told me to come back in three days. When I returned—application in hand—they rejected it again, saying I needed a letter of support from the British embassy. That letter cost me $61—money I barely had—but I paid up and waited two more days.

A week after first arriving in Tehran, I was finally handed my prize: a Chinese visa. Port of entry—any—so I duly cancelled my flight to Beijing.

With another week to kill before I was due to collect my five-day Turkmenistan transit visa in Mashhad, I decided to return to Esfahan. I hadn't planned on company, but, as ever, the road had ideas of its own.

I met three fellow travellers at my hostel in Esfahan. There was Anastasia, a sharp-witted Russian backpacker with cool eyes and a dry sense of humour. Alberto, an excitable Italian who was never far from either a strong opinion or a strong coffee. And John, a laid-back Canadian who let the experience wash over him like he was on holiday from real life.

"We should start at Naqsh-e Jahan Square," Alberto declared over breakfast. "The biggest in the world."

"I thought that was Tiananmen?" John said.

"*One* of the biggest," Alberto amended, shrugging. "But it's definitely the most beautiful."

He wasn't wrong. The square was vast—an ocean of stone bordered by architectural masterpieces. The Shah Mosque, its blue-tiled dome gleaming in the sunlight, loomed over one end. As we approached, the detail became dizzying. Each tile, each curve—it all felt impossibly precise.

Inside, our footsteps echoed off the cool marble. The silence was immense.

"Imagine the effort it took to build this," Anastasia whispered. The history felt so present that even our breath seemed too loud.

Next came the Sheikh Lotfollah Mosque—smaller, quieter, originally built for the royal family. No courtyard, no call to prayer. Just a single dome, the colour of peach skin at sunset, laced with swirling arabesques.

"So... private mosque?" John mused, craning his neck at the ceiling. "Not bad."

From the terrace of the Ali Qapu Palace, Esfahan sprawled out beneath us: the bazaar in one direction, the Si-o-Seh Pol bridge snaking across the Zayandeh River in another. Grace in every direction.

The bazaar, with its domed ceilings and lanterns swinging gently overhead, was a sensory assault. There were piles of saffron, dried rose, and turmeric. Vendors smiled behind mounds of nougat, nuts, and pistachios.

"Try this," a seller said, grinning, handing me a piece of *gaz*. It was chewy, sweet, and flecked with pistachio. Esfahan in a bite.

"I could live here," I said, half-serious.

"Alberto's already setting up a carpet shop," Anastasia said, pointing to where he was haggling passionately over a rug.

As dusk approached, we walked to Si-o-Seh Pol, the famed 33-arch bridge. Locals gathered beneath the arches—drinking tea, strumming guitars, singing softly into the golden air. It was a beautiful place to be young and hopeful.

That evening, Anastasia and I sat side by side watching the last light fade over Naqsh-e Jahan Square. We swapped stories about our old lives—we were both ex-lawyers who had stepped off the career treadmill. She had been in Paris, I in London. The similarities were strange and comforting. She'd been travelling through India and Myanmar, and hoped to return to India soon. I hoped we'd cross paths again—assuming I made it that far.

The next day, the four of us were swept into a house party hosted by some Esfahani students. Behind locked doors, there was dancing, quiet flirtations and laughter under curfew. I realised, not for the first time, that young Iranians weren't so different from anyone else—they just had to play a better game of hide and seek.

Shortly after, Alberto and John left for the UAE. Anastasia and I stayed on for a few more days, drifting lazily through Esfahan's best sights. I liked her. My ex had moved on; contact had dwindled. I longed for some connection, but I was never anywhere long enough for anything to begin. I told myself not to think too much.

When it was time for me to return to Tehran, Anastasia and I caught a bus together. I managed to wedge Shirley and my panniers into the luggage hold—but that's where the smoothness ended.

When we reached Tehran, the driver refused to release my bike without a $20 "fee"—more than twice the ticket cost. Normally, I'd argue, but I was out of patience and nearing the end of my tether. He refused to give me a receipt and laughed off my protests. Furious, I climbed onto the bus, got behind the wheel, and turned the key. Was I about to *drive* the 48-seater away?

Instead, I pocketed the keys.

Shouting erupted. Someone called the police. I calmed down—just enough to avoid being hauled off in cuffs. The officer, to my immense relief, found the whole episode hilarious. Eventually, I handed over the keys. The driver, now flustered and with his pride dented, offered me my bike for five dollars. I paid. He gave me back the money a few minutes later, sheepishly.

The incident killed whatever time Anastasia and I had left. She was off to the airport, and I needed to rest before heading east to collect my Turkmen visa.

We hugged outside the hostel and swapped email addresses.

"I hope we meet again," I said.

"India?" she smiled.

"India."

And then she was gone.

***

Mashhad—my next stop—was the holiest city in Iran. A city of pilgrims, its streets pulsed with quiet reverence, every step purposeful, every face set with belief.

At the Haram-e Razavi, I watched pilgrims circle the golden dome of Imam Reza's shrine, hands outstretched toward the latticed silver walls. Inside, the mirrored mosaics caught every flicker of candlelight, casting shimmering stars across the ceiling.

Later, at the quieter Torghabeh Mosque, I breathed in cool pine-scented air and listened to birdsong from nearby orchards. It felt like a pause button had been pressed.

Back at the hostel, Vali, the Afghani owner, gave me some unexpected advice: "Why not cycle into Afghanistan? It's quicker. Afghans are even more hospitable than Iranians."

I nodded politely. I didn't tell him I thought it was mad. Afghanistan was not an option. The country was at war, and the foreign office advised against all travel.

I collected my visa and continued with my plan to head east toward the Turkmen border.

The road to the Iranian border city of Bajgiran was a long, two-day climb through Martian terrain—red, rocky hills with barely a scrap of green. As the altitude rose, the warmth vanished. I pedalled through cold air, and thoughts of everyone I'd left behind came to mind: Reza's smile, Anastasia's quiet nod at the airport, Vali's wonderful hospitality.

By the time I reached the border—perched somewhere between 1,600 and 1,800 metres above sea level—the temperature had plunged.

Despite the gruelling cycle and harsh conditions at the border, when I arrived, I was told that I wasn't allowed to cross. No explanation. Just a vague wave toward nowhere.

I later found out it was simply that the border had closed for the day, and it would be open again the next morning at 7:00 a.m. I pitched my tent on the pavement, where it was exposed to the wind. The only accommodation was several kilometres back down the very steep hill I had tried so very hard to ascend that day. That night, the temperature dropped to minus six. As I lay there, shivering, watching my breath cloud the thin air, it dawned on me that I was woefully underprepared for the kind of winter riding that lay ahead.

CHAPTER 15

Five Days of Dust

Number of days on the road: 142
Total distance covered: 6,998 km

I was up at 6:00 a.m., eager to press on and finally cross into Turkmenistan.

The first light of dawn spread across the horizon, casting a golden glow over the vast, empty landscape. As I pedalled north from the border, the sheer surrealism of my surroundings took hold of me. The jagged, rocky outcrops and endless barren plains looked almost unearthly, as though I had been dropped onto a distant planet. The land was silent in a way that felt unnatural—no birds, no wind, just the crunch of tyres on gravel and the hollow sound of my own breathing. It felt like pedalling through a forgotten dream. The land was stark, stripped of excess, yet it carried an undeniable beauty—one that was both haunting and mesmerising.

Ashgabat, the Turkmen capital, came as a shock. The city was modern, immaculate—far more so than I had expected. Turkmenistan is one of those places that many people have barely heard of, let alone pinpoint on a map. Perhaps that was why I had imagined it to be stuck in a bygone era. Instead, I found a city gleaming with polished white marble, grandiose architecture, and vast, empty boulevards that felt more like a film set than a lived-in capital.

Walking through Ashgabat felt like stepping onto a meticulously curated stage set—everything shone, everything was symmetrical, but it was eerie like there was something missing. Where were all the people? The empty roads and pristine, but soulless perfection made me feel more like an outsider than I had anywhere else on this journey.

The first order of business was cash. Once I'd worked out where to withdraw money, I treated myself to a proper meal—something more substantial than the bread and cheese that had sustained me for three meals a day for the past week. The taste of something hot and freshly cooked was an indulgence in itself. That, and my first beer in weeks, which I savoured slowly, knowing it might be a while before the next passed my lips.

Ashgabat's skyline was dominated by white marble buildings, an architectural signature that gave the city an almost surreal, artificial sheen. The National Museum, the Monument of Independence and the Ashgabat Central Mosque were among its most recognisable landmarks, but Turkmenistan's rigid policies toward tourists meant my time here was severely limited. With only a five-day transit visa, I had little choice but to keep moving. Time was already slipping away—it was day two and, if I wanted to reach Uzbekistan in time, I needed to push forward without delay.

Beyond the city, the Karakum Desert spread out before me—a vast sea of shale-rich sand, covering nearly 70 per cent of the country. The road carved through an unforgiving yet strangely hypnotic wilderness.

It was the first time in weeks I hadn't felt the weight of decisions. No visa stress. No emotional baggage. Just sand, sky, and the rhythm of wheels on tarmac. I was a ghost crossing a ghost country—and for a little while, I found peace in that.

Rolling dunes sprawled out into the distance, interrupted only by scrubby vegetation and occasional oases. At one point, I stopped beneath a lone tree, barely more than a twisted branch, and shared a bottle of warm cola with a man in a tractor who offered no words, just a quiet nod before disappearing into the sandstorm behind him. The landscape felt lifeless at first glance, yet, as I whizzed through, I spotted signs of resilience—camels plodding in the distance, a lone gazelle darting across the sand, an eagle circling high above, scanning for prey.

The desolation of Turkmenistan was immense, but it had a quiet majesty, a raw and unfiltered kind of beauty that few would ever see.

Time was against me, and I felt a deep disappointment at not being able to see more of Turkmenistan. Of all the places I had hoped to visit, Merv was at the top of my list. Immortalised in 'The Great Game' in Rudyard Kipling's novel *Kim*, this legendary Silk Road oasis had been one of the most important cities in the region—a place where merchants, scholars, and travellers converged, exchanging goods, ideas, and cultures.

Its ancient ruins, scattered across the desert, told the story of a civilisation that had flourished for centuries before being swallowed by time and conquest. I had imagined wandering through its crumbling citadels, standing beneath the remnants of its palaces and mosques, and picturing the caravans that once passed through, laden with silk, spices, and stories about its role as a crossroads of civilisation. I had dreamt of Merv the way some people dream of Petra or Machu Picchu—not for the photo, but for the silence among the stones. To walk its ruins, I imagine, would have felt like shaking hands with history. But my time here was a sprint, not a slow pilgrimage, and I had to pass right through with nothing but a glimpse.

As I approached the Turkmen-Uzbek border, the landscape remained unchanged—flat, featureless, and dust-choked—but my mind had already shifted forward.

Turkmenistan had felt like a place that kept its secrets close—offering just enough to stir the imagination, but never enough to truly understand. There'd been no time to linger, no detours, just five days of sand, sweat, and relentless pedalling.

I watched as the border guards examined my passport, the sun beating down on their crisp, Soviet-style uniforms. Beyond them lay Uzbekistan, the next chapter of my Silk Road journey.

CHAPTER 16

Bukhara and Beyond

Number of days on the road: **147**
Total distance covered: **7,876 km**

I continued the Silk Road route into Uzbekistan and towards the city of Bukhara, following the auspicious path taken by intrepid explorers of the Great Game.

It was late when I arrived in Bukhara, but as luck would have it, I ran straight into Connor, a New Zealander I had first met in Baku who was travelling through the region by train and bus. He greeted me with an easy grin, clapping me on the back. It was like running into a familiar face in a dream. After the desolate quiet of Turkmenistan, even a single known smile felt like a floodlight in the fog.

"Mate, I was starting to think you'd disappeared off the face of the earth," he said. "What took you so long?"

"Let's just say Turkmenistan wasn't the most relaxing ride," I replied, shaking my head. "Five days through a desert with barely a chance to stop and look around. I don't think my water bottles have ever worked so hard."

He laughed. "I reckon you need a proper meal then. There's an Italian place nearby—it's not exactly Tashkent, but it's got beer and pizza."

That was all the convincing I needed. Before long, we were sitting in a cosy restaurant, tucking into large slices of margherita pizza. The smell of baked dough and tomatoes filled the air, and the first sip of beer was like liquid gold after the long ride.

"I ran into Chris and Sara earlier," Connor said, between bites. "They're here in Bukhara, too. Do you remember them from Georgia and Azerbaijan?"

"Of course! They still going strong?"

"Yeah, still pedalling. Meanwhile, Matt, Jack, and Keith are about a week ahead of you in Tashkent, jumping through hoops for their Chinese and Kyrgyz visas." He smirked. "Which I'm sure is a total nightmare."

"I bet. Sometimes shopping for visas seems like playing administrative Russian Roulette."

We shared a bottle of wine, a few more beers, and swapped tales of our travels. The hours slipped by in the warmth of the restaurant, the city of Bukhara humming quietly beyond the windows, its ancient walls and minarets standing watch over another night.

At this point, I was delighted to discover, by receipt of an email from the British Consulate in Pakistan, that they had contacted the police in Gilgit, close to the border, who had confirmed that the pass was still open. It felt like the first crack of sunlight after weeks of cloud. For the first time in days, I let myself believe again—maybe this journey wasn't doomed after all. Fragmented plans seemed to be finally coming back together. I missed Chris and Sara by a few hours, who had moved on to Samarkand, but there was a good chance I would catch them up in the coming days.

I stayed in Bukhara for a few days, and I was utterly captivated by the city. The usual tourist crowds had long departed, chased away by the arrival of bitter autumn winds, leaving the streets serene and atmospheric. The cold air sharpened the outlines of the ancient fortresses, mausoleums, and towering minarets, their brickwork and blue-tiled domes standing stark against the pale winter sky. It was no surprise that Bukhara was a UNESCO World Heritage site—every winding street and weathered façade seemed to hold the whispers of a long and storied past.

Bukhara was once at the heart of the Great Game, the covert 19th-century struggle between the British and the

Russian Empires for control of Central Asia. This city, with its labyrinthine alleys and shadowy caravanserais, had witnessed the cloak-and-dagger intrigue of spies and emissaries who navigated its dangerous political landscape. Arthur Conolly and Charles Stoddart, two young British officers, learned this the hard way. Sent to negotiate with Nasrullah Khan, the Emir of Bukhara, they were thrown into a rat-infested pit for months, accused of espionage and ultimately beheaded in June 1842, their deaths sending shockwaves back to London.

Standing before the Ark of Bukhara, the grand fortress where they had been held captive, I found myself contemplating their incredible bravery. To venture into this part of the world in their mid-twenties, navigating treacherous alliances, tribal conflicts, and the merciless rule of despots, all for the sake of imperial intelligence—it made my own journey seem almost leisurely in comparison.

Yet, despite its bloody past, Bukhara today exuded a quiet dignity, its ancient landmarks casting a golden glow as the sun dipped below the horizon. The Ark of Bukhara, once the seat of the Emir, stood as a formidable relic of power, its thick walls and high battlements silhouetted against the evening sky. The Kalyan Minaret, an architectural masterpiece from the 12th century, rose from the heart of the city, spiralling skyward, a beacon that had guided weary travellers for centuries.

As night fell, the Po-i-Kalyan Mosque became a dreamlike vision, its azure tiles and sweeping arches bathed in the glow of lantern light. A handful of locals and pilgrims knelt in silent prayer, their murmurs drifting on the crisp night air. Even in the stillness, the city pulsed with an energy that seemed to bridge centuries—its history alive in every worn stone and whispered call to prayer.

I could have stayed in Bukhara for weeks, wandering its dusty alleys, drinking strong tea beneath the shade of its grand madrasas, and tracing the footsteps of explorers, spies, and scholars who had passed through before me. But the road called, and my journey had to continue. Even so, I knew I was leaving behind one of the most mesmerising cities I had ever encountered—a place that made history feel close enough to touch, and solitude feel sacred rather than lonely.

***

I rode a relatively easy day's ride to my next stop, the ancient city of Samarkand. I found myself standing in the Registan Square at the heart of the city and, for a moment, everything else faded into the background. I had imagined this place, but nothing could have prepared me for the sheer magnificence of it in person. Three colossal madrasas rose around me, their façades alive with carefully crafted tilework, swirls of deep blue and gold forming hypnotic geometric patterns. The arches extended impossibly high, swallowing the sky, and the domes twinkled with the last of the daylight. I walked slowly across the worn stone square, trying to absorb it all—the weight of history, the whispers of ancient scholars who had once studied here, the grandeur that time had not managed to erase. It felt almost surreal, standing in the same place where traders, poets, and astronomers had passed through for centuries.

Still caught in the spell of the Registan, I made my way toward the Bibi-Khanym Mosque, its massive turquoise dome dominating the skyline. The closer I got, the more I could see the cracks in its walls, the scars left by time and earthquakes, yet even in its weathered state, it was humbling. I stepped through the towering entrance, my footsteps echoing in the cavernous interior. The air was cool, laced with the scent of old stone and incense, and high above me, calligraphy inscribed across the domed ceiling.

Later, as I wandered through Samarkand's winding streets, I was pulled in by the sights, sounds, and smells of daily life. The sizzle of kebabs on open flames, the sharp, floral scent of saffron drifting from spice stalls, the clink of metal as craftsmen shaped jewellery and decorative plates. Market traders called out their wares—handwoven silk scarves, carved wooden chess sets, deep bowls of pomegranates split open like rubies.

Eventually, I crossed paths with Chris and Sara at the hostel. Seeing familiar faces after weeks on the road felt comforting. Something familiar in a place that was so different. We sat in the courtyard, wrapped in warm layers to stave off the creeping chill of late autumn, swapping stories over steaming cups of chai. The place had a quiet charm—cushioned benches lined the walls and vines crawled up the brickwork, their leaves rustling in the wind. A small fountain trickled in the centre, adding to the sense of calm that came after long days of travel.

"So, how many times have you been dragged into an English lesson now?" Chris asked with a grin, stretching out his legs.

"At this point, I could probably put 'unofficial English teacher' on my CV," I laughed. "Everywhere I went, they were ready to hire me on the spot."

Sara chuckled. "Not a bad side hustle. Just don't start giving geography lessons—'cause if one more person asks us if Spain is next to Russia, I might lose my mind."

We spent the afternoon at a sprawling bazaar on the outskirts of the city, a labyrinth of stalls that seemed to go on forever, each alley bursting with colours, textures, and the hum of haggling voices. Silk scarves billowed from wooden beams, their patterns catching the light. Traders called out from behind pyramids of dried fruit and nuts, offering samples of sticky dates and tart dried apricots.

But while we had set out looking for gifts, practicality took over. The biting cold was making itself known, and we all ended up with thick fur hats pulled low over our ears.

Chris wrapped himself in his new coat, flexing his arms. "Well, I was hoping to go for style, but I think I've landed somewhere between 'local shepherd' and 'wandering philosopher.'"

Sara smirked. "More like 'guy who hasn't done laundry in two weeks.'"

The market was a reflection of Tashkent's place on the Silk Road, with bales of fine silk stacked next to stalls, the city's past as a vital trading hub still woven into every corner.

Despite the company, I couldn't shake a sense of urgency.

Sara, Chris and I travelled together to Tashkent, hoping to reunite with Keith, Matt, and Jack, who were tackling the infamous visa hunt. But when we arrived in the capital, the news was already stale—they had secured their visas and moved on.

"Damn," I muttered, "It would've been good to see them before heading into the mountains."

Chris sighed, shaking his head. "Typical. They move fast when they want to."

Sara nudged me. "And you move slowly when there's free tea involved."

We laughed, but the realisation was sinking in. Chris and Sara's journey was ending here—they were flying to India, their path splitting from mine for good.

As Chris and Sara packed up their gear for their flight, I felt an unexpected heaviness settle over me. Saying goodbye on the road was nothing new—but this time it hit harder. Maybe it was the shared history, or maybe I knew that from here on, things were about to get lonelier, colder, and harder in every sense. The Silk Road had connected us across multiple countries—Georgia, Azerbaijan, Iran, Uzbekistan—yet now, our paths were finally diverging for good.

"So, this is it?" I asked, forcing a grin as I adjusted the straps on my pannier.

Sara smiled, but there was a flicker of something else in her eyes. "Yeah. Unless you're suddenly planning on flying to India?"

I shook my head. "Not yet."

Chris clapped me on the shoulder, his usual easy-going demeanour masking the finality of the moment. "You'll be alright, mate. You've made it this far—Kyrgyzstan's just another challenge."

I nodded, but I wasn't sure I believed him.

We hugged, and then, in the way of all goodbyes on the road, it was over in an instant. No lingering, no prolonged farewells—just a final wave as they disappeared into the flow of people, leaving me alone in the cold.

For the first time in months, I felt the familiar weight of isolation pressing in around me.

The road ahead felt different now. The horizon had changed. It wasn't just distance—it was altitude, and ice, and consequence. The road would soon rise and, with it, the stakes. Less of an adventure, more of a test. The closer I got to Kyrgyzstan, the more the landscape turned wild and unforgiving. The mountains I had read about—the towering, snow-covered peaks of the Pamirs and Tian Shan—were no longer distant ideas. They were waiting for me.

The window to cross the border pass before winter slammed it shut was shrinking fast. The thought of being caught in an early blizzard, alone, without proper winter gear, was a constant, nagging presence in my mind. I had survived desert heat, relentless headwinds, and border bureaucracy, but this was different. This was nature, indifferent and absolute.

Every mile I pedalled eastward brought a new question I didn't yet have the answer to: Would I make it in time? Would my gear hold up? Would my body?

There was only one way to find out.

My Kyrgyz visa was processed in just two days, leaving me with time to explore Tashkent by bike. Independence Square, the beating heart of the city, was framed by imposing Soviet-era government buildings, including the Parliament and Cabinet of Ministers. Unlike the older, more atmospheric parts of Uzbekistan, this area had a sleek, modern aesthetic—a reflection of the country's post-Soviet identity, still evolving since gaining independence in 1991.

Wanting to get a broader perspective of the city, I cycled towards the Tashkent Television Tower, a futuristic steel structure that had dominated the skyline since 1985. From its observation deck, the city unfolded beneath me, a blend of wide boulevards, Soviet-style architecture, and pockets of old Uzbek charm.

Below, Amir Timur Square stood proudly, a space dedicated to the fourteenth-century Turco-Mongol conqueror better known in the West as Tamburlaine. Later, I wandered through the national museum.

Uzbek cuisine is unapologetically hearty and was exactly what I needed. I sampled *plov,* a fragrant pilaf-style rice dish, its saffron-infused grains mingled with slow-cooked lamb, caramelised onions, and ribbons of carrot, all soaked in the deep flavours of cumin and barberries. Another favourite was *laghman,* a steaming bowl of hand-pulled noodles, thick and chewy, swimming in a robust tomato and lamb broth. It was comfort food at its best, the kind of meal that sticks to your ribs and fuels long days on the road.

But time wasn't on my side. Winter was closing in fast, and I had a narrow window to reach China and cross into Pakistan before the Khunjerab Pass became unnavigable with snow and ice. Leaving Tashkent behind, I pedalled eastward, the rhythmic undulations of the Fergana Valley slowing my pace. The roads twisted through rolling hills and fertile plains, where farmers wrapped in thick woollen coats drove herds of sheep along the dusty verges.

The sense of urgency weighed on me, but so did the reality of what lay ahead. I wasn't sure if I was ready.

I had navigated my way across Europe and the Middle East, through deserts and border posts, reunions and heartbreaks. Now it asked something new—endurance, resolve, and a willingness to ride into silence.

CHAPTER 17

High Roads to the Border

Number of days on the road: 155
Total distance covered: 8,840 km

I crossed into Kyrgyzstan in the afternoon, but Osh, the nearest city, was still some distance away. By the time I arrived, darkness had settled over the streets, making the search for accommodation more of a challenge than I had anticipated. Just as I was beginning to feel the strain of exhaustion, I was approached by two, round, middle-aged Kyrgyz women, their kind faces framed by colourful headscarves.

They spoke rapidly in Kyrgyz, with a few words of Russian thrown in, and though I couldn't understand much, their gestures and warm smiles made it clear—they were determined to help. Despite my protests, they waved away my concerns, motioning for me to follow as they marched ahead with the confidence of locals who knew every street and shortcut in town.

We wound our way through quiet, dimly lit backstreets until, eventually, we arrived at a small, cosy hotel, where the women took charge of negotiations with the owner. Their voices rose and fell in animated haggling, a theatrical exchange of raised eyebrows, folded arms, and exaggerated sighs, until finally, they turned to me with beaming grins and triumphant nods.

"*Five dollars*!" one of them declared, holding up five fingers.

Five dollars—for a warm bed, a hot shower, and a roof over my head. I couldn't believe my luck. As I settled in for the night, I found myself grinning at the thought of my two unexpected guardians. Their generosity and motherly insistence had turned what could have been a frustrating night into a memorable, heartwarming welcome to Kyrgyzstan.

The next morning, feeling refreshed, I stocked up on supplies at a small supermarket, preparing for the remote mountain stretches ahead. I had hoped to catch up with Keith, Matt, and Jack, but there was no sign of them. Given the distances between towns in this part of the world, it was entirely possible they were a day or two ahead, or even behind.

Osh, Kyrgyzstan's oldest city, was lively but unpretentious, home to around 250,000 people. It sits at the foothills of the Pamir Mountains, resting at an elevation of roughly 1,000 metres.

The surroundings were stunning, with a patchwork of rolling hills, dense forests, and fast-flowing rivers, all set against presence of distant, snow-dusted peaks.

By midday, I was back on the road, the landscape transforming rapidly as I climbed towards the Chirchyk Pass, towering at 2,408 metres. The road snaked through dramatic valleys, past solitary yurts and herds of livestock, their bells clanging softly in the crisp mountain air. The higher I went, the more the air thinned and cooled, but the effort was worth it—the scenery was spectacular.

I pushed on, passing through the rugged terrain of Gulcha and Kyzyl-Korgon, where red cliffs stood like sentinels over winding riverbeds. Eventually, I reached the mountain village of Kung Elek, a tiny, weather-beaten settlement nestled into the heart of the Pamir Mountains. At night, the wind howled like an animal, and the sky was a riot of stars. I hadn't felt small in this way since my time in the Alps—but, somehow, this was different. This wasn't dramatic. It was vast. Unfeeling. Elemental.

The remoteness here was staggering. Soaring peaks loomed overhead, their jagged ridges carving shadows into the valley floor. The land had an untamed beauty, where nature was both majestic and unforgiving. I had been warned that bears roamed these parts, but the only wildlife I spotted were mountain goats perched precariously on sheer rock faces and eagles soaring effortlessly in the icy updrafts.

This was true wilderness, the kind that made you feel small and insignificant, yet deeply alive.

Here, I stayed with a wonderful Kyrgyz family, whose warmth and hospitality were beyond anything I had expected. The father was short and broad-shouldered, his face weathered by the mountain air, a thin black moustache neatly trimmed above a strong, serious mouth. His handshake was firm, his grip like iron, a man used to hard work and harsher winters. His hair was cut in the typical Kyrgyz style, short at the sides, slightly longer on top, giving him a stoic, almost warrior-like presence.

His wife, wrapped in layers of thick wool, bustled into the room carrying a steaming bowl of Kyrgyz stew, the aroma of slow-cooked mutton and potatoes filling my nostrils. She placed the earthenware bowls before me and gestured enthusiastically for me to eat, eat! I needed no encouragement—it was exactly what I needed after a freezing day on the road.

The children, wide-eyed and endlessly curious, were fascinated by my strange clothes, my bike, and especially my guitar. I strummed a few simple chords, and their faces lit up with laughter, their little hands clapping in delight. Even the stoic father cracked a smile, nodding approvingly. We snapped photos, capturing the bizarre but wonderful energy of the evening, a gathering of people who shared no common language, yet had no trouble understanding each other. I showed them pictures of my home and my family. Gestures, laughter, and expressive faces replaced words, and somehow, that was enough.

This village, Kung Elek, was the most out-of-the-way place I had ever visited. As I lay down to go to sleep, I felt grateful to have experienced a piece of Kyrgyz life that few travellers ever would.

I woke up at eight, the cold biting at my exposed skin as I packed up my gear, my breath hanging thick in the morning air. After a final round of handshakes and grateful smiles, I set off into the brittle dawn, the world around me silent except for the crunch of snow beneath my tyres. The road ahead was treacherous—thick with ice, rutted and uneven. More than once, I was forced to dismount and push Shirley uphill, my boots slipping on the packed snow as I fought against the incline.

Further along, I came across a flatbed truck struggling for traction on the frozen road. The driver, wrapped in layers against the cold, waved me over. Together, we heaved heavy rocks into the back of his truck, their weight intended to press the tyres down for grip. It was slow, bone-numbing work, but after a few final shoves, the truck lurched forward, sending up a shower of ice and grit as it disappeared into the distance.

The climb over the Taldyk Pass was brutal, the air thinning with every turn of the pedals. At 3,615 metres, the wind cut through my clothes, sharp and merciless, but the views were staggering. Snow-dusted peaks spread out endlessly in every direction, their jagged forms bathed in the pale light of an overcast sky. The descent was no less punishing—the road still slick with ice—but eventually, I rolled down into Sary Tash, the small settlement sitting quietly in the vast, frozen expanse of the Alay Valley.

Sary Tash felt like the edge of the world. A scattering of low houses, their roofs sagging under the weight of fresh snow, lined the streets. Smoke curled lazily from chimneys, twisting into the crisp, high-altitude air. The stillness was profound, broken only by the occasional bark of a distant dog or the muffled sound of hooves as a horse trudged through the frost. Icicles hung in dagger-like formations from every eave, glistening under the pale winter sky.

As I cycled out of town, gangs of excited children swarmed around me, their eager voices calling out as they jogged alongside my bike. "Pen! Pen!" they pleaded, their hands outstretched, their cheeks flushed from the cold. I laughed, shaking my head, knowing I had only one and needed it myself. They grinned regardless, running beside me until I picked up speed and left them behind, their laughter still ringing through the frosty morning air.

The temperature plunged with alarming speed. It was the end of November, and the cold was no longer a creeping discomfort but an unforgiving force, sapping the warmth from my body with every pedal stroke. As I rounded a bend exiting Sary Tash, a brutal headwind slammed into me like a physical wall. I gritted my teeth and pushed forward, but the icy blast cut through every layer of clothing, turning my fingers into lifeless blocks of pain.

The air was already freezing at -13°C, but with the wind howling mercilessly across the barren landscape, the chill factor plummeted to a deadly -26°C. My breath crystallised the moment it left my lips, and the skin on my face burned from the relentless exposure. Every movement felt slower, heavier, as if the cold itself was leeching the energy from my limbs.

Desperately searching for shelter, I huddled behind a mound of snow-covered rock, trying to escape the full force of the wind. But the cold was inescapable—it gnawed through my layers, burrowing deep into my core. My fingers were numb, my toes beginning to throb with the warning signs of frostbite. The realisation hit me hard: if I stayed here, I wouldn't last the night.

Panic clawed at the edges of my mind. I had no choice but to press on, to make the long, gruelling ride to Erkeshtam before darkness swallowed the landscape. There was no room for hesitation. Survival depended on movement, on keeping my blood flowing and my mind sharp. Steeling myself, I pushed back onto the road, fighting against the wind, knowing that each frozen kilometre along the ice-covered road was the only thing standing between me and the very real possibility of perishing in the vast, indifferent wilderness.

I arrived at the border at 5:00 p.m. on a Friday. The border with China sits at 3,005 metres above sea level. I was utterly exhausted and certain I had missed the last chance to cross that day. To my immense relief, the guards let me through—just me. The truck drivers had to wait in line until Monday, stranded in no-man's land for the weekend. Stupidly, instead of trying to find somewhere to stay in the tiny border zone, I convinced myself I could make it to a lower altitude before nightfall and pressed on downhill.

For a short while, I made good progress, but the days were short, and as the sun dipped below the horizon, so did the temperature. The wind picked up, carrying with it a biting chill that sliced through every layer of clothing. Suddenly, I was in trouble. There were no towns in sight, no signs of shelter. Erkeshtam, the nearest settlement on my map, was behind me, uphill, and the thought of turning back was unbearable. The temperature plummeted faster than I'd anticipated, my breath forming thick clouds in the frigid air.

I had no choice but to camp.

By the time I set up my tent, the temperature with wind chill was at -36°C[1]. I tried to light my stove to cook some noodles, but the fuel refused to burn in the freezing air. My water was already solid ice, so I wrapped the bottle in my sleeping bag, hoping my body heat would thaw it out. An hour later, it remained a slush of stubborn ice chunks.

I layered up: thermal base layer, t-shirt, long-sleeved cycling jersey, fleece, down jacket. Gloves, Russian hat, two pairs of socks, fur boots. I burrowed deep into my sleeping bag, but it was rated for only -5°C. The cold wasn't something I could fight against—it seeped into my bones, stole my breath, and made my muscles shudder involuntarily.

Then came the realisation that I wasn't just cold. I was scared.

My body refused to sleep. Not because of discomfort, but because some primal part of me understood that falling asleep in these conditions might mean never waking up. Panic flickered at the edges of my mind, but I pushed it down. There was nothing I could do but wait. Slowly, the fear gave way to exhaustion. My body relaxed, my mind quieted. This is okay, I thought. If I sleep, I sleep. And if

---

1 Whilst I was deeply aware it was extremely cold at the time, it was only later when I researched the temperatures that I actually found out how cold it was.

I don't wake up... well, so be it. I no longer felt afraid. I only wanted to rest.

But I never did fall asleep. And that, perhaps, saved my life.

***

The first grey light of dawn leaked through the tent like a whispered promise.

I stirred slowly. My fingers, swollen and useless. My toes burning back to life. I breathed shallowly, as if even the air could shatter.

But I was alive.

Alive.

The sky had turned a soft pinkish-blue. The wind had stilled. The silence no longer felt like death—it felt like mercy.

I unzipped the tent and looked out.

The mountains, silent sentinels, watched without comment. The world was still. I stood, wincing, stretching, shaky-legged and half-frozen.

But I was still here.

CHAPTER 18

Arrival in Kashgar

Number of days on the road: 161
Total distance covered: 8,972 km

I descended from my camping spot near the Erkeshtam Pass slowly towards Kashgar.

Every movement was cautious. My limbs were stiff, my brain sluggish, and the road unforgiving. Ice patches waited like traps hidden within the snow-covered road. The soft snow was easy to manage and provided reasonable grip, but the ice patches—well, they were evil.

More than once, I lost control and slammed down hard. My shoulder throbbed. My knees were raw. My confidence was threadbare.

It took two full days to reach Kashgar, travelling just over 200 kilometres.

At lower altitudes, the world softened. The cold relented, and the snowy road returned to asphalt. By the time I wheeled Shirley through the outskirts of the city, it was hard to believe how close I'd come to not getting here at all.

I found a hotel—not one from my guidebook, all of those were closed—but a clean, warm place with a thick quilt on the bed and boiling hot water.

I stood under the shower until my skin prickled and turned pink.

Then I ate. Noodles. Meat. Beer. Tea. More noodles. The kind of hunger that feels bottomless.

And then, at last, I slept.

Not the panicked half-sleep of a man whose life was at risk, but the deep, dreamless sleep of someone who had made it through.

After resting and refuelling at the hotel, the staff, curious about my journey, kindly phoned around to see if they could track down Keith, Matt, and Jack. No luck. They had most likely encountered the same punishing conditions and taken public transport into Pakistan. The thought was disappointing—our group had thinned, and now, I remained alone.

I ate ravenously, devouring bowl after bowl of steaming noodles, my body desperate for fuel. Later, I wandered to a nearby bar for a beer, allowing myself, finally, to feel relief. I had survived a very terrifying ordeal up in the mountains. I sank into another deep, undisturbed sleep —safe, warm, and infinitely grateful.

The early morning sun streamed through my window and flooded the waking streets of Kashgar. The city was already alive with the sounds of motorbikes humming past. Feeling restless, I rose quickly, determined to untangle the uncertainties surrounding my next move. My biggest concern remained unresolved—the elusive Pakistani visa. It had lingered in my thoughts ever since my brutal camping ordeal at the Erkeshtam Pass.

I set off through the maze of narrow alleys and broad avenues, heading for a travel agency where I hoped to find answers. With a mix of apprehension and hope, I explained my predicament to a woman behind the counter. She listened patiently, then, to my astonishment, offered an unexpected glimmer of hope.

"It is possible to reach Sost without a visa," she said, her tone reassuring. "You can obtain a visa on arrival at the border."

I felt a weight lift from my shoulders. Nowhere had I read that this was possible other than on the occasional travel blog I had stumbled across. I had never managed to find any official resource confirming that this would be possible. If this were true, it could spare me the long and frustrating visa application process. However, another problem loomed large—the Karakoram Mountains and passing over the highest paved road in the world in the middle of winter. The thought of tackling them, never mind alone–and after everything I had endured—gnawed at me. Sensing my hesitation, she suggested an alternative: taking a bus over the border.

"It's a two-day journey," she explained. "You'll stop overnight in Tashkurgan before crossing into Pakistan."

Grateful for the advice, I hurried to the bus station to make sense of my options. As I reached the ticket counter, a woman behind the glass glanced up at me.

"Are you with the group of four?" she asked, smiling.

"No?" I said, slightly confused. "But hang on a moment," I muttered to myself as I fumbled around for my camera. I located a picture of Keith and his unmistakable beard and showed it to the woman.

"Is this the group?" I asked. "Yes, that is them," she said politely.

It was fantastic news. She instructed me to return at 9 a.m. and I did, waiting anxiously as the minutes crawled by. Then, suddenly, through the shifting crowd, I saw them—Keith, Matt, Jack, and another traveller I hadn't met before, a jovial German named Christian.

Relief and excitement surged through me. After so many solitary miles, it was a joy to be reunited with familiar faces.

As we gathered, the bond we had forged earlier in our journeys along the Silk Road rekindled instantly.

"We must have hit the Erkeshtam Pass just a few days before you," Keith said, shaking his head. "I swear, it was like cycling into a frozen wall."

Matt groaned. "I still can't feel my toes properly. I think they gave up somewhere on that mountain."

Indeed, they had encountered the same freezing temperatures that I had and had been forced to throw their bikes on a truck and hitchhike over the pass.

I wandered through the streets of Kashgar, the uneven cobblestones beneath my feet worn smooth by centuries of traders and travellers passing through. Stalls lined the narrow streets. I witnessed iron workers making cooking equipment and bowls and stoves. A butcher, his cleaver coming down with rhythmic precision, worked through slabs of meat as customers haggled over prices. Nearby, a craftsman hammered tiny patterns into a copper teapot, his fingers blackened from years of work, while a group of elderly men sat cross-legged on a low wooden platform, sipping tea and watching the world go by.

But just as we were preparing to leave for Pakistan the next morning, news spread that the road ahead was blocked by a landslide. Officials muttered about the possibility of it remaining closed for days, weeks or even until the spring thaw. The idea of being stuck in Kashgar was frustrating, yet with our old cycling crew unexpectedly reunited, there was something strangely fitting about it.

"So, looks like we're all stuck together again," Matt said, grinning as I checked into their hostel.

"At least there's beer," I replied.

That evening, we crowded into the hostel's communal living room, the flickering light of a single lamp casting long shadows on the walls. We sat cross-legged on the floor with steaming cups of hot chai.

Matt stretched out, shaking his head. "You know, the last few months have been a real test of my sense of direction. Turns out, it's about as reliable as a compass in a washing machine."

Keith stroked his now-infamous beard. "Well, I can't go anywhere without someone calling me 'The Bearded Nomad'. I should start charging for photos."

I laughed. "And as for me, I think I've developed a unique skill—ordering food in every country without speaking the language. Point, nod, and hope for the best. Works every time."

The room filled with laughter, we were a bunch of guys who didn't take ourselves too seriously. And for now, Kashgar—unexpected and unpredictable—was exactly where we were meant to be.

The road was still closed the next day, and frustration started to creep in. We asked around, trying to figure out our options, and the hostel workers, ever resourceful, managed to arrange a 4x4 for us in case the bus remained a no-go the following day. It was a relief to have a backup plan, but none of us liked the idea of waiting indefinitely.

***

After much back and forth, Christian, Keith, and I made the call—we would attempt to cycle up to Tashkurgan.

A part of me screamed to take the easy route—to avoid the cold, the exhaustion, the sheer punishment ahead. But another part—the part that had brought me this far—couldn't back down. This road, this challenge, was what the journey was all about. And besides, with Keith and Christian by my side, it felt more doable than facing the elements alone.

I wasn't entirely sold on the idea. The memory of my near-fatal night at Erkeshtam was still fresh in my mind, and the thought of getting caught out in those brutal temperatures again unsettled me. But Keith, ever the optimist, grinned and waved a hand dismissively.

"We'll be fine," he said. "We've got three of us now—we'll figure it out."

Matt and Jack, on the other hand, made the more sensible decision. Without the right gear, they weren't about to risk the cold and opted to wait for the bus instead.

Determined to at least give myself a fighting chance, I made a beeline for a local army surplus store. I picked up a pair of thick Chinese army gloves, some fur-lined military boots that looked like they belonged in a 1960s Siberian campaign, and a heavy woollen blanket. The whole lot cost me about $10, which didn't exactly instil confidence in their quality.

I held up the gloves and turned to Christian. "Reckon these will keep my fingers from falling off?"

He gave them a sceptical once-over and smirked. "They'll probably keep your hands on, but you might lose a few fingers."

I wasn't entirely convinced that any of these last-minute purchases would stop me from freezing to death in my tent, if it came to that. But at least now, with three of us, we could help each other out, pool resources, and improvise if things got rough.

It was a better plan than taking on the elements alone.

The three of us were up at first light, the sky still a murky blue as we pulled on layers against the morning chill. Over a quick breakfast, we said our goodbyes to Matt and Jack, who, still snug in their sleeping bags, seemed quite content to wait for the bus. Then, with a final handshake and a few words of encouragement, we pushed off, weaving through the chaotic outskirts of Kashgar. Trucks blared their horns as they thundered past, and electric scooters, near-silent but deadly, zipped by unpredictably. Soon, though, the city faded behind us, and we found ourselves on a long, straight road stretching to the horizon.

At first, the ride felt almost too easy. The incline was barely noticeable, and we laughed at our earlier concerns about the journey being impossibly tough. The road was eerily empty, cutting through a vast, flat expanse with no mountains in sight. It didn't seem like the fabled Karakoram Highway at all. Had we taken a wrong turn?

"Shouldn't there be, you know… mountains?" Christian mused, scanning the horizon.

"They're probably just hiding in the smog," Keith replied, grinning. "Or we're cycling the wrong way back to Kashgar."

Despite our doubts, we pressed on and soon reached the dusty town of Upal. We ducked into a small roadside café, where the air was thick with the scent of frying onions and spices. A large log-burning stove radiated a welcome warmth in the centre of the room, and we thawed out our gloves as we hungrily devoured steaming bowls of *laghman* noodles. The chewy hand-pulled noodles, tangled in a spicy broth with chunks of lamb and vegetables, were exactly what we needed. As we ate, we congratulated ourselves on covering 50 kilometres already without encountering any major climbs, though the thick haze had robbed us of any distant views.

That was about to change.

An hour later, as we pedalled beyond Upal, the mountains suddenly materialised. And they were sheer. The road had been gently lulling us into false confidence. Now it began to rise steeply, winding its way up towards the towering, snow-covered peaks ahead.

It was gruelling, slow work. The air grew thinner with each passing kilometre, and after seven hours in the saddle, both Keith and Christian started to struggle. It was unexpected. Keith, who had mostly outrun me in Azerbaijan, was usually the stronger rider. Perhaps, after too much time lingering in Kashgar, his legs needed a day or two to warm up. We kept pushing forward, looking for a settlement marked on our maps, but as darkness fell, exhaustion crept over all of us.

"We must be close now," Keith panted.

"Just round the next corner," I said, though I didn't believe it. We'd been saying that for the last hour.

The Karakoram Highway—one of the highest paved roads in the world—was living up to its fearsome reputation. This legendary route, connecting China and Pakistan, climbed to a dizzying 4,700 metres above sea level. It was a marvel of human engineering, carved through one of the most extreme landscapes on the planet. And we were beginning to feel its full force.

By now, it was pitch-black. The only thing keeping us from plunging into unseen ditches was Christian's dynamo-powered bike light, a steady white beam cutting through the darkness. Our pace slowed to a crawl, our bodies screaming for rest, but we had no choice but to push on. There was nowhere to stop. No towns. No shelter. Just an endless road winding into the abyss.

Finally, after what felt like an eternity, we rolled into the tiny settlement of Ghez. The whole place was barely more than a scattering of buildings, but we found a shopkeeper who offered us a place to sleep. For $5 each, we got dinner, breakfast, and a room—if you could call it that. It was essentially the back of the shop, with thick blankets laid out on the floor. But it was warm and, after 133 kilometres of relentless uphill climbing to an altitude of 2,250 metres, it felt like luxury.

Collapsing onto the blankets, full from a simple but hearty meal of rice and mutton, we were asleep in seconds.

Visibility remained poor despite a promising start in the morning. The air was heavy with mist, and the road ahead faded into a bleak, colourless haze. The gradient steepened with every kilometre, and it became a slow but relentless climb that tested our endurance. By the time we reached 2,700 metres, the first snowflakes began to fall—light at first, melting instantly on contact with the road. But within minutes, the snowfall thickened, swirling all around us.

Several times, truckers stopped to warn us against continuing. Their faces, weathered and serious, carried the weight of experience. Some even turned their rigs around, retreating to safer ground.

At one point, a grizzled driver leaned out of his cab, squinting through the snowfall. He jabbed a finger toward the pass. "Too dangerous," he said in broken English, shaking his head. "No go."

We hesitated. Christian glanced at me. "Do we listen to them?"

I swallowed hard, staring up at the white abyss ahead. Every rational part of me screamed to turn back. Instead, I tightened my grip on the handlebars. "Let's just see how far we get."

Keith groaned, muttering something about how we were all idiots, but he followed.

We layered up—extra thermals, raincoats on top to fend off the wet snow—and pressed on. Often, the road became impassable, forcing us to push the bikes through the snow, the sound of it crunching beneath our boots. My feet felt like blocks of ice, numb from the cold despite the effort of trudging along. The air grew thinner as we climbed to 3,300 metres, and the wind howled through the mountains, stripping the warmth from our bodies as fast as we could generate it.

As we approached our intended place of refuge near Lake Karakul, all we found was a frozen, abandoned workers' camp in a wasteland that had closed for the winter.

We took refuge behind the cracked concrete wall. We huddled together as the wind ripped through the exposed landscape. Our fingers barely functioned, and frost was forming on our clothing. Keith stomped his feet, trying to get some feeling back. "This isn't ideal," he admitted, his earlier reluctance now fully justified. "We need a plan B."

As if on cue, a 4x4 rumbled into sight, headlights glowing faintly through the blizzard. The driver pulled over, rolled down his window, and spoke in rapid Mandarin, gesturing to the back of the truck. We didn't need a translation. He was telling us, in no uncertain terms, that we were getting in.

Christian hesitated, looking back at his bike. "We're really doing this?"

I didn't hesitate.

With our bikes strapped to the back, we climbed into the truck's cab, shivering and exhausted. The driver, a no-nonsense man with a thick coat and a cigarette permanently perched on his lip, pushed on without a word.

We watched as darkness fell all around, and before long, we rolled into Tashkurgan, where Keith—always on the lookout for the cheapest deal—sniffed out a basic but warm guesthouse. We cleaned up, ate bowls of *laghman* noodles, and relished the simple joy of sitting indoors with functioning fingers and toes.

Morning arrived, and with it, the final push towards the border. Excitement mingled with frustration as we rode up to the customs office, only to be met with an immediate roadblock: we weren't allowed to cycle across.

"We'll have to take the bus," Christian groaned, rolling his eyes. "Of course."

Annoyed but resigned, we formulated a plan. We would bribe the bus driver to drop us off at the top of the pass, allowing us to cycle down into Pakistan. In theory, brilliant, except the officials had clearly seen this trick before—our bikes were deliberately loaded onto a different truck. Foiled.

Despite our initial irritation, the bus was more comfortable than expected, and as we climbed higher, I realised how lucky we were to be inside. The weather was worsening–the road was now a treacherous ice track winding through the mountains. By the time we reached the Pakistani side, it became clear just how close we'd come to disaster—the road ahead was gone. It had been completely wiped out by a landslide.

We stared in disbelief. The road had simply... vanished. A gaping chasm of rock and debris blocked the path, the remains of a violent landslide. My heart sank. After everything, after freezing nights, blizzards, and endless climbs—this was how it ended? We had no choice but to wait, watching as an army of workers and bulldozers attacked the rubble with brutal efficiency. Minutes stretched into hours. Would we be stranded here for days? Then, like something out of a fever dream, the road began to take shape before our eyes.

Had we been on bikes, we would have been stuck indefinitely—or worse.

As we finally descended towards Sost, the realisation hit: we had made it. After all the cold, the warnings, and the exhaustion, we were in Pakistan. It wasn't a triumph. It was survival. My body ached, my brain felt like it had been wrung dry, and still, I couldn't believe we were here. The mountain hadn't let us conquer it—it had simply let us pass.

CHAPTER 19

The Descent into Pakistan

Number of days on the road: **164**
Total distance covered: **9,267 km**

The delay caused by the landslide earlier that day meant that, yet again, we arrived in the pitch-black of an Asian winter night. Sost, as far as we could make out, barely seemed to exist. There were no streetlights, no neon shopfronts—just an eerie quiet and the faint outlines of buildings against the starlit sky. A power cut had wiped out what little electricity the town had, making the customs process feel more like a scene from a bygone century than an international border crossing.

We fumbled our way through the gloom, locating our bikes where they had been unloaded from the truck, propping them up outside the customs office, where a single weak candle burned on the desk, casting long shadows on the walls. An immaculately dressed customs official in a neatly pressed uniform stepped forward from the shadows:

"Passport," one of the officers said, his voice measured and polite. He flicked through my pages, squinting at the dimly lit stamps, as if he was willing the light to be brighter.

With a dull thump, my passport was stamped. No questions, no inspections—after all, what could they really check in this light? There were nods all around, the officials thanked us with a warmth I hadn't quite expected, and just like that, we were in Pakistan.

Pushing our bikes down what we assumed was the town's main road, we soon found the Asia Hotel and Restaurant, a battered little guesthouse that suited us perfectly. For $2.50 a night, it offered beds, shelter, and—most importantly—food. A steaming bowl of spicy lentils appeared in front of me not long after we arrived, accompanied by freshly made chapati, still warm from the griddle. The food was simple but rich with flavour, the kind that warmed from the inside out.

Our rooms, though basic, were sufficient. The temperature inside was a relatively balmy two degrees Celsius, which, after everything we'd endured, felt almost indulgent. I curled into my sleeping bag, relishing the fact that I wasn't shivering, and drifted into the best sleep I'd had in a while.

Morning arrived with a glow that revealed the true magic of where we were. Sost had been nothing but shadows the night before, but now, bathed in early light, it was astonishing. Frosted summits loomed above the valley, towering and sharp against the crisp blue sky. These were the kinds of mountains you read about in adventure books—the ones that seem to touch the heavens.

Breakfast was a simple omelette, fried in ghee and served with a wonderful chapati. As I ate, my heart felt full—full of relief, excitement, the simple pleasure of knowing that, at long last, the hardest part was behind me. At 3,000 metres, I was still high up, but for the first time in a long time, I would finally be descending.

I glanced at the road ahead, winding and dipping into the valleys beyond. It was easy to believe that with every kilometre south, the air would grow warmer, the days more forgiving. After weeks of bitter cold, that thought alone made me eager to get back on the saddle.

This was going to be a ride to remember.

The Hunza Valley, which has an affectionate nickname of 'Heaven on Earth' across Pakistan, is breathtakingly beautiful. Our descent into it was not on a smooth, paved highway but a rutted gravel track, pockmarked with potholes that forced us into slow, careful riding. The road twisted and plunged through a landscape that was both humbling and exhilarating—on either side, the valley walls rose into towering peaks, many surpassing 5,000 metres, the tallest exceeding 8,000 metres. Below, vertiginous drops plunged into deep gorges, where the Hunza River carved its way through the rugged terrain like a thread of liquid turquoise.

As we entered deeper into the valley, the sheer majesty of the mountains held us spellbound. Rakaposhi, Ultar Sar, and the slender, needle-like Ladyfinger Peak dominated the skyline, their icy summits glowing in the sunlight. Glaciers sprawled across the high passes, their crevasses glinting in shades of white and blue, while lush pockets of greenery clung to the valley floor, an oasis of life in this formidable landscape. The images were striking—white blanketed mountaintops above, emerald-green terraces below, and a sky so clear it felt painted onto the world.

The valley is home to the indigenous Hunza people, a group renowned for their longevity and deep connection to the mountains. The six tribes of Hunzakuts have preserved their way of life for centuries, their traditions shaped by the land they inhabit. Travellers speak often of their warmth and hospitality, and we found this to be true at every turn—a friendly wave, an offer of tea, or a child beaming up at us with curiosity.

Progress was slow, but not just because of the terrain. We were constantly stopping—compelled to take in the raw splendour of our surroundings. Every few minutes, one of us would pull up in sheer awe, dismounting to capture yet another shot of the surreal landscape. The mountains demanded attention, their presence so commanding that it was impossible to simply cycle past them.

I scrambled down a rocky embankment to refill my water bottles at the river's edge. The moment I cupped my hands and took a sip, I knew I'd never taste anything like it again—icy cold, crisp, and pure, as if the very essence of the mountains had been distilled into this one drink.

The road, rugged and unforgiving, led us onwards towards Passu, where the jagged spires of the Passu Cathedral—also known as the Passu Cones—pierced the sky. Rising abruptly from the valley floor, these towering peaks looked as if they had been carved by the gods themselves. They had been formed over thousands of years by glacial movement—the immense forces that had shaped this land. Their serrated edges and icy ridges seemed impossibly sharp, their presence both ominous and awe-inspiring.

We stood beneath them in silence, momentarily overwhelmed by their grandeur. Against the deep blue sky, the sunlight illuminated their snow-dusted summits, turning them golden in the afternoon glow. It was hard to tear ourselves away.

Eventually, we came across a series of rickety wooden suspension bridges, strung precariously across the river like relics of a bygone era. The planks creaked underfoot, with some missing entirely to reveal dizzying gaps through which the rushing glacial water thundered below. They weren't particularly safe—nor solid—but that didn't stop us from larking about like reckless teenagers. We took turns inching across, arms outstretched for balance, pausing to snap photos and admire the breathtaking views of the valley from our precarious vantage points. The thrill of the crossings, the sensation of the bridge swaying beneath us, was exhilarating.

We scrambled up the rocky slopes for even better views, climbing with childlike enthusiasm. The valley spread out endlessly, an ever-shifting canvas of towering peaks and plunging gorges, the river snaking through its depths like a silver thread.

Our laughter echoed off the cliffs—until Christian lost his footing on a loose rock. For one heart-stopping second, he teetered on the edge, arms flailing, as we watched helplessly. By some miracle, he caught himself, gripping onto a jagged outcrop, his face drained of colour.

"Bloody hell," he exhaled, scrambling back onto safer ground.

We all stared at him in stunned silence before the realisation sank in—he had come inches from a sheer drop of several hundred feet. After that, our playful antics took a back seat to a more cautious approach, and we continued along the riverbank with renewed diligence.

A few days into Pakistan, we started noticing truck drivers leaning on their horns as they passed. We laughed at first, assuming it was just another case of chaotic road etiquette, until the penny finally dropped—we were cycling on the wrong side of the road. It had been six months and 10,000 kilometres since I had last ridden on the left back in Dover, and the muscle memory had completely slipped. No wonder they were beeping at us.

Further along, we made a stop at the colossal Batura Glacier, one of the longest ice flows in the world outside the polar regions. As we climbed towards it, the landscape transformed into something otherworldly —jagged ridges of ice, like frozen waves, spread out before us, their fractured surfaces reflecting the afternoon sun in dazzling hues of white and blue. It reminded me of old school geography lessons, only now, instead of textbook diagrams, I was standing on a living, breathing mass of ice, shifting imperceptibly beneath my feet, reshaping the earth one slow, grinding movement at a time. The sheer scale of it was impossible to comprehend.

By now, local residents began warning us of dangers ahead, advising us with some seriousness not to venture past Gilgit. They spoke of bandits, of Taliban factions lurking in the valleys beyond, of travellers robbed or worse. Their warnings were unsettling. Even the British Consulate, in my sporadic email exchanges, had been firm—tourists were not advised to travel between Gilgit and Islamabad due to 'dangers'.

At Karimabad, Keith, Christian, and I sat down to discuss it, voices low over cups of chai. "We'll reassess when we get to Gilgit," Keith decided, ever the optimist. "No point worrying about it now."

I wasn't so sure, but what choice did we have? The road only went one way.

Then, just as we were weighing up risk and reason, Matt and Jack caught up with us. Our five-strong group was reunited in one of the most spectacular settings of the journey so far—perched on the west bank of the Hunza River, framed by the snow-capped Karakoram Mountains. The town, with its narrow lanes and houses built from stone and carved wood, felt like a timeless resting place, which, in fact, it had been for centuries. Caravan traders had paused here on their long journeys down from the Hindu Kush or en route to Kashmir. It felt only fitting that we, too, stopped for a short break to celebrate our reunion.

We visited Baltit Fort, a medieval stronghold that had loomed over the valley since the eighth century, its sturdy walls standing defiant against time. The Mirs of Hunza had only abandoned it in 1945, leaving behind an air of quiet grandeur. From its vantage point, we gazed out across the valley, where golden autumn trees clung to the steep hillsides, their leaves shivering in the high-altitude breeze.

The food in Pakistan was proving to be a constant source of comfort. The simplicity of mutton curries, rich lentil soups, and stacks of hot chapatis made every meal feel hearty and rewarding. The variety was limited, but it didn't matter. At this altitude, food wasn't just sustenance—it was survival.

Sitting in Karimabad, staring out over the valley, I realised something—I had been on the road for exactly six months. Six months since I had left behind my job, my family, and everything familiar. I allowed myself a moment of quiet satisfaction, wondering what was happening back home. I had not had the opportunity to contact anyone for a long time. The next real connection to the outside world would be in Gilgit.

Moving southward, we passed through Chalt, a small town where accommodation set us back all of £0.33 per night. The roads remained brutal, the scenery breathtaking. In every village, children played cricket—on the streets, in the fields, anywhere that had the space for a pitch. One game was too tempting to resist. I put my bike down, joined in for a few overs, and revelled in the sheer joy and laughter of it. It struck me as unfair that this region had such a forbidding reputation, even among its own nationals. From what I had seen, the people were warm, hospitable, and full of life.

Eventually, we reached Gilgit, the largest town in the region, where we finally reconnected with the modern world. Here, we replenished supplies, withdrew cash—we were all running low—and finally enjoyed a break from the saddle. I found an internet café, logged in for the first time in weeks, and sent messages home: I'm alive. All is well. Still moving forward.

We explored the town, visiting the carved Buddha of Kargah, a towering seventh-century rock relief that had only been rediscovered in 1939. With a local guide, we clambered up narrow goat trails that wound high above the valley, looking down over the sprawl of Gilgit and the fast-moving river below.

We sat with maps spread across a table, running our fingers along the winding line of the Indus River that led south.

By now, almost everyone we met told us—in no uncertain terms—do not continue. It was too dangerous for tourists. The warnings had intensified, but so too had the pull of the road ahead.

Perhaps it was stubbornness. Perhaps it was the sheer magnetism of what lay before us. But we decided to continue with our plan. If we had known what lay in store for us, perhaps we would have reconsidered.

CHAPTER 20

Escorted South

Number of days on the road: 177
Total distance covered: 9,572 km

After much deliberation, we decided to plough on, and just a few kilometres into the ride, armed soldiers were now a real presence, and military checkpoints started popping up regularly. At one checkpoint, the soldier beside me adjusted his grip on the rifle. He didn't look at me. Just scanned the horizon. I tried to pretend it was normal to be cycling through armed checkpoints every few kilometres or so.

We left Hunza behind and cycled towards the Indus Kohistan, the valley narrowing as we rode, the river surging below. This was the point on the Karakoram Highway where three of the world's greatest mountain ranges meet—the Himalayas, the Karakoram, and the Hindu Kush. It felt momentous, as if we had reached the centre of the earth.

And rising before us was Nanga Parbat—the "Killer Mountain"—the ninth-highest peak on the planet. It loomed over the valley, impossibly vast, the white mantle of the mountain lost in the clouds. One of only 14 mountains in the world that reaches over 8,000 m, it is a place of legend and tragedy, where climbers have risked—and often lost—their lives.

As we came into Chilas, the atmosphere changed. In Gilgit, we were met with polite curiosity, but as we moved further south, the stares grew colder and unreadable. At a chai stall, a bearded man eyed us from across the table, his gaze unwavering. He said nothing, just sipped his tea, watching. A few minutes later, he muttered something to the stall owner, who glanced at us before looking away. I didn't understand the words, but I understood the weight of the silence that followed.

Then came the stones. It started with just one—a child, barely ten, threw a rock that landed harmlessly on the road beside us. Then another. By the time we reached the centre of town, we had to weave through a scattered barrage of pebbles, some striking our panniers, others bouncing off the road in sharp, unpredictable bursts. It was a stark contrast to the warmth we had felt in Hunza and Karimabad. Here, we weren't just strangers. We were outsiders. And not entirely welcome. It was the first time I truly felt vulnerable—not just exposed to the elements, but to the possibility that not everyone wanted us here.

It gnawed at the edges of my confidence. The same road that had once felt like liberation now felt like risk.

As we stopped on the main road in the centre of the village, we suddenly became surrounded by a swarm of children—dozens of them—shouting, pushing, and jostling around us. Their expressions were difficult to read. Some were curious, some excited, but there was also an unmistakable edge to their energy. As one boy hurled a stone that struck my leg, my unease deepened.

Keith took out his camera. Instantly, the atmosphere became more volatile as the levels of excitement increased. The town's population had lived under the weight of foreign scrutiny and military presence for decades, caught in the long-standing dispute between Pakistan and India over Kashmir. Western involvement—real or perceived—was often viewed with suspicion, a legacy of both colonial history and contemporary geopolitics. In these remote areas, visitors from outside were rare, and those from the West were often associated with journalists, spies, or foreign intervention.

I urged Keith to put the camera away. That night, I struggled to sleep, my mind racing through the events of the day. My unease wasn't unfounded. The next morning, we were assigned an armed escort to take us through and out of the region. The regular checkpoints continued. The military 4x4 followed us slowly, trundling along, wheels crunching on the gravel. It was now hot. Dry.

Tense. Dust hung in the air like suspicion. We were no longer alone, but not entirely safe either, and it took much of the enjoyment out of riding through this beautiful region.

As we approached Abbottabad, our movements were no longer our own. The Pakistani military forbade us from cycling further, loading us and our bikes onto the truck bed of the 4x4.

The soldiers didn't offer an explanation, nor did they encourage conversation. One of them, a thickly built man with a rifle slung over his chest, barely looked at us as he motioned us into the vehicle. "Get in," he said. No argument, no discussion. This was an order.

It dented our pride. At least when we had an escort following behind, it felt like we still had the freedom of moving under our own steam. But strangely, it was also comforting—like danger had finally made itself visible.

As we drove through Abbottabad, the atmosphere felt charged. It was tense in a way I couldn't quite place. The number of military checkpoints intensified, with soldiers stationed on rooftops and eyes scanning the streets.

The 4x4 dropped us about 10 kilometres outside Rawalpindi without ceremony. There was no explanation, no warning. Just a nod from one of the officers before they turned back towards Abbottabad.

I had the strangest feeling that we had been ushered out of somewhere we were never meant to be. For months, I had been crossing borders like pages in a novel. But this wasn't a story I was meant to read. It felt like I'd brushed too close to something classified.[2]

We cycled the final 10 kilometres into Islamabad, weaving through the smog-filled streets as the honking of rickshaws, cars, and motorbikes created a chaotic, almost rhythmic, soundtrack to our arrival. The city sprawled in every direction, the complete opposite of the rugged, untamed landscapes we'd come from.

After some aimless wandering, we stumbled upon a youth hostel—if you could call it that. The concrete-block rooms were bare-bones, windowless, and eerily quiet, making the place feel more like a low-security prison than a backpacker's retreat. Still, at 140 rupees a night (about £1.90), it was cheap and after the frozen nights up in the Karakoram it felt like a palace.

---

[2] Only later would we come to understand just how close we had been to one of the most significant covert operations in modern history. At the time of our visit, Abbottabad was unknowingly harbouring Osama bin Laden, the elusive founder of al-Qaeda. It was an open secret in intelligence circles that he was hiding somewhere in Pakistan, but his exact location would remain unknown for another year and a half.

Looking back, it made perfect sense why we had been hurried through Abbottabad under armed escort. We were much too close for comfort.

Dumping our gear, we made a beeline for an internet café in a dusty market square where a jumble of open-air stalls sold everything from freshly fried samosas to used car parts. We sat at a row of yellowed computer screens, clicking away on sticky keyboards, backing up photos and replying to messages from home. To my delight, I had a message from Anastasia, the quick-witted Russian girl I had met in Iran. She was asking if I wanted to meet at Christmas in Amritsar. She said she was excited to meet up. I tried to play it cool—but the flicker of joy I felt reading her message caught me off guard. After all the remoteness and road grit, it was a reminder that someone, somewhere, was waiting.

Back at the hostel, out of nowhere, a news crew turned up at the hostel, asking for us by name.

"Wait... what?" I blinked. "Who the hell called the press?"

One of the hostel workers grinned proudly. "We did! You foreigners—cycling all this way, no fear? Pakistan needs to see this!"

Jack snorted. "Bloody hell. One minute we're nobodies, next minute we're national celebrities."

Within hours, we found ourselves in front of a cameraman, giving interviews for Pakistan's national TV network. *The Dawn*, one of the country's biggest newspapers, even printed a photo of us grinning outside the hostel. Watching ourselves later on the hostel's fuzzy old TV screen was both hilarious and surreal.

"Hey Jack," I grinned, elbowing him, "your smile should come with a health warning."

Jack raised an eyebrow. "Oh yeah? What d'you mean?"

"Warning: May cause extreme happiness within a ten metre radius."

Laughter filled the room.

The Indian visas were issued surprisingly fast, and the next morning, Matt, Jack and I cycled to the diplomatic enclave to collect them. With no panniers to weigh us down, we raced through the empty embassy streets, enjoying the rare freedom of light bikes.

Once we had our visas in hand, there was nothing urgent left to do. The afternoon unfolded lazily before us, so we made our way to Rawal Lake, a peaceful oasis away from the city's noise. Sitting under the shade of a scruffy old tree, I let out a deep breath, watching boats drift on the calm water.

"It's weird, isn't it?" I said, staring at the horizon.

"What's weird?" Matt asked, skipping a stone across the lake.

"How far we have come," I said.

Matt leaned back on his elbows. "Yeah. And somehow, despite all the near-death experiences, we're still here."

We checked the tyre pressures, oiled the chains, and tightened every bolt. After the chaos, even these small rituals felt grounding.

On 19th December, I set off with Matt and Jack for Lahore. Keith and Christian decided to take an extra day before collecting their visas and catching us up later. The morning ride was smooth, and by lunchtime, we pulled into a market to refuel. We squeezed into a small roadside eatery for a snack, where I also bought a traditional *chador* from a nearby stall.

The roads were busy, so we made good use of slow-moving trucks, grabbing onto their rear ladders and letting them drag us effortlessly for kilometres at a time. We dubbed this "truck surfing". With this shortcut, we clocked up 80 kilometres by late afternoon and rolled into Sohawa, where we found a basic roadside hotel for the night.

Not long after settling in, there was a knock on the door.

Jack opened it to find a young Pakistani guy standing there, grinning.

"Alright, lads—need anything?" he asked.

We all stared at him, caught off guard. His Geordie accent was unmistakable.

"Hang on—what?" I said, laughing. "You're from Newcastle?"

"Aye," he nodded, stepping inside. "Well, half-and-half. My family owns this place, but I study back in the Toon. Just home for the holidays."

Over the next few days, we began to notice that many families in this part of Pakistan had relatives in the UK—particularly in the North East. It was surreal hearing broad northern accents from people in traditional salwar kameez.

By then, Matt had fallen ill, and Jack decided to stay back with him while he recovered. But I was keen to reach India in time for Christmas and to meet up with Anastasia. She had made all the arrangements, booked a hotel and planned to be there from the 22nd December.

As I pedalled into Lahore, a strange wave of relief, exhaustion, and exhilaration washed over me. The last few weeks had been relentless—freezing mountains, political tensions, military escorts. Here, the air was warmer, the streets louder, the chaos almost welcoming in its familiarity. I had pushed through some of the most dangerous and isolating parts of my journey, and for the first time in weeks, I felt like I could finally breathe.

Lahore was chaos and colour in equal measure. Though not the capital of Pakistan, it felt like the beating heart of the country, a place where history, culture, and modernity clashed in an intoxicating whirlwind.

Amid the frenzy, I set out to unravel Lahore's treasures.

At the Lahore Fort, a UNESCO World Heritage site, I stepped through the colossal gates, and inside, there were marble-carved archways and frescoes adorning the walls of the hallways.

Just beyond the fort stood the Badshahi Mosque, its domes and minarets dotting the skyline. The courtyard was a vast expanse of red sandstone and white marble. Inside, it was surprisingly silent, blocking out the sounds of the city outside.

But history wasn't just confined to Lahore's monuments—it pulsed through its markets too. I weaved through the narrow lanes of Anarkali Bazaar, dodging carts piled high with embroidered shawls and glinting bangles. Shopkeepers haggled with customers in rapid Urdu. At Liberty Market, I admired the hand-stitched fabrics, while vendors beckoned me over, eager to make a sale.

By evening, my hunger led me straight to Lahore's famed street food. I perched on a small plastic stool by a roadside eatery, watching as a cook skillfully turned marinated tandoori chicken over hot coals, the air thick with smoky, spiced aromas. I dug into a plate of Lahori biryani, the saffron-infused rice bursting with rich, layered flavours, before finishing with a bowl of nihari, its slow-cooked tender beef melting in my mouth.

As the day faded, I retreated to my hostel's rooftop terrace, where the setting sun bathed Lahore in a golden haze. The city, always buzzing, hummed below me, its chaotic energy momentarily softened by the evening light.

The road from Lahore to the border was hectic but straightforward, a blur of rickshaws, lorries, and roadside vendors. At customs, the official pressed a tiny exit stamp into my passport, taking up an entire page in the process. I stared at it in disbelief, an irrational frustration bubbling up inside me. A whole page! For a single stamp!

Later, as I pedalled towards the Indian border, I chuckled at myself. Of all the challenges I had faced—frozen nights, treacherous mountain roads, border bureaucracy—this was what annoyed me? Not the armed escort, not the risk of frostbite, not the kids hurling stones at me. No. A poorly placed stamp.

Still, I made a mental note to be more protective of my remaining passport pages.

Crossing the border felt like crossing another hard, literal line drawn in the sand. It always felt meaningful and that real progress was being made. And somewhere down this road, the next version of myself was waiting.

CHAPTER 21

Amritsar & Northern India

Number of days on the road: 190
Total distance covered: 9,784 km

With my bags thoroughly searched by Indian officials and my passport stamped, I was finally free to cycle the straightforward 25 kilometres to Amritsar. The road was smooth and the ride effortless—a welcome change after the rugged terrain of Pakistan.

On arrival in the city, Anastasia stood waiting in the hotel courtyard, her arms crossed, a playful smile on her face.

"I can't believe it!" she called out as I pulled up. "You really made it!"

Before I had a chance to reply, she threw her arms around me in a warm embrace. The sensation of closeness, of familiarity, after all this time on the road, caught me off guard. I took a second to take the moment in—realising just how much I had missed this. It had been months since we last saw each other, yet it felt like no time had passed at all. So much had changed—my appearance, my mindset, my entire rhythm of being—but as we hugged, I remembered the version of me who first left London. That man felt far away, like an echo. And yet, in this moment, I wanted to bridge that gap. To remember who I was, and who I might still be.

She pulled back slightly, studying me with an amused smirk. "You look... different."

I ran a hand over my unruly beard. "Yeah... this thing needs to go."

She traced a finger along my jaw, teasingly shaking her head. "I don't know... I kind of like the dishevelled look."

Our hotel had an old-world charm, its imperial decor and high ceilings giving it a certain faded grandeur. We lit the log fire, the flickering flames casting shadows across the wooden beams, and poured ourselves a generous measure of rum. Outside, the streets buzzed with life, but inside, wrapped in the warmth of the fire and the soothing burn of liquor, we could have been in an English country house on a winter's evening—if not for the distant honking of rickshaws and the unmistakable aroma of Indian spices drifting in through the open window.

By now, my beard had taken on a life of its own, thick and unkempt after months on the road. It was time for it to go. As I lathered up in front of the mirror, Anastasia watched with a mischievous grin.

"I think I preferred you as a wild man," she teased.

I gave her a look. "Well, it was either this or start looking like a yeti."

With one final stroke of the razor, I watched as months of travel disappeared down the sink, leaving behind a face I barely recognised.

We visited the Golden Temple in Amritsar, and it was nothing short of breathtaking. The Sri Harmandir Sahib, the holiest shrine in Sikhism, shimmered under the sunlight, its gold-plated domes gleaming brilliantly against the deep blue sky. I felt an inexplicable pull towards it—something beyond aesthetics, beyond history. Pilgrims moved with quiet reverence, their heads bowed in devotion, their hands clasped in prayer.

Stepping barefoot onto the cool marble pathway, a shiver ran through me—not from the temperature, but from the sheer weight of presence in this place. The hum of devotional hymns, sung in endless rotation, wrapped around me like a mantra. It wasn't just a temple. It was something alive, something breathing.

Within the gurdwara complex, the air vibrated with the soothing sound of hymns being continuously recited from the Guru Granth Sahib, the Sikh holy scripture. Pilgrims moved reverently around the temple, heads covered, their footsteps gentle on the polished stone. The architecture was a harmonious blend of Hindu and Islamic influences, carved marble inlays, floral motifs, and golden domes.

Despite its grandeur, there was an overwhelming sense of peace and welcoming warmth. The temple is open to all—regardless of faith, background, or status—and at its heart lies the Sikh principle of *seva* (selfless service). Nowhere is this more evident than in the *langar,* the community kitchen that serves free meals to thousands of visitors daily. We joined the volunteers, from elderly men to young children, working to chop vegetables, roll chapatis, and stir enormous pots of dal, ensuring that no one left hungry. Not yet trusted with cooking, we washed trays and plates ready to feed hungry mouths.

While in Amritsar, Anastasia and I were approached by a local Indian family who, with beaming smiles and warm gestures, invited us to their home for their son Arjan's dastar bandi (or turban-wearing) ceremony, a significant milestone in the life of a Sikh boy as he officially dons his first turban. Their kindness was immediate, and we gratefully accepted. As we entered their home, we were welcomed into their colourful living room, awash with family photos. Sitting cross-legged on floor cushions, we sipped on steaming cups of masala chai, its blend of cardamom, cinnamon, and ginger warming us from within.

Arjan's father, a tall man with a proud but kind face, explained to us that the turban, or dastar, represents discipline, respect, and a commitment to the Sikh faith. This was not just a cultural tradition but a spiritual rite of passage, marking his son's journey into adulthood and responsibility.

The ceremony took place inside a modest courtyard, where family and friends had gathered in celebration. Arjan, who was 12 years old, sat patiently in the centre, his hair neatly combed and tied in a topknot. His uncle then took a long length of cloth, folded it meticulously and then began the process of wrapping it around Arjan's head. Each layer was carefully placed, smoothed out, and adjusted, ensuring the turban fit snugly while maintaining its graceful folds.

Family members beamed with pride, snapping photos. Arjan though initially serious, couldn't help but smile when his little sister poked his side, giggling as she tried to help adjust the turban. Once completed, the deep blue turban sat perfectly on his head, its pleats sharp and symmetrical. He stood up, looking nervous before the room erupted in claps, and his father hugged him, whispering something into his ear that made him nod solemnly.

Out on a balcony at the side of the house, the children excitedly introduced us to the art of kite flying. Their eyes sparkled with excitement as their hands worked deftly to untangle the strings.

I was handed the kite, but my first attempt was laughably disastrous—the wind caught it briefly before it spiralled down in an undignified crash. Anastasia giggled at my struggles, covering her mouth as she watched me try and fail again. The children, sensing both my determination and incompetence, rallied around me like patient teachers, offering enthusiastic instructions in rapid Punjabi and exaggerated hand gestures.

Even with their guidance, I don't think I can say I mastered the technique, but with a well-timed release, my kite caught the wind and stayed in the air for at least a short while. I handed the kite back over to the boy next to me and realised that I would be better placed to stick to cycling.

Reluctantly, and with grateful farewells to our gracious hosts, we ventured back out into the cool night air and slowly walked back to the hotel.

In the room, we had a log fire. The flames danced in the hearth, their golden light flickering across Anastasia's face as she curled up in an armchair opposite me, her fingers wrapped around a glass of rum and Coke. The scent of woodsmoke mingled with the night air drifting through an open window.

We sat there for hours, letting the conversation flow effortlessly. There was something about the way she listened. A moment of silence settled between us, but it wasn't uncomfortable. Instead, it was charged with something gentler, warmer—an anticipation neither of us needed to voice. As the flames crackled softly, Anastasia reached over, brushing her fingers lightly against mine.

"We should get some rest," she said, her deep blue eyes fixed on mine, and she took me by the hand and led me to the bedroom.

***

The following day was Christmas Eve, and we decided to mark the occasion with something truly unique—a trip back to the India-Pakistan border for the famous Wagah border-closing ceremony. It was as theatrical as it was electrifying, an experience unlike anything I'd ever seen before.

As the sun began to dip below the horizon, the grandstands on either side of the border filled with an enthusiastic crowd, a mix of locals and tourists alike. The energy was palpable. A master of ceremonies worked the

Indian crowd into a frenzy of patriotic chants, while across the gates, the Pakistani crowd responded in kind. It was a duelling display of national pride, each side trying to out-cheer the other.

Then the ceremony began. Tall, impeccably uniformed border guards—with their towering turbans and crisp, starched attire—strode onto the tarmac with exaggerated confidence, their chests puffed out, their movements sharp and deliberate. What followed was a display of military pageantry unlike any other. The soldiers executed a series of high-kicking marches, their boots slamming onto the ground in perfect unison, sending echoes bouncing through the grandstands.

The two sides locked eyes across the border, their expressions fierce, their posturing designed to intimidate—but the whole thing had an almost theatrical flair, like a choreographed dance of rivalry and respect. It reminded me of New Zealand's Haka before a rugby match, an aggressive yet strangely ritualistic performance.

As the flags of both nations were slowly lowered in perfect synchronisation, the crowd fell momentarily silent, watching as the respective colours descended with solemn precision. And then, just as suddenly as it had begun, the gates clanged shut for the night, and the cheers erupted once more, a final roar of patriotic energy before everyone dispersed into the evening.

It was brilliant, bizarre, and completely unforgettable—a uniquely subcontinental spectacle, where pride, rivalry, and tradition blended into one extraordinary display.

Christmas Day was one I'll never forget, as it was utterly hilarious. Somehow, Anastasia had organised for a Santa outfit to be made for me and, before I could talk my way out of it, I found myself cycling around Amritsar dressed as Santa Claus. At first, I was dubious. With Punjab being predominantly Sikh, I wasn't sure how the costume would be received. But any hesitation vanished as soon as we hit the streets.

The reaction was pure joy. People waved, cheered, and laughed, delighted by the sight of a foreigner in full Santa attire wobbling through the streets on a bicycle. Children ran up to me, eager for photos, their wide grins infectious. Even the rickshaw drivers and market traders stopped what they were doing to clap and shout festive greetings. It quickly became obvious that, despite its Christian origins, Christmas had transcended religion—it was simply an excuse for people to celebrate, laugh, and share in the festive spirit.

That evening, we found a hotel serving a proper roast dinner with wine—a rare and wonderful luxury so far from home. We clinked glasses, toasting to an incredible year of adventure, and savoured each bite of the meal that, just for a moment, transported us back to family Christmases of years past.

The days that followed were a whirlwind of movement. We took a bus to Delhi, where Anastasia had arranged for us to meet some of her Indian friends.

They were fantastic hosts, eager to show us the hidden side of the city—not through museums or tourist sights, but through its street food culture. Our new friends took us straight to Chandni Chowk, the heart of Old Delhi, where food stalls lined the narrow lanes like a never-ending feast.

We started with *aloo tikki,* crisp golden potato patties fried on a huge griddle and drenched in tamarind chutney and cool yoghurt, then moved on to *pani puri*—small, hollow, crispy shells filled with a tangy, spicy water that exploded in the mouth. I watched Anastasia's reaction as she bit into one, her eyes widening as the burst of flavour took her by surprise.

"Wow," she gasped, fanning her mouth. "That is... intense!"

The group laughed, and I handed her a napkin. "Told you! Now try not to let the next one dribble down your chin."

To finish up, we had *jalebi,* deep-fried spirals soaked in sugar syrup, which left our fingers sticky and our stomachs pleasantly full. As we stood by a steaming chai stall, sipping on milky, cardamom-infused tea, the warmth of the moment settled over me.

"You're definitely not going to lose weight in India," Anastasia teased, nudging me playfully.

I laughed, licking syrup from my fingers. "At this rate, I'm just going to have to cycle faster."

But soon, it was time to say goodbye. At Delhi airport, Anastasia and I stood in silence for a moment, and the reality that we were parting began to sink in.

"I wish you were coming to Moscow for New Year with me," she admitted, squeezing my hand.

"And I wish you were cycling through India with me," I replied with a weak smile.

She laughed, but there was a tinge of sadness in her blue eyes. "Maybe in another life?"

"Maybe," I nodded.

We embraced tightly, neither of us wanting to let go too soon. Finally, she turned towards the departure gates, giving me one last look over her shoulder before disappearing into the crowd.

I stood there for a moment, watching the space she had occupied just seconds before.

The road had a way of pulling people in and then scattering them like leaves in the wind. Maybe we'd meet again. Maybe not.

***

Rather than head straight back to Amritsar to collect my bike, I booked a return bus trip from Delhi to Agra to see the Taj Mahal—a sight I felt almost obligated to visit, though I nearly refused on principle. The entry fee was exorbitant—it was enough to sustain me on the road for several days, possibly even a week. But in the end, I caved. It felt wrong to come all this way and not see one of the world's most iconic landmarks. I'm glad I did.

To avoid the crowds, I arrived early, just as the first light of day cast a soft golden glow over the ivory-white marble façade. The sheer scale was staggering. It wasn't just beautiful—it was perfect. Its symmetry is so precise that every angle seems designed for the ideal photograph. I took shot after shot, though in truth, the Taj Mahal does all the work for you. Its reflection shimmered in the long pools of water leading up to it, the morning mist adding a dreamlike quality.

Inside, however, was a different experience—dim, solemn, and largely unadorned. But that made sense. It was, after all, a mausoleum, built by Mughal Emperor Shah Jahan in memory of his third and most beloved wife, Mumtaz Mahal. The story behind it was as tragic as it was romantic. The emperor, once the most powerful man in India, was later betrayed by his own son and imprisoned in Agra Fort. From there, he spent his final years gazing out through a tiny window at the Taj Mahal, the monument to his lost love, before dying alone in miserable conditions.

I visited Agra Fort next—another of Shah Jahan's legacies. It was a city within a city, its massive red sandstone walls enclosing palaces, courtyards, and labyrinthine corridors. The intricate carvings and design reminded me of Lahore Fort, which I'd later discover was also built during his reign. From one of its balconies, I caught a final, hazy glimpse of the Taj Mahal, framed by the smog that seemed to cling to Agra.

Beyond those two architectural masterpieces, the city itself couldn't have been more different. Agra was chaotic, overcrowded, and filthy—the dirtiest place I had encountered so far. The streets were lined with piles of rubbish, stray dogs scavenged through heaps of waste, and the acrid stench of stagnant water clung to the air. The relentless noise, dust, and sheer volume of people became overwhelming. India was testing me. Despite the wonders I'd seen that day, I found myself longing for the open road once more.

I returned to Amritsar by train, and by the time I arrived, Keith, Matt, Jack, and Christian had also turned up. They'd only been a few days behind me and had spent Christmas in Lahore, where their holiday had been a bit more subdued. I couldn't help but feel relieved I'd spent it with Anastasia.

The next day was New Year's Eve, and we felt it was only right to mark the occasion with a few drinks. We headed to the Grand Hotel—only to discover, to our horror, that the bar closed at 10:00 p.m.

"What kind of bar shuts early on New Year's Eve?" Keith groaned.

"Welcome to India," Matt grinned. "What now?"

We exchanged glances, then jumped into tuk-tuks and launched into a frantic search for somewhere—anywhere—that was still serving. After a few failed stops, we finally stumbled upon a hotel bar just in time to order beers, grab a deck of cards, and settle in for the night. It was hardly a wild celebration, but as we laughed over games and reminisced about the year, I realised I wouldn't have wanted to be anywhere else.

At midnight, we raised our glasses in a simple but meaningful toast.

"To another year of adventure," Jack said, clinking his bottle against mine.

"And to actually finding a bar that's open next year," Christian added, grinning.

We all laughed. A new year, a new day, and new plans to make.

New Year's Day was spent scouting out shops for maps, gathering supplies, and plotting our onward journeys. I made copies of my India photos and sent them home—a small way of preserving moments before they slipped too far into memory.

The road was calling once again.

It was also time to say goodbye to Christian and Keith. They were heading north to Dharamshala, hoping for a glimpse of the Dalai Lama.

"You sure you don't want to come?" Keith asked, adjusting the straps on his panniers.

I glanced at the road ahead. North meant mountains, cold air, and uphill battles. South meant warmth, sunshine, and beaches. It wasn't a difficult choice.

"Tempting," I said, shaking my head with a grin. "But I think I'll let you two freeze while I go work on my tan."

Keith chuckled. "You'll regret it when you hear I've had tea with His Holiness."

"If that happens," I shot back, "I'll cycle back just to shake your hand."

We exchanged a firm handshake and a pat on the back, and with that, they were gone—riding off towards the mountains while I turned my sights southward.

CHAPTER 22

Punjab to Rajasthan

Number of days on the road: 202
Total distance covered: 9,784 km

Leaving Amritsar, I felt a quiet thrill stir in my chest—the return to the road. Jack was sick, Matt had stayed to look after him, and I was itching to head off again. Freedom.

The morning mist hung low over the Punjab plains, softening the edges of trees and buildings. Dew clung to my panniers like silver sequins. My breath came in faint clouds, and the cold nipped at my fingers, but the stillness had a kind of grace to it.

As the sun climbed, the land brightened. Fields of mustard flowers burst into view, bright yellow against the green, swaying like tiny flags of optimism. The roads were quiet, lined with eucalyptus trees and the occasional bullock cart trundling along to its own slow rhythm. Children ran out from doorways, waving and shouting,

"Hello, Mister!" with such joy that I couldn't help but grin and wave back.

There was something comforting about the landscape. In the distance, I could see tractors moving methodically across farmland. The air smelled of cow dung and woodsmoke, with the faintest trace of sugarcane on the breeze. At times, it reminded me of home—some quiet corner of Norfolk or Cambridgeshire, perhaps—if you squinted past the buffalo and the mango trees.

Somewhere near Kotkapura, a small car pulled up beside me, the driver matching my speed with surprising precision. He leaned out, smiling, and shouted over the wind, "You should go to Muktsar! There's a temple there—not as famous as Amritsar, but very holy. You'll be welcomed."

I nodded, waved, and watched the car peel away. The name lingered in my mind like a breadcrumb on the trail. Muktsar. It sounded right.

The road narrowed. Fields rolled gently by. The horizon shimmered in a late-afternoon haze. By the time I reached the Darbar Sahib complex, the sun was beginning to lower behind the temple domes, gilding the white marble in soft gold.

Muktsar, known as "The Pool of Liberation", was where Guru Gobind Singh made his final stand in battle, where

40 Sikh soldiers who had once abandoned him returned to fight and die at his side. Their sacrifice is remembered here. It was humbling to stand on such sacred ground, dusty and road-worn, my thoughts too tangled for words.

Inside the temple, the rhythmic cadence of scripture floated across the water. Volunteers welcomed me with quiet warmth. I was given a room—simple, clean, with a single bed and a tap with a plastic bucket. It cost the equivalent of £1.

Later, I joined the *langar*. Cross-legged on the marble floor, I ate dal and chapatis, passed down the line by silent, smiling volunteers. Afterwards, I helped wash trays in the steaming kitchen, sleeves rolled up, hands plunged into hot soapy water. The act, small as it was, filled me with an odd sense of calm.

That night, I slept well.

A few days further down the road, the next guesthouse wasn't nearly so welcoming. I barely noticed the threadbare sheets and the mosquito buzzing somewhere above my head. I should've paid more attention. But fatigue won out.

In the mirror the next morning, my face looked like a failed science experiment. Bed bug bites dotted down my face in a near-perfect line. I cursed under my breath and packed quickly.

I approached the edge of Rajasthan a week after leaving Amritsar. The rich greens of Punjab faded into drier tones. The landscape flattened and stretched. There was more dust in the air and more heat in the wind. I was tired—physically and emotionally— and my face was itching from the night before.

As I passed through a customs checkpoint between the two states, a man in a khaki uniform stepped out, one hand raised in greeting, the other already reaching for the kettle.

"Chai?" he asked.

I nodded and unclipped, grateful for the pause. Two tin cups were placed on the wooden table before I even sat down. The tea was strong and sweet, fragrant with cardamom. We sipped in silence for a moment, the occasional truck growling past in the distance.

"Where are you from?"

"England," I said.

He gave a small nod, then looked out toward the fields. "In Punjab, everything grows," he said. "Water, wheat, people's hearts." He turned slightly, gesturing east. "Rajasthan is different. Less water. But we are used to it. The people here are strong, proud. But sometimes, they are a little harder."

He smiled, not unkindly. “You’ll see.”

We sat quietly a little longer. No more words were needed.

When I stood to leave, I thanked him. He nodded once more, already refilling the kettle.

Sometimes, that’s all you need. A cup of chai, and someone who understands the road ahead better than you do.

***

I rested in Deshnok for a few days, which allowed Matt and Jack to catch up, although they admitted they’d taken a bus to do so.

Deshnok is home to a famous Rat Temple. Shocking-pink walls stand vivid against the flat, dusty plain. It’s a beacon of strangeness. Inside, thousands of rats darted through the temple, their tiny feet skittering across the marble. Here, the rats are sacred. They are reincarnated souls, fed bowls of milk and grain by devotees hoping for blessings.

At first, I baulked as the rats wove between our bare feet. But they didn’t behave like pests. They weren’t fearful or frenzied. They just were—part of the temple, part of the story. It was surreal and oddly moving. India in a single frame: reverent, chaotic, alive.

We continued south, pedalling under a warming sun. After weeks of piling on layers, it felt liberating to ride in nothing but a t-shirt and shorts.

As we headed deeper into the Thar Desert, the dunes rose and fell like sandy waves frozen in place. The air was dry and clean, the sun kind but never cruel, and a soft wind pushed gently at our backs. In the late-afternoon light, the sand took on a pink hue, the sky shifting through watercolour shades as the temperature dropped.

Each evening, we turned off the road and pushed our bikes into the dunes, tyres sinking into the powdery sand, seeking a hollow or ridge to shelter us from the wind. It always took longer than we expected, but we were getting good at this—three riders, three routines, working in quiet synchronicity.

One night, Matt was off collecting firewood while I knelt beside the stove, coaxing a flame from our dwindling fuel supply. The sand made everything harder—it was slower to move and harder to anchor things—but we got there. Sparks caught. The fire flickered into life, throwing gold light across the dunes.

The first sip of rum burned when it went down, but it warmed my chest like a second fire.

"This," Matt said, stretching his legs towards the flames, "is the life."

Jack, watching the sparks rise, smirked. "Yeah... until we run out of rum."

"We ration it," I said, passing the bottle. "Like the responsible adults we definitely are."

The fire crackled, sending up embers that vanished into a sky thick with stars. The Milky Way curved across the heavens like a brushstroke—unbelievably vivid, as if someone had switched the world to high definition. We lay back on our roll mats, the cold creeping into our sleeves and socks, but none of us moved.

The silence of the desert was rich. Not empty—never empty—but full of presence. Full of memory.

"Ever wonder," Jack said quietly, "how many people, centuries before us, sat around fires in this same desert doing exactly this?"

"Traders. Travellers. Soldiers," I murmured. "This place has seen them all."

Matt nodded. "And now... us."

We let the idea hang there.

Then I said, "I still can't believe Jack takes a shit standing up."

Matt burst out laughing. "Oh my god, I *know!*"

We all broke down, the silence shattered by stupid, glorious laughter.

But as the fire died down and the rum thinned out, the desert settled over us again. We lay back and watched shooting stars carve through the black, each of us quiet now, alone with our thoughts.

It was moments like this when I felt the full weight of where we were. What we were doing. Who we were becoming.

***

After days in the desert, Jodhpur felt like a reward. We arrived sun-blasted and brittle, our clothes stiff with dust, our muscles aching from the long, dry push across Rajasthan. The city greeted us with colour and noise and welcome shade. We checked into a modest hotel, and for just over a pound each, collapsed onto dorm beds that felt absurdly luxurious after nights sleeping on sand.

Jodhpur moved at its own pace—unhurried, sun-drenched, humming just beneath the surface. We ate like kings at the famed Omelette Shop, a shack on a street corner where thick golden omelettes crackled on a street-side griddle and were folded over tomatoes, onions, and fresh green chillies, served with slabs of toasted bread slick with butter. The lassis were almost a meal in themselves—ice-cold, heavy with yoghurt, lightly spiced with cardamom and sweetness.

One morning, we climbed through the twisting backstreets toward Mehrangarh Fort, which rose above the city like a battleship run aground. Its walls, hewn from the same red sandstone as the hill beneath it, seemed to grow out of the land itself. Inside, the heat bounced off stone courtyards and echoed through high archways. Spiked wooden doors stood guard over wide gates, once there to stop war elephants from charging through. And from the ramparts, the whole of the Blue City unfolded below—a patchwork of indigo rooftops shimmering under the midday sun, stretching into the haze like a mirage of water in the desert.

Evenings belonged to the rooftop terrace. It became our ritual— cold beers accompanied by the low hum of the city below. As dusk settled, the sandstone glowed amber, and rickshaws buzzed through the alleys like insects under glass. Somewhere, faint music drifted through the warm air—tabla, sitar, the static of an old radio. The chaos felt far away now, softened by height and distance.

On our final night, we lingered longer than usual.

Jack leaned back in his chair and exhaled. "Reckon we've done this place justice."

Matt nodded, swirling his drink. "I'm going to miss omelettes that cost less than a Mars bar."

I smiled, watching the lights shimmer below. "Time to get moving again, though."

Jack stretched. "Back to sleeping on rocks and being eaten alive by wildlife?"

"Something like that," I said. "Can't let things get too comfortable."

Nobody moved. The moment didn't need ending.

***

The morning warmth was a welcome change. Even at first light, it felt like the height of summer, and I relished the chance to start the day in sandals, shorts, and a t-shirt. As the sun climbed higher, I stripped down to just my shorts, letting the heat soak into my skin, finally giving my pasty, road-worn body a bit of colour again.

We chose the smaller back roads over the bustling highways, winding through tiny villages where our presence caused wide-eyed stares and whispered conversations. Women in dazzling saris worked the fields, their bright colours striking against the dusty earth. Some balanced heavy bundles on their heads, moving with effortless grace, while others wielded crude tools with remarkable strength. Life here was hard, but there was rhythm to it—a steady pulse of work and community that was both humbling and fascinating to witness.

The arid landscapes of the past weeks gave way to a lush, undulating paradise of valleys, scattered acacia trees, and winding roads. It was slow, tough cycling at times, but the scenery made every uphill stretch worthwhile. Vibrant green terraces clung to the slopes, swollen from recent rains, and snaked through the valleys below. Pools of water glinted like liquid silver in the midday sun. Every so often, a break in the tree line offered us breathtaking panoramas of the distant plains beneath the blue sky.

Lulled by the tranquillity of the road, I lost focus for just a second. That was all it took. I looked up just in time to see a slow-moving tractor looming ahead. There was no time to swerve. I crashed into it hard, hitting the ground at around 25 km/h. Pain tore through me as I landed awkwardly, taking a chunk out of my hand and scraping my knee, wrist, elbow, and shoulder. Blood trickled from my palm, and my bike clattered onto the road beside me.

Matt and Jack skidded to a halt behind me.

"Shit, mate! You alright?" Matt asked, hopping off his bike.

"Yeah... yeah, I'm fine," I muttered through gritted teeth, but the stinging sensation said otherwise.

Jack squatted down, inspecting the damage. "That's a fair bit of skin gone," he observed. "Could've been worse though. You could have landed on your face."

I let out a wry chuckle, shaking off the pain. "Reckon I'd have cracked the road before it cracked me."

With my pride as bruised as my body, I dusted myself off, sucked it up, and soldiered on. There was no choice but to keep going. By nightfall, we found a patch of trees to camp beneath, setting up just off the road. In the distance, a village was alive with the sounds of a wedding celebration—drumming, laughter, bursts of cheering. It was the kind of noise that makes you wish you were a part of it, but I was too busy nursing my aching body to do much more than lie awake, listening.

We took a longer but quieter route to Udaipur via Ranakpur instead of sticking to the main highway. It turned out to be one of the most rewarding choices we made. The ride through the hills was sublime—twisting roads, green valleys stretching into the horizon, and, along the way, magnificent Jain temples that seemed to rise out of the jungle itself. The most famous of them was the Adinatha Temple. It was a white marble structure housing over 1,400 carved symmetrical pillars.

It was here, in the temple parking lot, that Matt had an unfortunate run-in with a troop of monkeys. At first, it was just one, creeping towards his bike with beady eyes locked on his bananas. When Matt turned to shoo it away, the monkey lunged, baring its teeth and screeching in defiance.

"Oi! Piss off!" Matt shouted, waving his arms.

Instead of retreating, the monkey went into full attack mode, yanking at the straps of his pannier, tearing it open with alarming ease.

"Bloody hell, it's got my food!" Matt yelled, spinning in circles, trying to fend off the thieving beast.

I wasn't sure whether to help him or laugh. The monkey bared its teeth like a pint-sized bandit and yanked at the straps of his pannier with the skill of a seasoned pickpocket.

Jack and I were absolutely no help. We were doubled over in laughter as Matt waged war against his tiny, furry nemesis.

Then, as if summoned by some primal monkey battle cry, reinforcements arrived. Two more monkeys leapt onto Matt's bike, one making a direct grab for the bananas while the other gleefully rummaged through his handlebar bag.

"Bloody hell, it's an ambush!" I cackled, wiping away tears.

Just as things were spiralling out of control, a temple attendant appeared, wielding his belt like a whip. The monkeys scattered, screeching in protest, their stolen goods clutched triumphantly in their tiny hands.

Matt, panting, wiped his forehead. "That's it," he huffed. "I'm getting a 'monkey stick'."

When we arrived in Udaipur later that day, we checked into a budget hotel and immediately set out to satisfy our hunger, stumbling upon a place that served surprisingly decent veggie burgers. After days of dhal and chapatis, it felt like a small indulgence.

Udaipur exuded an effortless charm, a city that seemed to breathe romance and tranquillity in equal measure. Mornings were particularly enchanting. I lingered over breakfast on the rooftop of our hostel, cradling a steaming cup of chai while gazing out over the glassy expanse of Lake Pichola and "The Palace in the Lake". The iconic palace, floating in the lake's midst like something conjured from a dream, was bathed in a soft golden light. Its white façade reflected perfectly in the still water, and I found myself captivated, watching as the lake sparkled and rippled with the occasional boat gliding across its surface. I reached for my camera, hoping to preserve the moment. I took dozens of photos, but none of them could do the moment justice.

The days in Udaipur passed in a gentle rhythm, the kind that travel gifts you when you stop chasing destinations and let a place settle into your bones. I spent my time meandering through the city's winding streets, getting lost in its hidden alleyways and sun-dappled courtyards. I allowed myself the time to do nothing—to simply exist in a place without a checklist. My days revolved around slow breakfasts, idle strolls, and moments of quiet observation, soaking in the hum of daily life around me. Evenings were a ritual of their own—gathering on the hostel terrace, sharing travel stories over rounds of cards, and sipping on a rum and Coke as the city lights glowed in the distance.

It was here in Udaipur that I finally decided to cut my hair. It had been 220 days since I left the UK, and nearly 10,000 kilometres since I had last seen the inside of a barbershop. My hair had grown wild, constantly falling into my eyes, tamed only by an Alice band or the occasional top knot. Enough was enough. Digging out a pair of scissors, I took matters into my own hands, hacking away at the overgrown mess in front of a hostel mirror. The result wasn't exactly professional, but it felt liberating—a shedding of months on the road, of dust and sweat and the weight of the journey so far.

That evening, as I strolled back onto the rooftop terrace, Matt and Jack barely looked up from their drinks. Then Matt did a double-take.

"Bloody hell!" he exclaimed, eyes widening. "Who the hell are you?"

Jack squinted at me, confused, before breaking into laughter. "Mate, I thought we had a new roommate!"

I grinned, running a hand through my newly uneven hair. "Figured it was time for a fresh start."

"Fresh is one way to put it," Jack smirked, shaking his head.

But Udaipur also marked an ending. For Matt, the journey was almost over. He was running low on money, and the time had come for him to return home, find work, and slot back into the life he had left behind. But not just yet. Before stepping back into reality, he wanted a few weeks of nothingness—beach days, cold beers, and warm seas. He had heard from Chris and Sara, who were whiling away their time in Gokarna, and decided to take a bus south to join them before flying home.

Jack and I accompanied him to the dusty, chaotic bus station, standing together amid the honking rickshaws, hawkers shouting over one another, and the low hum of idling engines. As the departure time neared, our easy conversation faded into the inevitable silence that lingers before goodbyes.

Matt slung his bag over his shoulder, shifting his weight. "Well, that's it then."

"See you back in England, mate," I said, shaking his hand before pulling him into a hug.

Jack followed suit, clapping him on the back. "Try not to turn into a lobster in Goa."

Matt smirked. "Yeah, yeah. And you two—try not to get eaten by monkeys."

"We'll do our best," I laughed, shaking my head.

The bus doors creaked open, and Matt stepped inside, giving us one last wave before disappearing into the dimly lit interior. The engine rumbled to life, and just like that, he was gone.

CHAPTER 23

Desert to City

Number of days on the road: 216
Total distance covered: 10,639 km

After a few days of pleasant cycling from Udaipur through the rolling green hills of southern Rajasthan and into Gujarat, the open roads gradually gave way to heavier traffic, and the landscape shifted from vast rural stretches to a more urban sprawl. As we approached the cities of Ahmedabad and Vadodara, the traffic became more chaotic and the cycling far less enjoyable.

The romance of rolling into Mumbai died the moment we hit the outskirts. The sheer crush of humanity was unlike anything I had experienced—rickshaws darting unpredictably, cows wandering obliviously through traffic, entire families squeezed onto single motorbikes weaving between honking lorries. The air was thick with exhaust fumes, a chaotic cocktail of dust, heat, and relentless noise. My brain was overloaded—too much movement, too much sound, too many bodies, and wheels, and horns. The city didn't welcome you so much as consume you whole.

Every kilometre felt like an endurance test, which involved dodging potholes, swerving around overburdened trucks, and avoiding pedestrians who stepped into the road without warning. By the time we reached the city proper, sweat clung to my skin, and my patience was worn dangerously thin.

Finally, we conceded defeat, flagging down a bus that was willing to take both us and our bikes. As we heaved our tired bodies and dusty bikes aboard, we felt a wave of relief. Mumbai awaited— the city's buzzing streets and the promise of Maharashtra's sun-drenched beaches beyond them were tempting.

We were dropped off at a bus station not too far away from the centre of Mumbai and cycled the rest of the way to the Gateway of India. The grand stone arch is situated at the water's edge next to Mumbai Port, framed against the humid Mumbai sky. Built in 1924 to commemorate the arrival of King George V and Queen Mary, it had once been a symbol of colonial power but now stands as a defining landmark of the city, a meeting place for locals and tourists away from the centre of town.

Jack took a long look at the structure and let out a wide smile. "Bit excessive just for a doorway, don't you think?"

I laughed. "Well, when you've got an empire to show off, I suppose subtlety isn't the aim."

Mumbai was vast. The suburbs seemed to go on endlessly: there was mile after mile of chaotic streets lined with high-rise apartments. It had a cosmopolitan, almost Western feel in parts—sleek office buildings, luxury hotels, international restaurants, and a noticeable absence of the wide-eyed curiosity we had grown used to in the more remote regions.

Tourists were everywhere, particularly around the Gateway of India, where we found ourselves blending into the crowd for the first time in months. No one stopped us to ask where we were from or where we were going. There were no lingering stares, no enthusiastic invitations to chai, no questions about our bicycles or journey. After so long on the road as objects of curiosity, it was strange to suddenly be invisible. It felt liberating. But also disorienting. For months, I had been seen—really seen. Now, I could vanish into the crowd, and part of me missed the recognition, the curiosity, the way strangers made me feel like I mattered.

Accommodation was pricey, but Jack and I managed to find a room that was basic but sufficient. Mumbai felt expensive compared to where we had been.

The following day, we explored the city on our bikes, which were light and free of panniers. As we weaved through Mumbai's maze of streets, we hunted for a music shop where Jack could find a guitar or a ukulele like mine. He had been borrowing my guitar for weeks now, strumming away in the evenings, and had finally decided he wanted his own. The search took us through pockets of the city we might have otherwise missed—past tiny hole-in-the-wall shops, market stalls selling every oddity imaginable.

By late afternoon, we gave up the search and decided to reward ourselves with a drink. At a dimly lit bar tucked away in one of Mumbai's livelier districts, we fell into conversation with a couple of locals. Before long, we moved on to another bar together—this one sleek and modern, with polished wooden floors, low lighting, and an extensive cocktail menu.

Jack glanced at the prices and let out a low whistle. "One drink here costs more than our hotel room."

I raised an eyebrow. "Maybe we should just sleep on the bar floor and call it even."

The young, well-dressed Indians around us didn't seem to blink at the prices. They ordered rounds of imported whisky and craft cocktails without hesitation, laughing and chatting with the kind of effortless confidence that money buys. It was a stark contrast to what we had seen outside. The prices were higher than top end bars in

London and the price of one drink was equivalent to several days' budget so far on our travels in the country.

Later that night, as we made our way back to our hotel, the contrast became even more glaring. Just beyond the neon-lit bars and restaurants, the streets were lined with people sleeping on the pavement, wrapped in thin blankets or curled up on the bare ground. Families huddled together under makeshift shelters, their belongings piled beside them.

Jack shook his head. "How can a place like that bar exist right next to this?"

I wanted to say something—some profound insight into the cruel contradictions of the world—but there was no easy answer. This wasn't unique to Mumbai, of course. Every major city in the world has its divisions. But here, the contrast was sharper, more glaring, more impossible to ignore than I had been used to.

Over the following days, we stopped at the supermarket to stock up on noodles, bread and bottled water, and visited a bike shop as Jack needed a new switch for his gears. I took the opportunity to give my bike a once-over. I checked the nuts and bolts, but everything was welded on with dust and dirt accumulated over many months of cycling. I was less worried about nuts and bolts coming off now and wondering more whether they would ever come off if I need to replace anything.

We also ate plenty of good food. A mixture of Western food, including meaty burgers and doughy pizzas, and some local dhal. I located a set of scales and saw that I now weighed in at 68kg—a significant improvement from the gaunt figure I must have been in Pakistan. Still, I was very lean, and Jack and I made a pact to start a daily exercise regime of sit-ups and push-ups, determined to build a bit of strength in our long-neglected upper bodies.

We spent our final day in Mumbai at Chowpatty Beach, a stretch of golden sand that provided us with a rare moment of calm amid the city's relentless energy. It was a place where families gathered, children played cricket, and elderly men took slow, thoughtful strolls along the shore. We watched the sun dip below the horizon, casting the skyline in hues of orange and pink, the warm evening breeze carrying the scent of salt and street food.

It was there that we overheard a conversation about a ferry departing from the Gateway of India, offering a way to bypass the madness of Mumbai's traffic. Jack and I exchanged glances—escaping the city without battling the gridlocked roads? It sounded too good to ignore.

CHAPTER 24

Southern Shores

Number of days on the road: 223
Total distance covered: 11,142 km

The ferry turned out to be an inspired decision. As we disembarked in Mandwa, a quiet coastal town in the Maharashtra state of India, it felt like we had crossed into an entirely different world. The chaotic, congested streets of Mumbai were replaced by palm-fringed roads, the rhythmic sound of waves, and a languid coastal breeze that carried the scent of salt and tropical vegetation. The air was thick with warmth, almost humid, and it carried the unmistakable scent of the sea. It felt as though we had stepped onto a tropical island.

The scenery had transformed dramatically from the arid landscapes we had cycled through in Rajasthan and northern Maharashtra. Here, the greenery was lush and vibrant, the trees heavy with coconuts and mangoes, the roads narrow and meandering. Every so often, a tiny village appeared along our route, where life moved at an unhurried pace. Children waved as we passed while old men dozed under banyan trees. The heat radiated off the tarmac, bronzing our skin with every pedal stroke, but the occasional gust of sea breeze tempered its intensity.

By late afternoon, we had found the perfect camping spot—a secluded patch of sand beneath a cluster of swaying palms, with the Arabian Sea stretching endlessly before us. As the sun began its descent, painting the sky in hues of amber and pink, we gathered driftwood and built a small fire, its flames crackling softly as we stretched out on the warm sand. For the first time in weeks, I exhaled fully. My muscles melted into the sand.

We sat there, rum in hand, watching the flames flicker, casting shadows that were long and wavering across the sand.

Each morning began with the gentle rhythm of the waves, a natural alarm clock that stirred me from sleep as the first golden light beamed across the sky. We washed in the sea, letting the saltwater cleanse our skin before packing up camp and setting off along the meandering coastal road. The route was never straightforward—rivers frequently blocked our way, forcing us to take tiny, family-run ferries across tranquil estuaries where the water reflected the sky like glass. These crossings were an adventure in themselves. The ferries were little more than wooden rafts with a noisy motor, often overloaded with villagers, motorbikes, and livestock, while the ferry operators gestured for us to squeeze on our bicycles wherever we could.

I don't recall managing a full day's cycling during those days, not because of exhaustion, but because we kept stumbling upon beaches so perfect they felt like mirages. Each time we swore we would push on further, but then we would round a bend and find another crescent of untouched sand, another grove of palms swaying in the breeze, another cove where the sea was impossibly blue. We had no choice but to stay.

Our days became blissfully repetitive—riding, resting, swimming, and camping on beaches that felt like they belonged to us alone. Fires built from driftwood crackled into the night as we sat watching the sun sink slowly into the Arabian Sea, painting the sky in strokes of crimson and gold.

"I think I could live like this forever," I murmured one night, stretching out on the sand, feeling the warmth of the fire against my skin.

Jack grinned, poking at the embers. "Yeah, but we'd probably turn into a pair of leathery, half-naked old men who only communicate in grunts."

"Sounds like a decent retirement plan," I laughed, tilting my head back to watch the Milky Way stretch across the sky like a river of light.

Bathing in the sea became a ritual. The cool water was a perfect way to freshen up after long, sweaty rides. I used sand as an exfoliator, scrubbing away the grime of the road, and I always emerged feeling renewed.

We were making our way south towards Goa, but for the first time in months, there was no urgency. There was no rush. No visas to chase, no bitter cold or suffocating heat to endure, no harsh landscapes to battle. There were hills to tackle—the coast here was anything but flat—but nothing really mattered. Just the slow, deliberate movement of life on the road, where food, shelter, and adventure were always within reach.

We ambled along this peaceful way for almost two weeks. One night, though, something changed. We had pitched our tents on a heavenly stretch of sand, lulled into a false sense of security by its sheer beauty. But we hadn't calculated on the tide creeping in as we slept. I stirred slightly, half-conscious, listening to the familiar rhythm of the waves. But something felt... off. The sound was wrong—closer, deeper. It was like the sea had shifted in its sleep. It was inching toward us with each breath.

Then, cold. A sudden rush of water licked at the edge of my sleeping bag. My eyes snapped open. The moonlight reflected off the wet sand just inches from my feet. The tide had come for us.

"Jack! Get up!" I shouted, scrambling out of my sleeping bag.

In the darkness, we frantically grabbed our gear, hauling our bikes and belongings over a crumbling stone wall into the only available space—an overgrown garden thick with tangled vegetation.

"Watch out for snakes," Jack warned, shining his head torch into the undergrowth.

I grimaced. "Brilliant. Get washed away or get bitten by a snake. Great choices."

Jack, ever the pragmatist, decided to stay put in the garden, settling back down amongst the tall grass. I, on the other hand, refused to share my sleeping quarters with whatever creatures lurked in the shadows. I sat on the wall balancing my belongings and, as soon as the tide began to retreat, I dragged my belongings back onto the damp sand, content to wait it out under the open sky. It had been a close call, but as I lay there watching the waves, I couldn't help but laugh.

Paradise, it seemed, had its own way of keeping us on our toes.

A few days later, we approached the Terekhol River, the natural border between Maharashtra and Goa, and the scenery subtly shifted. Advertising boards for small hotels, beach huts, and bars began to appear, growing more frequent as we neared the ferry crossing. The laid-back, tourist-friendly atmosphere was unmistakable. It felt as though we were cycling towards a different world.

We stopped at a riverside stall for a lassi, a welcome refreshment in the midday heat. As we sat waiting for the ferry, I managed to slice open my big toe on a jagged sheet of metal, swearing loudly as blood trickled onto my sandal. Pulling out my medical kit, I cleaned the wound as best I could, bandaged it up, and shook my head at my own clumsiness.

Upon crossing the Terekhol River, we officially entered Goa. The change was instant. The number of Westerners multiplied, the air carried a distinct scent of sea salt and coconut oil, and the roadside shacks offered everything from sun hats to fresh fruit smoothies. It was a far cry from the quiet roads of Rajasthan or the sparse beaches of Maharashtra.

In Arambol, we stopped for a celebratory lunch—baked potatoes cooked in Goan spices and washed down with large, ice-cold beers. It felt well-earned. After months of hard cycling, we had reached India's most famous paradise for travellers. The thought of slowing down for a while, of taking a break from the road, felt intoxicating.

Feeling triumphant, we dragged ourselves down to the shoreline and waded straight into the sea, laughing as the waves crashed around us. A few tourists sitting on the beach watched in amusement, possibly wondering why two scruffy men were washing in the surf like a pair of shipwrecked castaways.

By evening, we had found a cheap residential beach hut tucked just behind the dunes, and relished the novelty of having unrestricted internet for the first time since Mumbai about two weeks earlier. I sent a few long-overdue emails home and flicked through my camera, marvelling at how far we had come.

And then, to my complete surprise, I bumped into Bill. Bill—the cyclist I had ridden across northern Turkey with.

"Bloody hell!" I exclaimed, spotting him in the internet café, with a beer in hand and a knowing grin on his face. "What are you doing here?"

"Waiting for you, obviously," he chuckled. "Took the easy route—hopped on a plane from Iran. Thought I'd line up a few beers for when you finally made it."

We laughed and slapped each other on the back. It felt surreal to see him again, here of all places. The cycling world, it seemed, was smaller than I had thought.

Goa's tourist towns had one undeniable perk—massive, indulgent breakfasts. After months of eating nothing but thali and curry for every meal, the sheer joy of being able to order a full plate of toast and jam, cereal, eggs, and even bacon was almost overwhelming. I imagined more sophisticated travellers eyeing me with quiet disapproval, sipping their masala chai while I wolfed down stacks of toast, but I didn't care. If they had spent months fuelling their bodies on rice and dal, burning through 6,000 to 9,000 calories a day in the saddle, they would have understood my gluttony.

Despite the Western comforts and the famously chilled-out atmosphere, I wasn't taken with Arambol. It was one of the original hippy enclaves of the '60s and '70s, but decades later, it felt like it had stagnated. The free spirits of yesteryear had been replaced by a new generation of wannabe hippies—people who spent half the year working regular jobs back home and the other half getting drunk, taking drugs, and preaching the virtues of peace and enlightenment in Goa.

I wasn't against the idea of taking time to escape the pressures of modern life—after all, I was on my own break from reality—but something about Arambol felt disingenuous. It wasn't a community of seekers; it was a playground for those who wanted to disconnect from responsibility without contributing much in return. The idea of "finding oneself" seemed to come with a side of cheap beer and an easy life, and I found myself wondering what, if anything, they were actually searching for.

Jack and I left Arambol behind, weaving our way through Anjuna and Calangute before reaching Candolim, where the River Princess, a rusting container ship, had sat beached in the bay for the past decade. For reasons unknown, the government had decided to leave it there, and so it had become an unlikely landmark—looming, forgotten, and slowly succumbing to the elements.

The further south we travelled, the more the tourist saturation of northern Goa grated on me. The unbroken stretches of empty road and wild camping spots we had once revelled in were a stark contrast to the crowded beach fronts and package holiday enclaves we now found ourselves in. It felt like India's answer to Benidorm—loud, commercialised, and entirely at odds with the freedom we had been enjoying. To top it off, our cheap guesthouse came with an unexpected guest: the biggest cockroach I had ever seen. It scuttled across the ceiling at speed before launching itself at Jack, who leapt out of bed with a yelp. I found the whole thing hilarious—perhaps because I wasn't the target.

Almost three weeks after leaving Mumbai, we left behind the well-trodden tourist paths of Goa and rolled into the quieter, more rural state of Karnataka.

The ride into the small beach town of Gokarna felt different—more relaxed, less developed, with the scent of salt and sandalwood in the air. The landscape was changing too, the lush palms giving way to rugged coastal cliffs and quieter, more secluded beaches.

As we entered the town, we were hopeful but uncertain. We had no idea where to find Matt, Chris, and Sara before they returned to the UK. But luck was on our side. That evening, as the sun set, we found them at a beachfront restaurant, deep in conversation around a low wooden table.

"Oi, look who finally made it!" Matt grinned as he spotted us approaching.

"About time!" Chris added, raising his beer in our direction.

I dropped my bike against the wall and slid into a chair beside them. "Wouldn't want to miss this, would I?"

I glanced around the table and felt an immediate pang of nostalgia. It was Matt's last night before returning to the UK, and they were gathered for a farewell meal—one final evening together before he headed home. The plates were already half-cleared, the flickering candlelight reflecting off half-empty glasses of rum and lime sodas.

Sara shook her head, a playful smirk on her lips. "You always seem to turn up just in time for the big moments, don't you?"

"Call it good timing," I said, reaching for a menu.

The evening unfolded with stories, laughter, and the occasional pause for reflection. We reminisced about the adventures we'd shared—the long desert roads, the freezing mountain passes, the hidden beach camps, and the meals wolfed down after brutal days on the bike. Matt, as always, was in good spirits, but there was no denying the weight of the moment. It was the end of an era for our little cycling tribe.

"Feels weird, doesn't it?" Matt said, looking around the table as he swirled the last of his drink in his glass.

"Yeah," I admitted. "You've been a big part of this trip."

He leaned back in his chair and exhaled. "I know I've gotta go back, but I'll miss this. The freedom. The madness. Even the bloody saddle sores."

We all laughed, but there was a melancholic edge to it.

The next morning, we walked him to the bus stop, awkward in the quiet weight of the goodbye. When the bus rumbled up, he shouldered his bag and grinned.

"See you back in England, mate," he said, pulling me into a firm hug.

I patted his back. "Try not to get sunburned on the Goan beaches."

"Yeah, yeah," he smirked. "And you lot try not to get eaten by monkeys."

With a final wave, he climbed aboard. The bus pulled away, kicking up dust as it wound its way out of town.

Over the next few days, I settled into a slower rhythm with Chris, Sara, and Jack. Gokarna had a quiet charm, a world apart from the tourist-heavy beaches of Goa.

The hottest parts of the days were spent swimming, reading or playing endless rounds of backgammon on a set I constructed out of bamboo. The wooden pieces clicked against the board as I lounged in the shade, lassi in one hand, dice in the other.

In the cooler afternoons, we would play Frisbee on the beach. My skin had started to tan, my body felt strong, and I realised that, for the first time in a long while, I was completely at ease.

Life here was simple: my beachfront hut cost me between £1 and £1.50 per night, my meals—delicious thalis, fresh fruit, and the occasional cold beer—totalled no more than £6 a day. It was, quite honestly, bliss.

Gokarna's beaches were a paradise. Unlike the party-driven sands of Goa, these were almost hidden from the outside world. Framed by lush green hills, they spread out in untouched golden arcs, the clear blue waters gently lapping at the shore. It felt as though I had stumbled upon a secret, a place where time slowed and life moved at a different pace.

After several weeks, the inevitable question loomed—what next? I spent the next few days debating my onward route, tracing my fingers over maps and weighing up the options. Eventually, I decided to break with my usual overland custom and take a flight to Kuala Lumpur in Malaysia. From here, I would cycle north through Southeast Asia. The thought of a new chapter was exciting, but it also meant leaving behind the comfort of familiarity and the friends I had come to consider family.

The next morning, I scurried to the "internet hut" to book my flight. The "internet hut" was a bamboo hut on the sandy beach containing two computers with a temperamental internet connection.

Just as I clicked "Confirm Booking", I saw it.

A cobra. A real, actual, hood-flaring cobra. It slithered in as if it owned the place, sliding under the rickety table, its beady eyes locked onto me like I had personally offended it. My hands froze over the keyboard.

Every muscle in my body screamed for me to move, but I stayed perfectly still. I was convinced it could smell fear.

The hut owner, a wiry old man sitting outside, peeked in at my panicked expression. He glanced down, nodded at the snake, and—without a flicker of alarm—reached for his flip-flop.

"Uh," I croaked. "I don't think that's gonna do much..."

But, before I could argue further, the snake gave me one last look, flicked its tongue dismissively, and slipped away as silently as it had arrived.

My heart hammered as I exhaled. Booking flights was stressful enough—add a venomous snake, and it became a near-death experience.

But as the confirmation email landed in my inbox, so too did the weight of the farewell ahead.

Saying goodbye was harder than I had anticipated. My ragtag group of travellers—Jack, Chris, Sara—had been more than just passing acquaintances. We had shared roads, meals, hardships, and endless laughter. We had found each other in the randomness of the journey, brought together by the slow rhythm of travel—by bicycles, and by the sheer unpredictability of the road.

On my last night, we gathered one final time on the beach, a small fire flickering between us. Jack strummed my battered guitar, its familiar chords carrying into the warm night air.

"So, Malaysia, huh?" he said, handing me back the guitar.

"Yep," I nodded. "Feels like the right move."

"Feels like the end of an era," Chris added, raising a beer in a mock toast.

"It's been one hell of a ride," I admitted, staring out at the waves.

There was nothing grand or dramatic in this goodbye—just a quiet understanding that this was the way of things. The road brings people together, and then it takes them apart. No promises were made, no grand speeches given. Just one last night of stories, drinks, and the kind of companionship that doesn't need words.

***

The flight to Kuala Lumpur almost went by without a hitch. I had spent the entire day weaving through the relentless traffic of Bangalore, dodging rickshaws and squeezing through alleyways in search of a suitable box to pack Shirley into.

Eventually, I stumbled upon a motorcycle shop that had exactly what I needed—an enormous cardboard box, seemingly tailor-made to house her.

As I bid farewell to India, a wave of nostalgia washed over me. Taking a flight felt like breaking a silent vow. For the first time since leaving England, I wouldn't be feeling every inch of the journey beneath my tyres. No gradual transitions, no slow unfurling of landscapes, just the blunt disconnection of air travel—one world blinking out, another blinking in.

I stared out of the tiny aeroplane window as India ebbed away below me, its roads, rivers, and mountain ranges shrinking into patchwork pieces of a world I had lived in so deeply. Eight months, 10,000 kilometres, and what felt like an entire lifetime of moments.

Shirley, tucked away in the cargo hold, was temporarily still. But the journey wasn't over. Not yet.

I was confident in ways I never could have imagined back in England. The unpredictability of the road no longer unsettled me. I knew how to navigate the madness of city traffic, how to read the land and find the best spots to sleep—whether hidden in the brush at the roadside, tucked under the shelter of a motorway bridge, or haggling for the best deal in a backstreet guesthouse. The things that might have fazed me before—language barriers, mechanical failures, sudden downpours—had become mere details, challenges to be met with a shrug and a solution.

CHAPTER 25

The Quiet Peninsula

Number of days on the road: 259
Total distance covered: 12,441 km

Kuala Lumpur reappeared like a memory half-remembered. I'd been here before, years earlier—jet-lagged, backpack slung over one shoulder, disoriented by the crush of humidity and neon. But this time was different. I rolled Shirley through the airport like a returning pilgrim, road-worn and salt-streaked, dragging with me thousands of kilometres of silence, sweat, and dust.

The contrast with India was immediate and jarring. Air-conditioning. Polite queues. Functioning infrastructure. It felt like someone had turned the volume down on the world.

I found a bike shop tucked in a side alley near Bukit Bintang, run by a gentle man whose fingers were permanently blackened with grease. He spoke little, but when he handed back Shirley with a new chain and freshly tuned gears, he offered a quiet nod that said more than a receipt ever could.

Then came the haircut.

I sat in the barber's chair watching curls fall to the floor like fragments of an old life. Months of sun and wind and grime vanished with each snip. In the mirror, I didn't see the same man I'd been when I left home, but I saw someone I recognised—less feral now, though still sun-dark and sharpened by the road.

My friend from back home in the UK, Jessica, had messaged. She was flying to Thailand for a backpacking trip. She didn't want to do it solo, and so we had agreed to travel around the country together. Her presence on the horizon stirred something restless in me: anticipation, uncertainty, a flicker of vulnerability I hadn't felt in a while.

I visited the Thai embassy to extend my visa, filled in forms, handed over passport photos, and waited in air-conditioned purgatory. Bureaucracy, yes—but also agency. A rare feeling on the road: the sense of being proactive, of shaping what came next.

Later, in KLCC Park beneath the Petronas Towers, I watched the late light slant through mist. Joggers passed. Children shrieked by the fountains. The scents of street food and cut grass mixed in the air. I sat beneath a tree and let it all wash over me. Malaysia wasn't thrilling, but that wasn't the point. It was still. Clean. Kind to my frayed edges.

I headed north along Malaysia's west coast, and the world softened around me. The roads were wide and smooth, stretching between small villages and fields of sugarcane and rice, the edges blurred by heat haze. Mosque minarets reached above the treetops. The call to prayer, drifting on the breeze, became a kind of musical punctuation to the day.

Cycling here was gentle. Measured. Not always exciting, but kind. Chickens scratched beside roadside *warungs*. Mango trees leaned lazily over wooden fences. The hills rolled in slow, green waves, and above them, the sky sat vast and white with heat.

Some mornings I would wake early and ride through dawn mist that clung to the paddies, the sun rising orange and swollen behind the palms. I stopped when I felt like it. Ate when I was hungry. Drank sweet, milky coffee and watched old men play checkers in the shade. Even the dogs here didn't bother to bark.

It was quiet in a way that made room for reflection. Not the heavy introspection of the mountains or the emotional rawness of India—just small thoughts, small moments. How far I'd come. What it had taken. The quiet pride of movement without drama.

I camped where I could: behind schools, beside plantations, in unused corners of dusty towns. I listened to frogs and fireflies, lay awake in the sticky night, and let the stillness settle into my bones.

By the time I reached Langkawi, the rhythm of the road had slowed to a near stillness. I checked into a cheap guesthouse tucked beneath swaying palms—a simple room with a fan that ticked all night and a view of the sea through salt-crusted shutters. It was enough.

After a week of long, quiet days crossing the Malaysian peninsula, I let myself lean into the island's softness. The days blurred: swim, read, eat, repeat. Meals were the reward—grilled fish still crackling from the coals, sticky rice wrapped in banana leaves, and icy lime juice that bit the tongue and cooled the blood. I ate barefoot at plastic tables, waves lapping at the shore, sand drying on my calves, the air thick with the scent of charcoal and seaweed.

Malaysia didn't ask for anything. It just let me be.

When the time came to leave, I packed slowly. I wheeled Shirley down to the harbour and bought a ferry ticket to Satun, Thailand.

As the boat pulled away from the dock, I stood out on the deck, wind tugging at my shirt, salt stinging my face. The island receded behind me—soft and green and half-unreal in the haze.

CHAPTER 26

Satun to Bangkok

Number of days on the road: 269
Total distance covered: 12,836 km

The border crossing into Thailand was as smooth as I could have hoped—no questions, no queues, no drama. I wheeled my bike past the customs booth, smiled at the sleepy border official, and just like that, I was in a new country.

There was no grand ceremony. Just a subtle shift in tone.

The air seemed softer somehow, the trees a deeper shade of green. Roadside shrines stood like tiny bursts of gold in the foliage, and the lettering on the signs curved and looped in unfamiliar patterns. Thailand already felt different—lighter, somehow. A country stretching itself open to the wandering traveller.

Satun was my first taste of Thailand. A quiet town far removed from the brashness of the country's more famous destinations. There were no backpackers here, no elephant-print trousers or reggae bars. Just morning markets spilling into the streets, the hum of mopeds, the scent of garlic frying in woks.

I found a café just off the main drag—a little place with plastic chairs and faded Coke signs. Locals sat nursing tiny cups of coffee, laughing softly, their pace unhurried. I lingered longer than planned, soaking in the calm.

The riding was blissful.

The roads were smooth, carved from perfect tarmac, with a dedicated hard shoulder that might as well have had my name on it. There was little traffic, and when there was, it gave me space. Drivers waved. Shopkeepers grinned. Kids yelled greetings from mopeds. After the madness of Indian roads, this was heaven.

While the everyday traffic was not as dangerous, there were still threats. The heat was one of them, and it was no joke. The midday sun struck like a hammer. I sweated through my shirt before breakfast, gulped down litres of water by lunch. I stopped at roadside stalls every chance I got—slurping icy sodas, chomping on watermelon, occasionally pouring water straight over my head to cool down.

Then came the kids on mopeds.

Two of them. No older than 12. They pulled up beside me on a battered scooter, giggling as they matched my pace.

"Hello, mister! Hello!" one of them shouted, grinning like a maniac.

They rode far too close, swerving just enough to make me nervous. At first, I smiled, waved, and humoured them. But after a few minutes, the fun wore thin. They weren't going anywhere, and their teasing grew bolder—laughing, shouting, reaching out towards my panniers.

Then one of them cut across my front wheel, almost sending me into the ditch. That was it.

I snapped.

I turned and delivered the universal sign of frustration—middle finger, raised high. A petty release of steam. They gasped theatrically, faces dropping like I'd slapped them, and with a burst of throttle, they were gone in a puff of smoke.

I sighed, shaking my head. It wasn't my finest moment.

But 20 minutes later, a motorcycle pulled up beside me. Older boys this time. Teenagers—lean, unsmiling, eyes locked on mine.

The passenger held up his hand and returned the gesture I'd just given. Then slowly, deliberately, he dragged his finger across his throat.

The air shifted.

I stayed calm, hands on the bars, legs moving steadily. I tried to convey peace. A nod, a raised palm, an apologetic smile. But they didn't leave. They rode beside me in silence, making gestures, watching.

Then, eventually, they peeled away.

I stopped at a roadside café an hour later, sweat drying on my back, nerves jangling. I told myself I was being paranoid. Coincidence. Just a weird encounter.

Then another motorbike flashed past. It could have been them. It could have been anyone.

I waited longer than I needed to, sipping a drink that I didn't want while scanning the road. Eventually, I convinced myself to push on.

That evening, as darkness was falling, I was aiming for Yan Ta Khao. I was close—just a few kilometres short—when it happened.

A motorcycle came up behind me. No headlights. No sound until it was on top of me.

Then—impact.

A sharp, jarring jolt to my side. One of the riders kicked out, striking my pannier and nearly sending me sprawling. I veered wildly off the road, barely keeping control, tyres skidding onto gravel.

Shirley stayed upright. Barely.

I shot down a narrow track parallel to the main road, heart thudding in my chest. *Or was it a drainage ditch? I thought.* Regardless, the motorbike riders had stopped. I looked back. One of them made the same throat-slitting gesture again.

Then they were coming.

Down the track. After me.

I stopped abruptly, bracing myself, bike between my legs. The pillion rider kicked out at me as they passed, but this time I was ready. The blow missed.

They skidded to a halt 10 metres ahead, and one of them pulled something from behind his back. A machete.

Adrenaline surged through me. I yanked open my front pannier and grabbed the heaviest thing I could find—my bicycle pump. It was solid aluminium, long and heavy. My only weapon.

I stood my ground.

No words. Just wild, electric silence.

Then a woman on a moped appeared on the road above. She shouted something in Thai, her voice sharp and urgent. A young boy, also on a moped stopped beside her, eyes wide. They could see what was happening.

The attackers hesitated.

"Go! GO!" the woman yelled, pointing down the road.

I didn't wait. I hauled my bike out of the ditch and threw my leg over the saddle. The woman took off ahead. The boy rode his moped just behind me, like an escort.

I pedalled hard. Legs burning. Heart in my throat. I didn't look back.

When we reached the edge of Yan Ta Khao, police were already there—two officers standing in the road, waving me down.

They had their guns drawn.

I skidded to a stop, breath ragged.

"You okay?" one of them asked.

"Two guys. Motorbike. They attacked me," I gasped.

They nodded. They'd already heard.

"Description?"

"Black clothes. Late teens. That's all I remember."

"Number plate?"

I shook my head. I hadn't even thought to look.

The officers exchanged a glance. One of them turned back to me. "Not safe. We take you."

They led me through town to a small, neon-lit hotel. The owner stepped out, looking confused. The police spoke rapidly in Thai, then turned to me.

"You stay here. Okay now."

Inside my room, I dropped my bags and sat on the edge of the bed, still gripping the bicycle pump. My hands were shaking.

The adrenaline gave way to something heavier.

That could've ended very differently.

I made noodles with trembling fingers, drank a beer without tasting it. My mind spun in circles: What if the woman hadn't stopped? What if she hadn't shouted? What if I'd fallen on the gravel?

That night, I didn't sleep. I lay in the dark listening to every sound outside the window, running over the moment again and again.

I'd been on the road for months. I'd dealt with traffic, cold, loneliness. But this was different.

This was fear. Real, close fear.

And I'd survived it.

The morning after the attack, I left Yan Ta Khao later than usual, exhausted from a night of near-sleep. My limbs were slow, my nerves raw, and for the first time since I'd started this journey, I didn't feel like riding. I felt like hiding.

Every truck that passed made me flinch. Every approaching motorbike sent a jolt of tension up my spine. My helmet, usually buried in a pannier, was now firmly strapped to my head. I pulled on gloves too, more for the comfort of protection than the grip.

I didn't listen to music. I wanted to hear everything—engines, footsteps, voices. Every sound became a potential threat, every shadow something to be scanned. It was irrational, but fear doesn't care about reason.

The road to Trang was short, just 40 kilometres, but it felt like 100. The sun blazed down, the air clung to me like a second skin, and my mind spiralled.

What if they followed me again?

What if it happened somewhere more remote next time?

What if they had a car?

But slowly, kilometre by kilometre, the landscape began to do its work.

Southern Thailand was lush and alive. The trees leaned in close to the road, casting patterns of dappled light that danced across the tarmac. Rice paddies shimmered under the sun, their green hue mirrored in still water. Cows wandered lazily through the shade of coconut palms. Birds darted across the road ahead, their wings slicing through the heat.

The land had no idea what had happened. It just continued. And slowly, so did I.

In Trang, I ducked into a shaded café and ordered a strong Thai coffee. The woman behind the counter offered a smile and a second glass of water without asking. Her kindness was quiet, instinctive.

I sat there for over an hour, watching the street, listening to the clink of cups, the rhythm of mopeds, the low hum of a radio. It was ordinary—and that was exactly what I needed.

Time passed. Nothing happened.

No angry teenagers. No machetes. Just locals getting on with their day.

My pulse began to settle. My hands stopped clenching. The dread began to loosen its grip.

Later that afternoon, back on the road, I began to feel something else—relief. The joy of the ride returned in small doses: a cooling breeze, the snap of tyres on smooth tarmac, the ease of movement that cycling always gives me. My legs were strong. My mind was still a little fragile, but it was healing.

I decided to veer east, crossing from the Andaman coast toward the Gulf of Thailand. A new route and a change of scenery.

The road out of Trang was fast, flat, and flanked by endless palm oil plantations. Monotonous but efficient. It gave my legs purpose and my mind space to wander again.

By the time I reached Surat Thani, the fear had been largely replaced by fatigue—and a sense of reorientation.

I'd last been here six years earlier, as a wide-eyed backpacker. I remembered Surat as a dusty ferry terminal with a single overpriced café. But now, arriving by bike, I realised just how much I must have missed the first time.

It was more developed than I remembered—streets lined with cafés and barbershops, stalls selling everything from mango sticky rice to spare motorcycle parts. It had a relaxed, local vibe. The kind of town that didn't care whether you stayed or went. I liked that.

I found a modest guesthouse and spent the evening wandering aimlessly, sipping iced coffee from a plastic bag and watching tuk-tuks weave through traffic.

A part of me—just a sliver—considered hopping on a ferry to Koh Phangan. I'd had fun there in my early twenties. But when I checked the dates and saw the Full Moon Party was just a day away, the thought vanished.

No thanks.

There would be no chance of getting accommodation and I was not in a state of mind to be anywhere near neon paint, deafening bass and buckets of Thai whisky.

I wanted calm.

So instead, I stayed put for another night. I ordered a bowl of steaming noodle soup, and let the day wind down without expectation or urgency.

And that night, I slept deeply—really slept—for the first time since crossing the border.

Leaving Surat Thani behind, I followed the flat ribbon of tarmac as it unravelled northward through the coastal plains of southern Thailand. The road was simple, fast. There were no dramatic switchbacks or jungle ascents, no vast temples or near-death incidents. Just movement. Just me and the bike, rolling under the late morning sun.

It was what I needed.

The further I rode, the lighter I felt. The unease that had followed me since the attack had not vanished completely, but it no longer sat on my shoulders. It drifted behind me like a shadow that no longer needed attention.

I passed endless rows of palm trees, their slender trunks swaying gently in the breeze. Roadside stalls offered bags of salted peanuts, fresh-cut pineapple, and icy drinks in plastic cups sealed with a straw. I stopped often—partly for the sugar, partly for the smiles. Thailand had a way of lifting your spirits even when nothing extraordinary happened.

By the time I reached Chumphon, I wanted to rest, but the guesthouse I'd been recommended was fully booked. I stood outside it for a while, staring at the reception door as if it might magically open, but no luck.

So I did what any good traveller learns to do: I kept going.

And that's how I found Thung Wua Laen Beach.

The road dipped gently towards the sea, revealing a long, quiet crescent of golden sand stretching far into the distance. No towers. No chains. Just palm trees, fishing boats, and the faint scent of salt and suncream carried on the breeze.

It was perfect. Too perfect to be real.

I rolled up to a small beach hut resort—wooden bungalows scattered among the trees, just steps from the surf. For a few quid, I had my own bamboo shack with a fan, a hammock, and a view of the sea through swaying branches.

I parked the bike, kicked off my shoes, and walked straight into the ocean. The water enveloped me, warm as blood, silk against sunburnt skin. I floated, eyes closed, weightless.

Later that evening, I sat at a little restaurant made entirely from woven palm leaves and bamboo, the floor sandy beneath my feet. I ordered a red Thai curry with beef—fiery and rich, with ribbons of meat melting into the coconut broth—and a Chang beer that was so cold that beads of condensation slid down the glass. It was, without exaggeration, one of the best meals I'd had all trip.

As I ate, the sun dipped into the sea in a flare of orange and gold. I could hear the quiet laughter of a few other travellers, the gentle splash of waves. A dog wandered through the restaurant, flopped down in the sand beside my table, and sighed as if it had also finally found peace.

That night, I sat on the porch of my hut, writing in my journal by headtorch, the pages curled from humidity. The ink smudged slightly as I recorded the day:

"No plans. No stress. Just a beach that feels like it belongs to no one. Just enough."

The next morning was even better. I took my breakfast—fresh mango, papaya, and pineapple with muesli and yoghurt—out onto the deck. The juice was sweet and sharp, and the fruit so ripe. The breeze rustled the leaves overhead. The tide had crept up during the night, leaving behind its wet signature—a dark line on the sand.

These were the moments that made cycle touring so strange and beautiful. One week, you're swinging a metal pump at machete-wielding teenagers in a ditch. The next, you're wiggling your toes in the sand, in the sunshine, eating tropical fruit by the sea.

I picked up my battered copy of Gandhi's autobiography, *The Story of My Experiments with Truth,* and read until the sky turned lilac.

I left Thung Wua Laen with reluctance. The place had offered something rare: silence, stillness, and space to breathe. But I knew I couldn't linger. Bangkok was calling—and Jessica would be landing in less than a week.

The road north was long, straight, and fast. There were no dramatic climbs, no border crossings, no great epiphanies—just kilometre after kilometre of easy motion. For a while, I let myself slip into the rhythm of it. A good road, a loaded bike, and the steady hum of tyres against tarmac. There's peace in that. A kind of cycling meditation.

I passed through small towns and villages that blurred together—places that barely registered on the map but pulsed with everyday life. Men lounged on scooters outside hardware shops. Women swept dust from front steps with woven palm brooms. Children shouted greetings from behind school gates, waving until I disappeared from view.

Every day followed the same pattern: early starts to beat the heat, a mid-morning food stop, and a long afternoon stretch under the harsh sun. I ate like a king — stir-fried morning glory with garlic and oyster sauce, bowls of pork noodle soup with lime and chilli, plastic bags full of chopped watermelon, sealed with a skewer. Food wasn't just fuel in Thailand; it was part of the ride.

By the time I reached Bangkok three days later, I was soaked to the skin with sweat, sticky with sunscreen and talc, and completely exhausted.

The final stretch into the city was madness. Motorbikes swarmed like hornets. The city throbbed with noise and energy. Horns. Shouts. Music.

Then, out of nowhere, I saw a small temple and watched a saffron-robed monk sweep fallen leaves into a perfect circle. Amongst all of Bangkok's chaos, everything felt still. I thought about how far I'd come—not in distance, but in resilience. Whatever lay ahead, I knew I had already changed.

I rolled into the city centre half-blind from the salty sweat in my eyes, grinning through clenched teeth. Somewhere behind the fatigue, a thought flickered: *This place is utterly insane. But it's alive.*

I checked into a guesthouse down a narrow side street, stripped off my wet clothes, and took the longest shower of my life. Afterwards, I wrapped myself in a towel and collapsed onto the bed, feeling every mile of the journey in my legs.

And then my phone buzzed with a message.

It was Jessica.

"Landing in two days. Can't believe it's happening!"

I smiled. After three weeks of cycling mostly alone since leaving India, the idea of seeing someone from home—someone who knew me before all of this—felt surreal. It felt exciting. Strange.

I stared at the message a moment longer, then rolled over and reached for my journal.

"Bangkok. Madness. Music. Chaos. But underneath it all, a calm excitement. She's coming."

I smiled and closed my eyes.

Tomorrow, I'd rest. The day after that, everything would shift again.

CHAPTER 27

A Friendly Visit

Number of days on the road: 279
Total distance covered: 13,581 km

The taxi to the airport crawled through Bangkok's backstreets, weaving between barricades and diverted traffic as the city writhed under the pressure of political protests that were in full swing in the city. I'd given myself plenty of time, but even so, I chewed my lip with every red light.

I hadn't seen anyone from *home* since I'd rolled out of England nearly ten months earlier. And now Jessica was about to step through the arrival gates. A familiar face from another life. And part of me wondered—were we still the same people?

I stood near the arrivals board, shifting from foot to foot, scanning every face. Then I saw her.

Blonde hair bouncing with each step, suitcase trailing obediently behind her.

“Oh my god, Rob!” she laughed, trotting forward.

I met her in a hug that felt both familiar and strange at the same time.

"Jesus Jess," I said, pulling back slightly, "you look—exactly the same."

"Rude!" She arched her brow. "I fly across the world and that's the best you've got?"

"Ok, fine, you look amazing!"

We grabbed a taxi back to the centre, her eyes wide with every chaotic turn of Bangkok’s streets. She laughed as a tuk-tuk blared past us at impossible speed, and I realised how numb I’d become to it all—the madness of the road, the noise, the smells. Seeing it through her eyes made it all new again.

Back at the hotel, we freshened up and found ourselves seated in the quiet courtyard, drinks in hand, the heat easing into evening.

At first, our conversation was cautious—friends catching up after too long apart. But soon the rhythm returned. The laughter. The shorthand. The ease. Like no time had passed at all.

“I still can’t believe you’re actually here,” I said, stirring the ice in my drink.

Jess tilted her head. "Well here I am. You look different, though."

"Different?"

"Tanned, obviously. Scruffier. Rugged."

"Hey."

"In a good way." She smiled. "You look like someone who's been *doing something*. You look alive."

I felt a quiet warmth bloom in my chest. "Thanks. That means a lot."

The next few days slipped into an easy rhythm—a blur of temples, tangled backstreets, sticky heat, and the hum of a city that never stood still.

We wandered through Bangkok like two people rediscovering the world, and maybe a little of each other, too.

We went to a street food spot that had been recommended, the kind of place you'd miss if you didn't know what you were looking for. Hawker stalls flickering under bare bulbs, smoke curling from makeshift grills, the scent of garlic, soy, and chilli thick in the air.

"We *have* to try this," I said, pointing at the menu.

She wrinkled her nose. "I don't know, Rob..."

"Oh, come on."

She rolled her eyes at me.

We ordered barbecued red snapper. The crisp skin crackled as I peeled it back, and steam carrying hints of char and lime wafted out. Her eyebrows shot up.

"Okay… that's actually amazing."

We sweated our way through the golden halls of Wat Pho, where the reclining Buddha—all 46 metres of polished gold—lay in impossible stillness. His expression was beatific, as though he knew something the rest of us hadn't quite worked out yet. The echo of bare feet on temple tiles and the low murmur of prayers added to the stillness.

Later, we stood before the Emerald Buddha at Wat Phra Kaew. It was smaller than we'd expected, but commanding. The temple was a riot of mirrored mosaics and steeply pitched rooftops that gleamed in the sun like dragon scales. We wandered in silence, sweating, awestruck.

"It feels like you could spend a lifetime here and still not understand it," Jess said quietly, eyes scanning the intricate murals.

"Yeah. But I wouldn't mind trying."

We booked Thai massages that nearly broke us both.

"They *walk* on you?" she hissed, eyes wide as we stepped into the lemon-scented calm of the studio.

"It's therapeutic."

She gave me a withering look.

An hour later, she emerged looking shell-shocked.

"I think I just got suplexed by a grandmother."

I laughed so hard I nearly pulled a muscle.

In the evenings, we nursed cold beers in dimly lit courtyards, watching geckos scurry up the walls and tuk-tuks cough past on the street beyond. The city softened at night, like it was exhaling.

One evening, as we sat in the shadow of a tangled banyan tree, Jess turned to me.

"You know, I wasn't sure about coming out here."

"Here?"

"To see you. I thought maybe you might not be the same."

"And?"

She shrugged, a slow smile tugging at her lips. "Turns out you're still you. Just a bit smellier."

"Charming."

"But... in a good way."

It caught me off guard. She had this way of getting under the surface with just a few words, whilst also being playful and funny.

The next evening, we boarded the overnight train to Chiang Mai. It was one of those wonderfully disorienting journeys—half sleep, half motion. We were rocked gently through the night, lulled by the rhythmic clatter of wheels over worn steel, the occasional rattle of passing food carts, the soft snores of strangers nearby.

I lay awake for a while, listening to the hum of the train and the noise of a city fading behind us, wondering what the mountains might hold.

Shirley had been left behind in Bangkok, secured in the underground car park of the hotel. It was time to let go for a while and just be a tourist and not a traveller.

Chiang Mai greeted us with morning mist and mountain air. It felt like a different country entirely. It was calmer, cooler, and quieter. The pace dropped a gear, and so did we.

Our hostel was tucked into a leafy side street, all teak wood and paper lanterns. We ditched our bags, stretched the train from our bones, and headed out to book a multi-day tour, something we'd both been looking forward to: a proper jungle trek.

The next day, a rattling pickup truck carried us out of the city and into the hills for the beginning of the trek.

The buildings gave way to farmland, then to forest. We wound higher and higher until the trees swallowed the road, and green was all that remained.

Our guide was a wiry, softly spoken man named Lek who wore flip-flops and moved through the forest like he'd been born in it. We followed him into the jungle, packs on our backs, sweat already trickling down our necks.

The heat was wet and immediate, like walking through a greenhouse. Ferns towered overhead. Vines curled from tree to tree like jungle punctuation. Somewhere unseen, birds cried out, high and mournful.

It was hard work. Slopes turned to climbs. Paths disappeared into root-choked earth. Jess slipped more than once and swore colourfully every time.

"Remind me why we signed up for this?" she gasped, wiping sweat from her brow as we scrambled up a particularly steep trail.

"For the view," I grinned and pointed ahead.

We reached a hilltop clearing just as the sun dropped behind the ridge, bathing the whole valley in gold. Below us, a river curled like a ribbon, wrapped in layers of mist and trees. Mountains rolled away into the distance like the spine of something ancient.

We just stood there for a while, breathing it in.

Our accommodation that night was a bamboo hut perched on the hillside—no electricity, no internet, no sounds but the rustle of leaves and the occasional thud of ripe fruit falling somewhere in the dark.

Dinner was cooked over an open fire. We ate by candlelight, spooning curry from enamel bowls and listening to the forest hum. Afterwards, we lay side by side on the bamboo floor, staring through the gaps in the slatted walls at a sky littered with stars.

There was something about being out here—surrounded by nothing but jungle and sky—that made everything else feel very far away.

On the second day, we hiked to an elephant sanctuary. There were no barriers, no ropes—just earth, jungle, and giants. Their skin was thick and cracked like old leather, their eyes dark and unreadable. We waded into a shallow pool beside it, scooping water over its massive back, watching the mud run in rivulets down its sides.

On the third day, we hiked through the jungle to the Taeng River. The energy shifted again when we found ourselves strapped into a bright yellow raft, helmets crooked, paddles ready, hearts pounding. The river was fast, white-tipped, furious. We bounced and spun and soaked ourselves in adrenaline, yelling over the roar, battered and buzzing, completely alive.

***

Back in Chiang Mai, we attended a cookery course.

"Are you ready to become a master chef?" Jess asked, as we arrived at a traditional wooden house tucked just beyond the city limits, surrounded by a garden thick with herbs, papaya trees, and impossibly vibrant chillies.

"Only if you're ready to lose," I replied.

We each had our own cooking station under a thatched-roof pavilion. Mortars and pestles, gas burners, woks. A jungle kitchen with a view.

"Let's make this interesting," Jess said, tying her apron. "Whoever cooks the best dish wins."

"High stakes," I nodded. "What's the prize?"

She smiled. "Winner gets bragging rights."

"Deal."

I tackled Pad Thai. Oil, garlic, chicken, tamarind paste, fish sauce, sugar, crushed peanuts. I tossed it all together with the theatrical confidence of someone winging it hard.

Jess went for a green curry—pounding fresh herbs into a paste so fragrant it made my eyes water. She was in the zone, brow furrowed, arms moving with surprising strength as she crushed lemongrass and chilli into oblivion.

When we finally tasted each other's dishes, we both grinned.

"Okay," I admitted, chewing slowly. "That curry is outrageous."

The sun was setting by the time we sat with our beers, feet bare, full of food and satisfaction. Lanterns swung gently in the garden breeze, casting soft light across the wooden table.

"That cookery school was honestly one of the best things I've done in Thailand," I said, tipping my bottle towards her.

Jess looked out at the silhouetted mountains. There was a long, warm silence. Then she softly said,

"Uh oh."

She didn't need to say anything else. I knew what she meant. It was a moment of realisation that we were no longer just friends.

***

We arrived in Koh Lanta by ferry, standing on the sun-drenched upper deck as the island came into view—a long stretch of green rising from the sea, fringed with white beaches and swaying palms. Compared to the buzzing islands like Koh Phi Phi or Koh Samui, it felt hushed, like it had been left behind by the tourism boom on purpose.

A few tuk-tuks loitered at the dock, but we opted to walk—dragging our bags down the sandy road until we found it: a humble bamboo hut tucked beneath the shade of coconut trees, just a stone's throw from the beach.

It was perfect. Rough around the edges, sure, but with a charm you can't buy. The kind of place you didn't just stay—you *exhaled* in.

In the mornings, we woke to birdsong and the gentle hiss of waves on sand.

"How are we ever supposed to leave this place?" she asked one morning, toes buried in the cool sand.

"We don't," I replied. "We write home, tell them we've joined a cult of coconut farmers."

She laughed, tilting her head back to soak in the sun.

Days blurred beautifully. We rented a scooter and zipped along the coastal road, stopping at hidden beaches, waterfalls, and roadside cafés that served grilled barracuda so fresh it practically leapt onto your plate.

We read books in hammocks, swam until our fingers wrinkled and played cards by lantern light. Occasionally, we just sat in silence, legs stretched out in the sand, letting the tide creep closer.

Evenings were our favourite.

One night, we watched the sun melt into the sea, the sky aflame with pinks and oranges. Jess leaned on my shoulder, drawing lazy shapes in the sand with her finger.

"You're going to keep going, aren't you?" she said softly.

I nodded. "Yeah... I think so."

"I knew you would," she said, not with sadness, but with understanding. Like she'd accepted it long ago.

There was a weight in her words, one I didn't quite know how to carry. A tenderness too big to speak aloud.

And yet, neither of us pushed for more.

We both knew this wouldn't last forever. That this was a moment, precious because it was fleeting. And that maybe, that was okay. We had spent three wonderful weeks together.

Back in Bangkok, we took the long, quiet route to the airport, speaking in half-thoughts, stretching out every step.

At the gate, she turned to me, smiling through glassy green eyes.

"This sucks," she said, laughing despite herself.

"Yeah," I said. "Definitely the worst bit."

We hugged. It was a real hug, the kind where everything unspoken folds into the space between two people.

"Take care of yourself."

"You too."

And then she was gone. Just another traveller disappearing into the blur of airport crowds.

I stood there for a while, watching the empty space where she'd been.

Eventually, I walked out into the heat, alone again.

***

Back in Bangkok, the city had exploded in celebration. *Songkran*—Thai New Year—was in full swing, and the streets had turned into a waterlogged warzone. Children with neon water pistols ambushed tuk-tuks. Teenagers with hoses rode in the backs of pickup trucks, dousing pedestrians. Buckets of icy water came flying from alleys and storefronts.

It was joyful chaos. For a while.

And then, it wasn't.

I couldn't go outside without getting drenched. Getting food became a mission. I was waterlogged, mildly annoyed, and craving quiet. But then, a message.

Bill was in town.

Bill. The cyclist from Turkey. We had sweated our way along the Black Sea coast together. Then, randomly, bumped into one another in Goa.

We met for lunch and picked up like no time had passed—the shorthand of shared hardship still intact. We swapped stories, compared maps, and laughed at our own madness.

"This your last stop?" I asked.

"Yeah," he said, finishing his beer. "Back to the UK tomorrow."

I grinned. "And you didn't think I'd still be at it?"

He shrugged. "Wasn't sure. But I'm glad you are."

So was I.

We parted with a handshake and a grin. It was a proper traveller's farewell.

Later that night, I sat alone on my bed, a map sprawled across my knees.

Cambodia? Vietnam? China? Korea? Japan?

My plan had always been to cycle overland through Cambodia and Vietnam into China. But my funds were dwindling. I was ten months in with just enough money for two more.

I stared at the map.

If I stuck to the plan, I might run out of money somewhere on a highway in rural China, and I had already travelled extensively through Vietnam on a backpacking holiday a few years earlier. But if I flew ahead to Hong Kong, maybe? I could get a visa there. I could save time and keep the journey alive—not in method, but in momentum.

It wasn't an easy decision.

But, eventually, I knew what I had to do.

This wasn't about the purity of the route. It was about the journey—the *whole* journey.

And I wasn't done yet.

CHAPTER 28

China Revisited

Number of days on the road: 299
Total distance covered: 13,581 km

The embassy in Hong Kong processed my visa with impressive efficiency, and after catching up with an old school friend who lived and worked in the city, I wasted no time boarding a train bound for Shanghai.

The journey was a lesson in modern Chinese engineering—the train was sleek, immaculately clean, and eerily smooth as it glided along the tracks. Settling into my seat, I let out a breath, finally allowing myself to relax. Outside the window, the scenery whizzed past in a blur, a far cry from the slow, meandering rhythm of cycling. Vast stretches of farmland and glinting rivers snaked through the landscape, and clusters of high-rise apartment blocks seemed to rise out of nowhere.

I reached into my bag and pulled out a bottle of chilled green tea, the condensation cool against my fingers. The first sip was earthy and refreshing, washing down the strange but oddly addictive rice crackers I'd picked up from a station kiosk. Around me, passengers dozed or quietly chatted in Mandarin. Occasionally, a uniformed attendant passed through the carriage, efficiently delivering hot meals in plastic trays to those who had pre-ordered. The faint scent of steamed rice and stir-fried vegetables drifted through the air.

Arriving in Shanghai, I reassembled Shirley on the station platform, shaking off the stiffness from the long journey. The city was alive with movement—crowds weaving seamlessly through the vast terminal and announcements crackling over the speakers. From the moment I rode off from the station, I had a great feeling about this place. Shanghai felt modern, dynamic, and full of energy.

With no map in hand, I set off, pedalling through the unfamiliar streets, letting instinct guide me. The city rose around me in gleaming towers and neon-lit storefronts, with small, rickety shops from centuries past tucked between them.

Eventually, I found my way to a main shopping district, where I spotted an internet café. Ducking inside, I scanned a digital town plan and browsed a list of hostels. One caught my eye—brand new, clean, and well-equipped. That would do. With the address scribbled onto a scrap of paper, I made my way over and checked in.

Over the next couple of days, I focused on recharging. I ate well—steaming dumplings and sizzling stir-fried dishes from hole-in-the-wall eateries—and let myself enjoy a slower pace. The city fascinated me—it was an intoxicating mix of old and new, tradition and progress. As I settled into Shanghai's rhythm, I fired off an email to Alberto, the Italian I had met back in Iran, who was now working at the Shanghai EXPO. Maybe we'd have a chance to catch up.

Feeling light and free without the weight of my panniers, I set off to explore Shanghai on two wheels. The city was a dream to cycle through—it had wide, well-maintained roads with dedicated bike lanes, and a surprising number of fellow cyclists weaving through the morning traffic. Without the burden of my full touring setup, I could glide effortlessly, taking in the sights and sounds of this vibrant metropolis.

My first stop was The Bund, Shanghai's iconic waterfront promenade. As I cycled along the sweeping curve of the Huangpu River, I was struck by the sheer contrast of the skyline. On one side, grand colonial-era buildings stood as a testament to Shanghai's history as an international trading port, while futuristic skyscrapers of Pudong —dominated by the needle-like Oriental Pearl Tower— sat across the river. It looked like something out of a science-fiction film.

The scene felt oddly familiar, and I smiled to myself as I realised why—it reminded me of the Liverpool waterfront back in the UK, where my family was from. The old stone façades, the sense of a proud maritime past, the energy of a city constantly evolving—it was all there.

Leaning Shirley against the railings, I stood for a while, watching cargo ships glide down the river and locals doing their morning exercises along the promenade. Elderly residents performed slow, deliberate tai chi movements, while groups of friends gathered to chat, sip tea, and enjoy the view.

Shanghai had an infectious energy, and I was determined to absorb as much of it as possible. After my morning ride along The Bund, marvelling at the stately colonial buildings set against the ultra-modern skyline of Pudong, I pedalled westward into the French Concession—a completely different world from the city's towering glass and steel skyscrapers.

As I entered its tree-lined boulevards, the pace of life seemed to shift. The streets were shaded by a dense canopy of London plane trees, their branches arching over the roads. It reminded me of Europe. Unlike the fast-paced hustle of central Shanghai—here people strolled rather than rushed—young couples held hands as they browsed bookshops, and groups of expats lingered over cappuccinos at outdoor cafés.

The architecture was stunning—red-brick townhouses with wrought-iron balconies, art deco mansions with intricate façades, and restored villas that now housed trendy boutiques and cocktail bars. It was the kind of place that made me momentarily forget I was on this mad, gruelling journey—a city where people sipped espressos, debated art, and seemed utterly at ease in their routines.

I couldn't help but wonder: What would my life look like if I stayed in a place like this? No more roadside instant noodles, no more sleeping in damp tents, no more aching legs and exhaustion at the end of every day. Could I do it? Trade the road for stability?

Needing a break, I stopped at a small, family-run café tucked between two vine-covered buildings. The smell of freshly baked pastries and brewing Yunnan coffee filled the air. I ordered a steaming latte and a flaky egg tart, a nod to the region's colonial influences, and sat outside watching the world go by. The mix of locals chatting animatedly in Shanghainese, French tourists admiring the architecture, and young creatives tapping away on laptops gave the place a cosmopolitan charm that felt miles away from the high-rise bustle of Shanghai's centre.

Alberto had replied to my email, and we met up. He brought along Alessandro, a close friend of his, and the two of them welcomed me with open arms.

"Rob! Finally, you are here!" Alberto beamed, as he affectionately slapped me on the back.

"You made it all the way from England on a bicycle," Alessandro said in awe. "I would love to do something like that, man!"[3]

They had a birthday party to attend and insisted that I join. It turned out to be a fantastic gathering, full of vibrant expats and locals, all curious about my journey. People peppered me with questions—what was the hardest part? What did you eat? Where did you sleep? I found myself reliving my trip through their excited reactions.

The dinner was an assault on the senses—in the best way possible.

Steam billowed from freshly pinched *xiaolongbao,* their delicate skins trembling with the hot broth inside. Alberto demonstrated the correct way to eat them—biting a tiny hole in one first, slurping the broth, and only then popping the rest into his mouth. I ignored his instructions and burned the roof of my mouth instantly.

"You see?" he grinned, shaking his head.

Plates of crispy duck, fragrant stir-fried greens, and a sizzling clay pot of tofu so hot it kept crackling when it reached the table. Laughter rose over the clinking of

---

[3] Alessandro did indeed embark on his own epic adventure cycling home to Italy from Shanghai several years later.

chopsticks and the constant refilling of tiny porcelain cups of *baijiu*—China's dangerously strong liquor.

Alessandro, deeply moved by my journey, leaned in at one point and said, "Rob, this... what you're doing... it's incredible. You're living the kind of adventure most of us only dream about."

Alessandro was as Italian as they come—effortlessly stylish, impeccably groomed, and with the kind of charm that turned heads wherever he went. He carried himself with an easy confidence, his sharp jawline and perfectly tousled dark hair making it abundantly clear that he had once worked as a model. And, if I needed further proof, the constant attention from women at the bar confirmed it.

I wasn't complaining, of course. With Alessandro in the spotlight, I happily found myself drawn into conversations with the women who gravitated toward our table. His smooth Italian accent and playful wit kept them engaged, but they were just as curious about my journey.

"You cycled here?" a woman asked in disbelief, her eyes widening.

"All the way from England," I confirmed, sipping my drink with a grin.

"*Ma dai*!" Alessandro interjected, shaking his head dramatically. "This guy—he's a legend. A lunatic, but a legend."

Fuelled by food, conversation, and laughter, we moved on to a bar with a rooftop terrace overlooking the Shanghai skyline, where we sipped on whisky and cocktails as the city twinkled below us. Eventually, someone suggested a club and, before I knew it, we were dancing the night away—a blur of pulsing lights, electronic beats, and carefree energy.

The night ended in the early hours, and as we stumbled out into the neon-lit streets, I realised how much I loved Shanghai. I could have stayed. I could have searched for a job here. Something about the city drew me to it and made me want to live here, but something stronger was also telling me I had to complete my journey.

As I left the towering skyline of Shanghai behind, the city gradually faded into a vast, open expanse of China's eastern heartland. I crossed the mighty Yangtze River, its slow-moving waters stretching wide beneath me. Beyond the river, Nantong welcomed me with its industrial outskirts, but soon enough, I pushed onward into Jiangsu Province, where the landscape transformed.

Jiangsu was startlingly different from the urban jungle I had left behind. The terrain was flat and fertile, a patchwork of endless rice paddies, waterways, and fields, occasionally punctuated by small villages with white-walled houses and red-tiled roofs. The region's wetlands, irrigated by the complex system of canals and rivers, had long made it one of China's most agriculturally rich areas, and it showed. Everywhere I looked, people were hard at work in the fields, their wide-brimmed straw hats bobbing among the crops.

Cycling through this landscape was peaceful, a contrast to the frenetic energy of Shanghai. The roads were mostly smooth and quiet, with the occasional rickety tractor trundling along or an old motorbike sputtering past. Locals stared curiously at me, their expressions somewhere between amusement and disbelief.

Aiming for Yancheng, I found modest lodgings—a simple guesthouse, the kind where the walls were thin, the mattress was hard, and the bathroom was little more than a tiled wet room. But for a weary cyclist, it was perfect.

The real adventure came when I set out in search of food.

Ordering a meal here presented a challenge. Unlike the more cosmopolitan cities I had passed through, English was practically non-existent, and my grasp of Mandarin was laughably insufficient. I fumbled through an awkward exchange of hand signals, hopeful gestures, and mumblings of what few words I had picked up.

Seated in a bustling eatery, I watched as steam swirled out of a bamboo basket set before me, the unmistakable aroma of pork, ginger, and rich broth drifting upwards. I had ordered *xiaolongbao* (the same soup dumplings that Alberto had patiently shown me how to eat without burning my mouth), and as I pried off the basket's woven lid, I was greeted by plump, delicate dumplings, their thin, translucent skins pulled taut over the hot broth inside.

Between bites, I dipped the next dumpling into a saucer of dark, tangy vinegar flecked with slivers of freshly sliced ginger. I washed it all down with a bottle of Tsingtao beer, feeling satisfied and slightly smug that, despite the language barrier, I had managed to secure an excellent meal.

As the days rolled on, I settled back into the rhythm of the road, though my legs burned with every pedal stroke—a stark reminder of my week-long hiatus in Shanghai. The initial discomfort was expected, but what I hadn't braced for was the quiet weight of solitude creeping back in.

The road opened up ahead, flanked by expansive fields and wide wetlands—a landscape that felt both endless and unchanging. It should have been liberating. But instead, a familiar longing gnawed at me. I found myself drifting back to warmer memories—the carefree days on Koh Lanta with Jess, the sound of her laughter over a game of cards, the way the sun had warmed our skin as we lazed on the beach, the effortless companionship that made everything feel lighter.

I shook the thoughts away. No. There was no room for homesickness now. I had come too far, had endured too much, and there was no way I was turning back just because I felt a little lost inside my own head. The only way to find my balance again was to push forward—mile by mile, pedal stroke by pedal stroke.

The open road lay ahead—an empty canvas with no one to share the painting with.

It should have been liberating. It had been before. But now, I felt the weight of every unspoken conversation, every laugh I wasn't sharing, every moment that would only be remembered by me.

I wasn't lonely.

But I wasn't sure I liked being alone anymore.

The city of Qingdao greeted me with a merciless downpour. Rain lashed against my face, soaking through my clothes and chilling me to the bone. This wasn't the warm, tropical rain of Thailand—this was a cold, relentless soak that seeped through every layer, making my fingers stiff and my body ache. The once-refreshing sensation of rain on my skin now felt harsh and unforgiving.

And then I saw it.

The golden arches of a McDonald's shone like a beacon through the storm. Should I? I hesitated, the tug-of-war between culinary shame and sheer desperation raging in my mind. But as another icy gust of wind whipped through my dripping clothes, the debate ended.

To hell with it.

I stomped inside, dripping onto the floor like a half-drowned stray dog, and ordered a double cheeseburger and fries without a second thought.

I settled into a booth and camped out there for hours—drying off, nursing a hot coffee, and indulging in the salty, familiar taste of home. It was ridiculous, really. I'd spent months immersing myself in local cuisines, discovering bold flavours and dishes I'd never heard of before, but right now, this cheap, greasy meal felt like the warmest embrace.

Once I'd thawed out enough to brave the rain again, I left the McDonald's and I stocked up at a nearby supermarket, stuffing my panniers with convenience-store Sichuan noodle pots, instant coffee, and a handful of snacks for the journey ahead. The plan was simple: find the ferry terminal, check the departure schedule for tomorrow, then locate a place to stay for the night.

But Qingdao had one last surprise for me.

As I arrived at the ticket office, dripping onto the counter, the attendant glanced up and casually dropped a bombshell.

"Next ferry to Incheon? Leaves in two hours."

I blinked. Wait, what?

I'd expected to spend the night here—explore a little, maybe have a final meal in China that wasn't a McDonald's.

Instead, the decision was being made for me. Two hours. That wasn't much time. But… wasn't this perfect? An overnight crossing with a bunk bed included—it was basically transport and accommodation rolled into one. It was a no-brainer.

"I'll take it," I said, barely hesitating.

I wheeled my bike onto the massive ferry, the smell of salt and diesel filling my nostrils as I secured my belongings. As I stood on deck, watching the lights of Qingdao flicker against the rain-drenched skyline, a wave of realisation hit me.

My mind flickered back to where it all started—the ferry from Dover. All those months ago, I had stood on deck, naïve and full of nervous energy, staring out at the English Channel with no idea what was ahead. Now, as Qingdao's skyline faded behind me, I was no longer that person. The fear was gone and it had been replaced by something quieter, steadier—an understanding of the road, of myself, of what it meant to keep going.

But something nagged at me. Had I lost some of the wonder along the way? The thrill of the unknown, the magic of each new place? Or had I simply become too used to the rhythm of movement?

I shook the thought away. This was no time for existential reflection—I had a bed waiting for me.

As I settled into my bunk, I listened to the gentle hum of the ferry's engine and the occasional creak of the metal hull as the ship moved through the dark waters. One last night between lands. The thought was oddly poetic.

With that, I closed my eyes, and sleep took me before I had the time to think any further.

CHAPTER 29

Korean Cuisine

Number of days on the road: 311
Total distance covered: 14,268 km

I wheeled my bike down the huge steel ramp of the ferry and into the rain-soaked Korean port city of Incheon. It was a grey, damp morning. Rain drizzled steadily, flooding the streets and slicking my jacket. Not again, I thought.

After the frenzy of China, Korea felt clinical in its quietness. Everything seemed cleaner. Sharper. Less forgiving.

As I was securing my panniers, a tall, bespectacled man with a perfectly round bowl-cut wandered over.

"Excuse me," he said, peering at my loaded bike with curiosity. "Where are you cycling from and to?"

His English was excellent, but there was a slight, deliberate carefulness to his pronunciation.

"From London to Japan," I muttered, shaking the rain from my sleeves. "I've just arrived from China. I've been cycling for over ten months now."

His eyes widened behind his square-rimmed glasses. "Wow! That is very impressive. You must be very fit and strong!"

I laughed, waving a hand. "Not really. More stubborn than anything else."

"Amazing," he said, shaking his head in admiration. "Listen, if you like, I can take you for some real Korean food later. Not the tourist food. Proper food. I would love to hear about your trip."

That caught my interest immediately. "That sounds brilliant!"

We swapped email addresses and agreed to meet up later near my hostel, and with that, I set off on my bike for the rain-soaked ride to Seoul whilst he took a train to the capital.

The 40-kilometre ride from Incheon to Seoul felt like a punishment. The rain, at first a gentle mist, turned into a relentless downpour, slapping against my face like icy needles. Water pooled on the roads, sending cars skidding dangerously close, their tyres hissing as they ploughed through deep puddles.

My jacket was useless. Rain seeped through every layer, trickling down my back, soaking into my socks. My fingers, stiff from the cold, barely gripped the handlebars as I powered forward, head down, teeth clenched against the wind-whipped droplets that stung my cheeks.

The ride itself wasn't particularly difficult—it was mostly flat, with well-maintained roads, but the rain sapped all enjoyment from it. By the time I reached Seoul, I was cold, sodden, and slightly irritable.

Finding the hostel was straightforward enough. I checked in and dropped my sodden bags in the corner, and took the longest, hottest shower imaginable. Feeling half-human again, I took stock of my surroundings.

Compared to China, Seoul was noticeably pricier—it was a far cry from the cheap street food and bargain hostels I'd experienced so far, but what was on offer was very different too. Everything was pristine—gleaming, spotless, precise. Even the walls of the hostel room were glossy.

Lee met me at my hostel, and we headed to a tucked-away, no-frills restaurant in a side street, far from the usual tourist spots. He greeted me with a broad smile and an enthusiastic handshake.

"You made it!" he said, eyeing my now-dry clothes. "You look much better than before!"

"It turns out hot showers solve a lot of problems," I chuckled. "Now, where's this amazing food you promised?"

Lee led me inside, where the air was thick with the mouth-watering smell of grilled meat, garlic, and sizzling sesame oil. The restaurant had low wooden tables, and diners sat cross-legged on cushions while plates of food covered every available surface.

A waitress came over and, without even asking, brought out a tray filled with small bowls of colourful side dishes.

"This," Lee gestured, "is *banchan.* Many small dishes. You eat with the main course."

I eyed the assortment of tiny plates. Fiery red *kimchi,* sweet and sticky braised potatoes, spicy pickled radish, soft tofu in a light soy dressing, and crispy, golden fish cakes.

"These are amazing," I said, popping a piece of kimchi into my mouth. The fermented cabbage exploded with garlic, chilli, and tangy vinegar—a sharp, addictive kick that made me reach for another.

Lee smiled approvingly. "You like kimchi? Very important for Koreans."

"I think I could eat a whole plate of this."

"Ah," he laughed. "Careful—too much, and your stomach won't be happy!"

The main dish arrived next. It was *bulgogi*, marinated slices of tender beef, glistening in a rich, soy-based sauce. The waitress set up a small grill in the centre of the table, and we watched as the meat sizzled, caramelising in its juices.

Lee handed me a piece with his chopsticks. "Try like this. Or wrap in lettuce."

I followed his lead, wrapping the smoky, slightly charred beef in a crisp lettuce leaf, adding a dollop of *gochujang* (spicy red pepper paste), and popping the whole thing into my mouth.

It was incredible.

The beef melted on my tongue, the *gochujang* adding a fiery heat, while the lettuce gave a cool, refreshing crunch.

We traded stories, and Lee listened to some of my exploits from earlier in my journey, whilst I listened to his tales of studying in Canada before coming back to Korea to work for a tech company. He promised to stay in touch by email.

Seoul was a melting pot of old and new. It was buzzing with energy in the best possible way. I weaved through traffic, passing towering glass skyscrapers adorned with giant digital billboards displaying everything from K-pop idols to financial updates. The streets were packed with pedestrians, while sleek bullet trains glided silently across overhead tracks. Yet, in between the rush of modern life, I found glimpses of old Korea—tiny traditional tea houses and wooden hanok buildings with curved roofs.

The palace complex of Gyeongbokgung was colossal. Built in the 14th century during the Joseon Dynasty, it had been burned, rebuilt, and restored multiple times over Korea's turbulent history. Standing at the main entrance, Gwanghwamun Gate, I watched as rows of guards in vibrant red and blue uniforms stood motionless, their expressions unreadable beneath their traditional black *gats* (hats).

As I stepped through into the palace grounds, the city noise faded. The complex opened up into wide courtyards flanked by pagoda-style buildings painted in deep greens, golds, and reds. The changing of the guards began with the low thud of a ceremonial drum, followed by a procession of soldiers in flowing silk robes marching in perfect synchronisation.

From Gyeongbokgung, I made my way towards Namsan Park, home to the Namsan Seoul Tower, perched high above the city. The climb up was a lung-buster, the road snaking steeply through dense woodland, but I enjoyed the shift in atmosphere—the scent of pine trees replacing exhaust fumes, the distant chatter of hikers echoing along the trail.

Viewing a city from high up had become my favourite way to really see a city. At the top, Seoul sprawled beneath me. The view was magnificent—a vast expanse of high-rise apartments, snaking highways, and the Han River winding lazily through the metropolis.

The next day, I bought the essentials, some bottled water and a bright turquoise hoodie, as I felt so dishevelled whenever I left the hostel in my travel-worn clothes.

Leaving Seoul was quite hectic. Buses roared past within inches, motorbikes weaved unpredictably. More than once, I had to swerve sharply to avoid becoming another casualty of Seoul's ruthless traffic.

Eventually, I found the Han River, and just like that, the madness of the city melted away. The transition was almost surreal—one moment, I was dodging taxis, weaving between motorcycles, heart pounding from the constant near-misses, and the next, I was gliding along a wide, smooth cycle path, where the only sound was the soft rustling of reeds and that familiar rhythmic hum of my tyres on the pavement.

The morning breeze was crisp, cool, and refreshing. It swept across my face like a gentle hand wiping away the stress of the city. Joggers passed by with relaxed nods, a couple strolled hand-in-hand, and birds skimmed across the surface of the water. The scent of damp earth and fresh blossoms lingered in the air. It was the kind of place that made you exhale without realising you'd been holding your breath.

Gradually, the towering skyscrapers of Seoul faded into the distance, replaced by rolling green hills, clusters of dense woodland, and expansive rice paddies. The road ahead led me out towards the hilly, verdant Korean countryside, promising a landscape of forested slopes, misty valleys, and slow, winding rivers.

A few days into the ride, just past the city of Chuncheon, I rolled into a picturesque mountain town nestled between rugged peaks and a glimmering lake. The streets were lined with wooden houses, their curved, tiled roofs—remnants of a time before Korea's urban explosion.

I pulled into a bustling eatery, where groups of friends sat cross-legged on the floor around low wooden tables, cooking their own meals on built-in tabletop grills. The restaurant owner, an elderly woman with an apron tied tightly around her waist, gestured for me to sit. Without a word, she lit the grill and tossed chunks of marinated chicken, rice cakes, and cabbage onto the sizzling pan in front of me.

"Spicy?" she asked, grinning.

I nodded. "Of course."

She smiled cheekily. "Foreigners always regret it."

I laughed. It was spicy, but I had been eating spicy food for the last six months, and it didn't overpower me.

"Good, right?" she said. I wondered if she was secretly hoping for me to start squealing with the heat.

I simply gave a thumbs-up between bites, and she patted my shoulder with a broad smile.

After days on the road near the city of Daegu, I found myself in a quiet rural town where time seemed to slow to a standstill.

It was there that I met an elderly woman. She was tiny, barely five feet tall, with short curly hair and a warm, toothy smile. As I paused to check my map outside her house, she stepped out, eyes filled with curiosity.

"*Kopi?*" she asked, making a drinking motion. Coffee.

I hesitated for a second before nodding. "Sure!"

She beckoned me inside her small wooden house, where the scent of freshly brewed barley tea filled the air. The walls were adorned with black-and-white photographs, faded with age, showing a young couple dressed in traditional *hanbok* , and others featuring family gatherings spanning decades.

With gestures and broken words, she insisted on giving me a quick tour of her home, pointing at objects with pride and nostalgia.

She motioned towards an old wooden chest and mimicked opening it. I nodded eagerly. Inside were neatly folded embroidered fabrics, which she carefully lifted, explaining in rapid-fire Korean that I could barely follow but understood just enough of: these were traditional clothes she had made by hand.

I felt a sudden wave of gratitude—this was no museum; this was her life, her history, her story laid out in fabric and photographs. As she carefully lifted a delicate *hanbok*, running her fingers over the embroidered silk, her face softened into something distant—a memory, perhaps, of the last time she had worn it, or of someone who once had.

When it was time to leave, she pressed a small paper bag into my hands, filled with homemade rice cakes. I thanked her the best I could, bowing deeply in gratitude.

As I pedalled away, I realised how these brief, fleeting moments of human kindness were some of the most profound experiences of my trip. They were unplanned, unscripted, but deeply real.

***

Busan—South Korea's second-largest city and its most important port—felt like the final stop before stepping into the unknown again. Unlike Seoul's electric, high-speed chaos, Busan had an unhurried, salt-tinged rhythm, shaped by the ebb and flow of the sea.

One of Busan's biggest draws is Haeundae Beach, a long stretch of golden sand on the city's eastern edge, famed for its sunbathing, water sports, and lively beachfront cafés. On any other day, I might have been tempted to kick back, stretch out on the sand, and stop for a well-earned swim. But Busan wasn't showing me its best side—the sky was grey and overcast, the wind whipped off the sea, and I could see the beach was a far cry from the summer hotspot it's known to be. The rows of closed umbrellas and shuttered beachfront stalls told me I'd arrived out of season.

I stood at the waterfront, watching the grey waves roll in under the heavy clouds, their restless energy mirroring my own thoughts. The city was built into the spine of the mountains, sloping down to meet the sea, its skyline a mix of towering apartments and neon-lit fish markets. There was a pull to it—a place where I could have stayed and lingered, let myself breathe. But the ferry ticket in my pocket said otherwise.

Maybe that was the hardest part of travelling like this. Everywhere held the potential to become home, but nowhere ever was.

Each country had fed me in its own way. Some filled me with noise. Some with kindness. Korea fed me quietly—with broth, with precision, with silence that somehow felt like a warm hug.

Japan beckoned, and I was nervous, terrified even. But I was also excited. A new culture. A new cuisine. A new chapter.

CHAPTER 30

The Beginning of the End

Number of days on the road: **321**
Total distance covered: **14,725 km**

I hadn't expected the reality of this being the final part of the journey to hit me so bluntly, but as the ferry docked in Fukuoka, a mix of elation and melancholy settled over me. The sun was blazing in the bright blue sky, and the air was warm and inviting. Yet, beneath the thrill of arriving in a new country, a nagging realisation gnawed at me—this was it.

Japan was the last country of my journey and the final chapter in an adventure that had shaped me in ways I was only just beginning to understand. The finish line was somewhere on the horizon, but as much as I had longed for the thrill of Japan, I wasn't ready for it all to be over.

I stood for a moment on the ferry deck, gripping the rail. I let out a slow breath. Enough dwelling. There was an entire country ahead of me.

I pedalled off the ferry ramp and into the immaculate streets of Fukuoka, where everything was in perfect order—cars obeyed traffic rules, pedestrians crossed at designated walkways, and there was no honking, no chaos, just quiet efficiency.

"Okay, Japan," I muttered to myself. "Let's see what you've got."

My first order of business was finding a hostel, and after a bit of navigating, I spotted a place down a quiet side street that had been recommended in my guidebook. I wheeled Shirley up to the entrance and barely had time to take off my sunglasses before a lively young man with spiky black hair and a beaming grin sprang from behind the reception desk.

"Ohhh, hello!" he greeted me in enthusiastic English.

I laughed at his energy. "Hello! I don't suppose you have a room for one person?"

He clapped his hands together. "Yes! Yes! Please, come in. You are… from?"

"England."

His eyes widened. "Ahhh, very good! You like Japan?"

"I think I'm going to love it!"

His name was Hiroshi. He led me through the clean, minimalist interior of the hostel, and he handed me a map of the city with a list of must-see spots. His eagerness was infectious and, as I dragged my bags upstairs and settled into my room, I felt a wave of appreciation.

Fukuoka was a small city by Japanese standards, but it was full of life, and I had arrived at the perfect time —*Ōgon Shūkan*—Golden Week. One of Japan's biggest celebrations, it consists of a series of national holidays that send locals into full-blown festival mode. My favourite highlight of the week was the Hakata Dontaku Festival, which was originally celebrated as a New Year event under the old lunar calendar and is a tradition that dates back centuries.

I found myself among throngs of people lining Meiji Street, where colourful processions of dancers, musicians, and performers paraded through the heart of the city. The beating of taiko drums filled the air, mingling with flutes, clashing cymbals, and laughter.

A group of elderly men in bright red happi coats waved their fans as they performed a traditional dance, while young children in dragon costumes playfully wove through the crowd. Some performers balanced lanterns on their heads, others twirled golden umbrellas, their movements perfectly synchronised.

I stood there, smiling widely, absorbing the sheer joy of it all. The energy, the colours, the sounds—it was invigorating. I found myself walking along to the rhythm of the drums, resisting the urge to dance.

I spent the days after Golden Week settling into Fukuoka, making friends with the hostel staff, and attempting to pick up some basic Japanese to help me through the rest of the journey. It didn't go well at first.

I sat in the hostel's common area with a scrap of paper covered in scribbled phrases while Hiroshi, the lively receptionist, shook his head at my pronunciation.

He sighed dramatically, shaking his head as if I were a lost cause. "You need more beer to learn properly."

The others laughed, and someone slid a cold Asahi across the table toward me. I took a sip, shrugged, and gave it another go.

By the end of the night, I could half-decently order food, and most importantly, say "please" and "thank you" properly.

I also studied my road atlas during this time, plotting the route that would take me from Fukuoka towards Hiroshima, Kyoto and then on to Tokyo. I felt a growing determination to make these final weeks count, to savour every kilometre before my adventure came to an end.

On my last night in Fukuoka, I was sitting on the hostel's rooftop terrace, sipping a beer, when Hiroshi and a couple of the other guests came up, holding a small chocolate cake with a single candle flickering on top.

"Rob-San," Hiroshi called out. "Surprise!"

I blinked. "Wait—what?"

A German backpacker named Lena grinned. "Hiroshi told us it's your birthday. So... happy birthday!"

I laughed in disbelief, feeling a swell of warmth in my chest. "You guys didn't have to do this."

Hiroshi clapped a hand on my shoulder. "Ahhh, but in Japan, a birthday is special. And you are our special guest."

We put on music, cracked open a few beers, and for the next few hours, we sat under the twinkling fairy lights, talking, laughing, and celebrating.

At one point, Lena raised her drink. "So, Rob—what's next after Japan?"

I hesitated, then shrugged with a smile. "Who knows?"

And with that, I took another sip of beer and let the night carry on, full of laughter and good company.

***

Leaving Fukuoka behind, I eased into a steady rhythm, the familiar hum of my tyres on well-maintained tarmac a comforting soundtrack to the road ahead and a far cry from some of the bone-rattling roads I had experienced since leaving the UK almost a year before. The early morning air was fresh and invigorating. Being back on my bike after a few days off always made me feel alive again as the endorphins slowly started to flood my body.

Just as I was settling into the ride, I spotted two cyclists up ahead, their panniers gleaming, their frames spotless, and their movements just a little too careful. Newbies.

As I pulled up beside them, they turned with eager but slightly nervous expressions. They were a couple from California, and this was their first cycling trip. Their shiny bikes, perfectly packed bags, and neatly folded maps reminded me of my own first day 11 months ago. Back then, I had set off with half my worldly possessions and lugged them across London, convinced I would need everything I'd packed into my panniers.

Since then, I had shed the excess, and now my gear included only what was truly essential. My bike was battered and caked in road dust, my once-pristine panniers scuffed and stained, and my clothing had stopped looking clean long ago.

"Where are you guys headed?" I asked.

The woman, Vicky, who was adjusting the strap of her helmet, answered with a wavering enthusiasm, "We're... uh... making our way to Kyoto. It's our first time doing something like this!"

"Nice one," I said, nodding. "Got everything you need?"

The guy, Kelly, chuckled, running a hand over his handlebars. "I think so? We, uh, probably over-packed."

"Probably," I grinned. "But that's part of it. You'll figure out soon enough what you need."

I didn't lecture them on what to bring; they had their own lessons to learn, just as I'd had—and, for me, that had been half of the adventure.

"Check the nuts and bolts on your racks every few thousand miles. Trust me, a loose bolt at 60 km/h downhill is no joke."

Their eyes widened, and I could see them mentally adding "bolt check" to their list of new habits.

We rode together for the next two days, exchanging stories, and adjusting to the gentle climbs and coastal breezes of Western Japan. They had a wonderful attitude—a mix of excitement and just enough fear to keep them pushing forward.

By the time we reached Shimonoseki, where the western tip of Honshu met the sea, it was time to part ways.

"I hope Kyoto is everything the guidebook says it is," I told them as we stood by our bikes, overlooking the calm waters of the Kanmon Strait. "Take your time there. Soak it in."

"Thanks, Rob," Vicky said, offering a warm smile. "And if we ever make it to England, you owe us a pub recommendation."

I laughed. "Deal."

With a final handshake and a pat on the back, we went our separate ways.

CHAPTER 31

Bridges & Shrines

Number of days on the road: 326
Total distance covered: 15,002 km

That evening, I found a quiet, secluded park just outside of a small town. With tall bushes for cover, I set up camp, boiled some instant noodles over my stove, and sprawled out under the clear night sky. It was a perfect, undisturbed night—just me, my tent, and the stars that had followed me everywhere I went.

Feeling recharged the next day, I managed a solid 125-kilometre ride, pushing through gentle hills and winding roads before rolling into the town of Iwakuni. As the sun set below the horizon, I found a quiet, dried-out riverbed to set up camp for the night. The sound of the water trickling in the distance, paired with the crisp evening air, made for a peaceful end to the day.

At dawn, I packed up and visited the Kintaikyo Bridge, a masterpiece of Edo-period engineering. Built in 1673, its five elegant wooden arches propped up by stone columns reach gracefully across the calm, reflective waters of the Nishiki River. Standing before it, I couldn't help but admire the craftsmanship—no nails were used in the construction, only interlocking wooden planks fitted together using ancient techniques.

Beyond the bridge, at the foot of Mount Yokoyama, Iwakuni Castle stands proudly at the summit. Originally built in the 1600s and reconstructed in the 1950s, it is one of Japan's revered "Hundred Great Castles". It has retained its feudal charm, and the climb up presented me with sweeping views of the surrounding countryside.

From Iwakuni, it was a short ride to Hiroshima. The Japanese city became known the world over when, on the morning of 6th August 1945, an atomic bomb exploded above it. The effects were devastating.

I checked into a hostel early enough to make my way to Hiroshima Peace Memorial Museum. It didn't sensationalise the city's history, nor did it dwell in anger or blame. The curators had presented the facts with stark honesty, weaving together the tragedy of Hiroshima with the broader horrors of war.

I moved through the exhibits slowly, taking in the accounts of survivors and the charred remnants of everyday life that remained after the bombings—a child's tricycle, a school uniform, a watch frozen at 8:15 a.m.

A lump formed in my throat. These weren't artefacts. They were people's lives, their stories. These objects belonged to people who had woken up that morning, never knowing what was about to happen to them.

Very little remained from the destruction. The bomb exploded 600 metres above the city. Intense heat and radiation spread instantly, surface temperatures soared to between 3,000 and 4,000°C, and the blast travelled at nearly 1,000 miles per hour.

The deaths were indiscriminate—old and young, rich and poor, Japanese nationals and foreigners alike. Around 80,000 people died immediately, while 140,000 had died by the end of the year. Seventy per cent of the city's buildings were destroyed.

I stood before a glass case displaying a single tattered lunchbox, its contents fused into an unrecognisable black mass from the heat of the explosion. The placard told the story of its owner: a teenage schoolboy who had brought his lunch to class, expecting to eat it at noon.

I stepped outside. I needed air. The Atomic Bomb Dome stood across the river—one of the few structures left standing after the blast. Its skeletal frame was silhouetted against the fading light, a haunting and defiant presence.

I found a park bench and sat down; my thoughts were tangled in the incomprehensible scale of destruction.

Life carried on here. People were picnicking in the park, and children were playing. Hiroshima hadn't just survived—it had transformed into a city of peace and renewal.

I left the next morning, following the Seto Inland Sea along quiet roads that hugged the coastline. The ride was gentle and beautiful—water that stretched to the horizon was dotted with emerald-green islands and bobbing fishing boats.

My next destination was Onomichi, a charming, sleepy town that is also the starting point of one of the most unique cycling routes in the world: the *Shimanami Kaidō* is a spectacular 60-kilometre cycling and driving route in Japan that connects the main islands of Honshu and Shikoku, running from Onomichi in Hiroshima Prefecture to Imabari on the island of Shikoku. It stretches across six small islands in the Seto Inland Sea, linked by a series of impressive suspension bridges—some of the most beautiful and cycle-friendly in the world.

I pedalled along the waterfront past moored ferries and rusting boats and reached the first of ten spectacular bridges.

The Kurushima-Kaikyō Bridge was the most staggering of them all. Spanning more than 4 kilometres, it's the longest suspension bridge in the world with massive steel towers that soar into the sky and cables that fan out like spider silk. Ahead of me, the bridge stretched endlessly across the sea. It looked like a highway in the clouds.

As I cycled across, I felt the wind tug at my jersey and push against me as I rode high above the water. Below, cargo ships carved slow arcs through the waves. The rhythmic hum of my tyres, the whisper of cables in the breeze, and the vastness around me created a surreal, euphoric quiet.

And that was just the beginning.

Each of the ten bridges had its own character—the graceful Tatara with its soaring stays, the low, arched silhouette of the Ikuchi Bridge. Some passed high over open water, others dropped close to tiny island harbours where boats gently rocked at their moorings.

Part way along the Shimanami Kaidō, the sun began to set on the island of Ōmishima. As the sky melted into amber and purple and long shadows stretched across the water, I needed somewhere to sleep before the last of the light vanished.

After a bit of searching and not finding anything for a few kilometres, I found an unlikely option: a public toilet block annexed to a visitors centre that was closed.

The disabled toilet room was immaculate—large, dry, and clean. I wheeled Shirley and my bags inside, unrolled my mat, and lay back. It had a toilet, a basin, and more room than many hostel dorms. In Japan's obsessively clean, minimalist way, it was more sanitary than plenty of places I'd stayed.

I chuckled to myself. I'd just spent the day crossing world-famous bridges—and now I was wild camping in a loo.

But it was dry. It was secure. In its own strange way, it was perfect.

I woke at first light to complete silence. No cars, no voices—just the soft hush of wind moving through the trees outside my unlikely "hotel". I stretched, packed up, gave the toilet block a quick tidy (it seemed only polite), and set off into the cool morning air.

Japan had been an unrelenting adventure so far. I had travelled in excess of 500 kilometres in a week, and I still had a long way to go. But first, I needed food.

Convenience stores in Japan are a thing of wonder. Neatly stacked bento boxes, iced coffees, *nikuman*—steamed pork buns, and a dizzying array of snacks I couldn't pronounce. Arriving in Imabari on the island of Shikoku, I stopped at the first convenience store that I saw. Inside, a young cashier watched me browse with amused curiosity. I greeted her with a cheerful "*Ohayō gozaimasu*!" and got a delighted smile in return.

It turned out she could speak a little English, and she gave me a tip: if I waited five minutes, the bento boxes would be marked down. Sure enough, just as she said, the discount bell chimed just a few minutes later, and I got a perfect breakfast for half the price. Rice, grilled salmon, and a bit of pickled radish. I sat on a bench under a cherry tree, unwrapped the box, and ate slowly, watching the town stir to life.

It was a moment that cost almost nothing, but felt utterly priceless.

Leaving the bridges behind, I continued cycling across Shikoku. It felt different here—older, quieter. To the north, the Naruto Strait churned with swirling whirlpools. To the south, the deep-green mountains of the island rose in waves, ridges stacking one behind another like folded silk.

I rolled through narrow valleys and past vine-covered bridges, rice paddies, and houses that looked like they hadn't changed in a hundred years. This was a part of Japan that many travellers missed, and I felt lucky to see it.

In Kotohira, I stopped to visit the town's famous shrine. Dedicated to the guardian deity of sailors, it sits high atop Mount Zōzu. To reach it, I had to climb 1,368 stone steps.

My legs, which were already knackered from the 70 kilometres I'd cycled that morning, were less than thrilled.

Still, I locked up the bike and began the climb. Step after step, through *Torii* gates and past stone lanterns, I wound upward, joined by elderly pilgrims who somehow managed to overtake me with ease. Every few hundred steps, I paused—ostensibly to admire the view, but really to stop my lungs from falling out.

It took about 45 minutes to climb all of the steps. At the top, the shrine opened out onto a broad courtyard with views stretching across the hills and rooftops below. The *honden* (Main Sanctuary) and *haiden (*Worship Hall*)* buildings stood quiet and dignified, framed by forest and sky. There was a serenity up here, the kind that made you want to speak in whispers.

On the way down, I stumbled into a tiny eatery at the base of the hill and collapsed onto a tatami mat. The owner, a kindly old woman with a face full of smile lines, brought over a bowl of *sanuki udon*—Shikoku's signature dish.

The noodles were thick, the broth light and fragrant, and it was topped with spring onions and a soft-boiled egg that melted into the soup.

I slurped, sighed, and nodded my thanks. "That hit the spot."

From Kotohira, I made my way east toward Takamatsu. The city felt both lively and unhurried—nestled between the sea and the hills, with just the right amount of bustle.

That night, sitting outside a small family-run *izakaya,* I struck up a conversation with two local women, Yuki and Asami, in their late twenties. They said they'd spotted me—a tired, road-worn foreigner—and decided to invite me to join them for dinner.

"Have you tried curry udon?" Yuki asked, eyes wide with excitement.

"Not yet," I said. "But it already sounds like my kind of thing."

They ordered for me, and soon a steaming bowl arrived —udon noodles bathed in a rich, spicy curry broth. It was heaven. Comfort food at its absolute best.

"You approve?" Asami asked, watching me with a grin.

"Wholeheartedly," I said, between mouthfuls. "I might never leave Takamatsu."

We talked for hours—about Japan, cycling, travel and everything in between. They told me where to go next, who to talk to and what to eat. I couldn't stop smiling.

Later, they introduced me to a group of "businessmen" deep into their post-work beers, and soon I had yakitori skewers and sake pushed into my hands. I was toasted, cheered, and quizzed. "To cycling!" someone shouted. "To adventure!"

By the time I left for the ferry terminal, I was full, slightly buzzed, and overwhelmed with warmth. I boarded the overnight ferry to Kobe feeling happy and refuelled.

Kobe was a brief stop. I arrived in the early morning, bleary-eyed from a night of ferry engines and salty air. There wasn't much time to linger. I grabbed a coffee, checked my emails, sent a message home, and studied the map. The route to Kyoto was direct but uninspiring—suburban roads, strip malls, convenience stores, and grey skies. I pushed on.

My legs were tired, but my mind was more so. Seven days on the road, 800 kilometres ridden, was beginning to press down on me. I needed a break.

Kyoto, Japan's cultural heart, was exactly the place for it.

I checked into a small hostel on the outskirts of the city, dumped my bags, and slept like the dead. When I woke, hunger hit with a vengeance. I headed out and did the only sensible thing: ate everything in sight.

Kyoto's food scene was a revelation. On every street corner, someone was grilling, frying or steaming something. I roamed the markets and alleyways like a man possessed—slurping noodles, biting into soft *yatsuhashi* (cinnamon rice crackers), picking skewers off smoky izakaya grills. I tried silken tofu, which was delicate and nutty. Crispy tempura. Chargrilled yakitori. The city fed me, body and soul.

I wandered with no real plan, letting Kyoto unfold around me. The city was like a living museum—temples nestled into hillsides, lanterns swung gently above narrow alleys, the air was thick with incense and age. Time moved differently here.

The next morning, map in hand, I set out to explore properly.

My first stop was Nijō Castle, a formidable complex of moats, thick stone walls, and carefully raked gravel. Built in 1603 for the Tokugawa shoguns, it was a place that exuded power—sharp edges, creaking "nightingale floors", and rooms painted with tigers and pine trees in gold leaf had been designed to sing out intruders. You could almost feel the presence of history, coiled and watchful in every corridor.

From Nijō Castle, I cycled across the city to *Kinkaku-ji*—the Golden Pavilion.

It stopped me in my tracks. It gleamed like a mirage, its surface covered entirely in gold leaf reflecting perfectly in the still waters of the surrounding pond. It shimmered under the midday sun, quiet and unearthly. It didn't feel real. It felt like something from a dream.

When I arrived, I was taken aback by the astonishing sight: a path of *Vermilion Torii* gates wound through the forested hillside, thousands of them forming a tunnel of colour and light. Each step took me deeper, the noise of the city falling away until it was just me, the soft crunch of gravel underfoot, and the quiet whisper of wind through the leaves. Fox statues watched from the shadows, their stone faces unreadable.

I walked slowly, reverently, letting each gate carry me further into a kind of meditative calm.

That night, back at the hostel, I sat alone in the courtyard with a beer and a thousand thoughts swirling in my head. The road was pulling again. I could feel it.

Tokyo was out there. And beyond Tokyo—home.

The journey was nearing its end.

The road to Nagoya was challenging. The weather turned foul—grey skies, slashing rain, and a cold wind that cut straight through my jacket. Urban sprawl stretched endlessly. Either on their own would have been fine, but the terrible weather and terrible traffic was an unpleasant combination.

I gritted my teeth and pressed on.

I camped in wet gear on a piece of development land and woke up damp and cold, before setting off again into more rain. It felt like a cruel test of endurance. I had known tougher days on the road, but there was something about this stretch, this final leg, that made it feel harder.

When I finally reached Shizuoka after two long days covering a total of 280 kilometres, I was physically and mentally drained. I needed somewhere—anywhere—to dry out, rest, and recharge. Salvation came in the form of a Japanese internet café.

For a few hundred yen, I secured a private cubicle for the night, which included a reclining leather chair, unlimited drinks from a vending machine, and a plug socket for my phone. The place even had showers. Luxury.

I stripped off my soaked clothes, took the longest, hottest shower imaginable, and collapsed into the chair like it was a five-star hotel bed. It wasn't glamorous. But in that moment, it was everything.

In the morning, I did what any sleep-deprived cyclist in Japan must do—I headed to a convenience store for breakfast, and I picked up a perfectly arranged bento box and hot coffee. I was ready for my final challenge.

Mount Fuji.

It had loomed in my mind for days—Japan's highest peak, 3,776 metres of stoic grandeur. I knew I wasn't going to cycle to the summit; that would require time, permits, and the right season. But I could cycle as high as the road would take me—the Fifth Station, which perched at 2,300 metres.

On the day, the weather didn't look promising. The summit was buried under thick, low cloud. I pushed on anyway.

The climb was relentless. The road coiled higher and higher in a slow-motion spiral, switchback after switchback, the gradient never easing. It was a battle of wills—me versus the mountain.

I thought back to the goodbye when I left home. Not with pain this time. The distance had softened any sharp edges. I had left chasing freedom and silence, maybe even chasing a version of myself that I hadn't met yet. And now, thousands of kilometres later, I realised I wasn't running anymore. I had become the man I'd been trying to find.

I dug deep and pedalled on.

Hours passed. The air thinned. My breath grew ragged. My thighs screamed. The temperature dropped, and mist clung to the trees. But I didn't stop. I couldn't.

At last, I reached the Fifth Station—exhausted and drenched.

The view?

It was a complete white-out. I was unable to see anything.

The mountain I had come to conquer was nowhere to be seen.

Then the rain returned. Cold, stinging sheets of it. There was no triumphant celebration. Just fatigue and frustration.

I descended carefully, soaked to the skin and utterly depleted. Somewhere halfway down, I spotted a tiny roadside park with a wooden shelter beside a children's playground.

It would have to do.

Too tired to pitch my tent, I threw my sleeping mat on the bench, climbed into my damp sleeping bag, and fell asleep to the sound of rain hammering the roof above me.

If I had known what awaited me in the morning, I probably never would have managed to sleep.

CHAPTER 32

The End: Fuji & the Pacific

Number of days on the road: 338
Total distance covered: 15,775 km

I stirred at dawn.

The rain had stopped, and a strange, perfect silence hung in the air—the kind that makes the world feel like it's holding its breath.

I sat up slowly, sore and stiff, rubbing the sleep from my eyes.

As the sun cracked the horizon, painting the sky in a palette I'd never seen before, I stood still. Wind battered my sleeping bag, but inside, something had settled. Not joy exactly—something quieter. A peace that felt hard-won. The kind that doesn't announce itself but arrives like a held breath that's finally exhaled.

Then I looked up—and froze.

There it was.

Mount Fuji.

Clear. Towering. Magnificent.

It felt strange, standing on the side of something I'd imagined so often. Mount Fuji—iconic, symmetrical, immortalised on postcards and prayer scrolls. But in this moment, it was less a mountain and more a mirror. I had come here not just to finish a journey, but to understand what the journey itself had done to me.

Mount Fuji's snow-capped summit glowed in the soft morning light, every ridge and fold bathed in golden-pink. The mist was gone. The sky was clear. The mountain I had battled so hard to reach had finally revealed itself to me.

I stared, breath caught in my throat. It was more than a view—it was a moment. A gift. A silent witness to everything I'd endured.

"Hello, Fuji-san," I whispered.

For the first time in weeks—maybe months—a tear rolled down my cheek. This wasn't just a reward. It was the embodiment of every hard-earned kilometre, every day on the road.

Twenty minutes later, the clouds returned and Fuji vanished again.

But I had seen it.

And that was enough.

I ran a hand along Shirley's frame—scratched, dusty, faithful. She had carried not just my bags, but my doubts, my grief, my hope. I'd called her my escape once. But now, she felt more like a witness to this wonderful journey.

I coasted down the mountain in near silence, letting gravity carry me. Past sleepy towns and pine forests, through quiet farmland, replaying the thousands of kilometres behind me.

Eventually, I reached the Pacific coast—the farthest east I could go without falling into the sea.

I stood at the water's edge, watching waves crash under a pale sky, and let it sink in.

I had cycled from London to the edge of the Pacific Ocean.

I could have stopped there. Part of me wanted to.

But I knew the story wasn't finished yet.

Tokyo awaited.

The final 75 kilometres were a blur—traffic, noise, chaos. Glass towers and neon lights. Lorries thundered past. People flowed across crossings in perfect, oblivious rhythm.

And in the middle of it all was me—just another speck in the sprawl, weaving through it all on a battered bicycle named Shirley.

There was no applause. No grand finale. Just me, Shirley, the wind, and the road curving downward again. But I didn't need a finish line. I had left with questions I couldn't answer. I returned with questions I could live with. And, maybe, that was the whole point.

I didn't feel lost.

I felt alive.

I started laughing. Then crying. Then laughing again.

I sang to myself. Shouted nonsense. Smiled at strangers. No one noticed. No one cared.

And I loved that.

I was completely anonymous again—just another soul in the great machine.

But inside, I was bursting.

I thought of that first day in London, over-packed and quietly terrified.

I thought of deserts and jungles, of freezing nights in Kyrgyzstan and sweat-drenched days in Southeast Asia.

Of food poisoning, storms, and kindness. The machete-wielding lunatics in Thailand.

I thought of every stranger who had offered me a meal, a bed, a smile. Every moment that had made the road feel like home.

I had cycled most of the way across the world.

And in doing so, I had learned the simplest, most powerful truth of all: that the world is generous.

The world is not something to fear. It's full of wonder. Full of good people. Full of moments that remind you what it means to be human.

I had spent a year chasing something across a map, thinking it was waiting for me at the end.

But it wasn't.

The journey itself was the treasure.

The people. The landscapes. The pain. The laughter. The silence. The chaos. The stillness.

All of it.

That was the gift.

I slowed to a stop.

I sat there on my bike, breathing it in, holding the final moment.

I thanked everyone. It might have been out loud, or it might have been my inner voice.

The strangers. The friends. The road. The world.

I was grateful.

I was ready.

It was time to go home.

THE END

Number of Days on the Road: **339**

Total distance covered: **15,880 km**

Acknowledgements

This journey was never mine alone.

To my family and friends back home—thank you for believing in me when I doubted myself, and for the messages that always seemed to arrive just when I needed them most.

To the strangers I met along the way—the drivers who waved, the shopkeepers who shared smiles, the men in tea shops who poured endless refills, and the countless people who offered kindness without expecting anything in return—this book is as much yours as it is mine.

I also want to thank the editors and proofreaders who helped me shape these pages into something worth sharing. Your sharp eyes and careful guidance made the story clearer and stronger, and I'm deeply grateful for the time and skill you brought to the work.

And finally, to Shirley, my long-suffering bicycle—thanks for carrying me every rough kilometre, even when I didn't always deserve it.

Printed in Dunstable, United Kingdom

68223413R00221